MOROCCAN MIRAGES
Agrarian Dreams and
Deceptions, 1912–1986

Ouzoud Waterfalls in the Middle Atlas. Fully harnessing Morocco's water resources for irrigation has been a central dream of policymakers since the 1930s.

MOROCCAN MIRAGES

Agrarian Dreams and Deceptions, 1912–1986

WILL D. SWEARINGEN

Princeton University Press
Princeton, New Jersey

Copyright © 1987 by Princeton University Press
Published by Princeton University Press, 41 William Street,
Princeton, New Jersey 08540
In the United Kingdom: Princeton University Press, Guildford, Surrey

All Rights Reserved

Library of Congress Cataloging in Publication Data will be found
on the last printed page of this book

ISBN 0-691-05505-X (cloth)
0-691-10236-8 (LPE)

Publication of this book has been aided by a grant from the
Whitney Darrow Fund of Princeton University Press

This book has been composed in Linotron Galliard

Clothbound editions of Princeton University Press books are
printed on acid-free paper, and binding materials are chosen
for strength and durability. Paperbacks, although satisfactory for
personal collections, are not usually suitable for library rebinding

Printed in the United States of America by Princeton University Press,
Princeton, New Jersey

Designed by Karen Stefanelli

In Memoriam
PAUL PASCON

Contents

Illustrations

Frontispiece: Ouzoud Waterfalls in the Middle Atlas
 1. Roman ruins at Volubilis
 2. Moroccan peasants
 3. Plowing by traditional means
 4. Rendezvous in Casablanca, 1931
 5. The California Dream in Moroccan colonial agriculture
 6. Colonial advertisement for Californian irrigation technology
 7. The El Kansera Dam on the Oued Beth
 8. The Bin el Ouidane Dam on the Oued el Abid
 9. Tadla irrigation landscape
10. Orange orchard of a French settler
11. Gharb village dispossessed by colonization
12. Field patterns in the Gharb
13. The Moulay Youssef Dam near Marrakech
14. Sugar cane in the Gharb
15. Traditional agricultural village
16. Hassan II, King of Morocco

Credits: Photo 2 by Robert K. Holz; photo 3 by Neal Artz; photo 4 from *LTM* 7 (1931): 22; photo 5 from *FPAN* 5 (1931): 138; photo 6 from *LTM* 12 (1932): 3; photo 16 by Jane Hammoud; remaining photos by author.

Figures

Tables

Acknowledgments

I am deeply grateful for assistance received during the more than six years that this research monograph has been in progress. The cast of those who have assisted is quite large; it includes mentors, friends, colleagues, librarians, funding agencies, family members, and various others. An enthusiastic thanks is issued to all. Those whose contributions were truly indispensable are the following. James A. Miller, now of Clemson University, first made me aware of the monumental scale of dam construction in Morocco, awakening my interest in the present topic. Paul Ward English, of the University of Texas at Austin, helped focus my early research ideas; most important, he prevented me from stumbling down a dead-end alley that then appeared inviting. Edmund Burke, III, of the University of California, Santa Cruz; Richard Lawless, of the Centre for Middle Eastern and Islamic Studies, University of Durham; and Robin Bidwell, of the Middle East Centre, University of Cambridge, each supplied valuable information about sources in France and Morocco and were encouraging at a crucial early stage. Salah Hammoud, now of the Defense Language Institute in Monterey, California, among other things helped me prepare an application for a Moroccan research visa; as a result of his efforts, this valuable document was issued in record time. Nejib Bouderbala and the late Paul Pascon of the Institut Agronomique et Vétérinaire Hassan II, Rabat, and Jean Le Coz of the Université de Montpellier, offered unique and penetrating insights into policy making in Morocco during both colonial and contemporary periods. Herman Henning, then assistant cultural attaché at the American Embassy in Rabat, and Abdellatif Benabdeslam, cultural attaché assistant, were warm friends during my sojourn in Morocco, lending a helping hand on many occasions. Abdelmajid Benyoussef and Abderrahim Bouanani of the Bibliothèque Générale et Archives, Rabat, were charming hosts during the many months when I was a regular visitor at their research center; they often went out of their way to help. Alan Baldry was the pilot from whose small plane I obtained splendid views of the Moroccan countryside and the aerial photos used in this work. Robert K. Holz, who served as dissertation advisor at the University of Texas, provided strong and generous support while I was running the doctoral marathon. He helped to nurture an earlier incarnation of this monograph to maturity. His many efforts on my behalf are deeply appreciated. Ian Manners, Robert Fernea, Robin Doughty, Claudio Segrè, and Bharat Bhatt, all dissertation committee members at the University of Texas, helped to find and plug holes in my arguments and provided indispensable inspiration. Malcolm Blincow, of York University, Canada, deserves special thanks for many hours of stimulating discussion during which he imparted unique insights from his deep knowledge of the Gharb. Rhys Payne, a doctoral candidate and Maghreb specialist at UCLA, shared many obscure and valuable references on Morocco. Dale Eickelman, of New York University, gave an earlier version of the book manuscript a careful and scholarly reading; his suggestions were extremely helpful in preparing the final draft. Margaret Case, of Princeton University Press, has gained my everlasting gratitude for her early faith in the manuscript, patience while I tinkered with it, and skillful oversight over its publication. I also wish to thank Sherry Wert of Princeton University Press for her cheerful and conscientious assistance, and Jane Van Tassel for her painstaking and expert copyediting. The College of Liberal Arts at the University of Texas, Austin, squeezed travel funds from a lean budget which enabled me to go to Morocco for preliminary research during the summer of 1980. A Fulbright-Hays Doctoral Dissertation Research Abroad Grant from the U.S. Department of Education allowed me to spend the entire year of 1982 conducting research in France and Morocco; without their munificent support, this book could not have been written. The Center for Middle Eastern Studies at the University of Texas provided a small grant that enabled me to hire the talented John V. Cotter to draft the figures in this book. To these institutions, and to John, my special thanks. Mohamed Ben-Madani, founder and editor of *The Maghreb Review*, kindly permitted me to reuse an article that appeared in vol. 9 (nos. 1–2), 1984, of his journal; in revised form, it now forms a portion of Chapter 5. The *International Journal of Middle East Studies*, likewise, generously gave permission to republish an article from vol. 17 (4), 1985; it now appears in revised form as Chapter 2. In conclusion, and above all, I wish to thank my wife, Jennifer. She has had unflagging belief in the merit of this undertaking and confidence in my ability to bring it to fruition; she has continuously rendered sage advice, expert editorial assistance, and essential material support; finally, she has been a warm fellow traveler throughout: no better companion for this scholarly odyssey could have been found.

Albuquerque, New Mexico
February 1987

Note on Transliteration

The primary vehicle for Western scholarship on Morocco has long been the French language. Unfortunately, conventional French transliterations of Moroccan place names and other common Moroccan Arabic terms are often imprecise and occasionally sloppy. This is primarily because these transliterations were accomplished early in the colonial period—to a significant degree, even before the start of the protectorate in 1912. Transliterators were commonly military officers, commercial agents, geographers, and others without training in linguistics or a firm grasp of Arabic. Their purpose was to come up with a functional lexicon as rapidly as possible for the *oeuvre de pénétration*, not to erect a foundation for future scholarship. Unfortunately, early pragmatic transliterations quickly became fixed in popular usage, perpetuated even by later French scholars who knew better.

The problem for Moroccan specialists writing in English today is double-edged. First, readers of such works as mine who do not have a functional knowledge of French will not know, for example, that Ouaouizarht and Ouerrha should be pronounced respectively as Wāwizaght and Wargha. Second, Moroccan place names and terms in the conventional French transliteration scheme, even if given correct French pronunciation, will occasionally be significantly off the mark. For example, Ar-Ribāṭ is transliterated in French as Rabat, Ṭanja as Tanger, Marraksh as Marrakech, and Malwiyya as Moulouya.

Despite these problems, I have decided for two reasons to keep place-name transliterations in their conventional French renditions. First, the early French investigators primarily recorded and transliterated what they heard; therefore conventional French transliterations are usually fairly faithful to colloquial Moroccan pronunciations—probably closer overall than would be precise English transliterations of the classical Arabic place names found on maps of Morocco. The French *oued* for watercourse, for example, is very close to the spoken Moroccan term, much closer than the English transliteration *wadi* from the written Arabic. Second, standard French transliterations of

Moroccan place names have now been in general use for over seventy years. A consistent scheme of transliteration was used in the literature consulted for the present research and continues to be used by the Moroccan government and most Moroccan scholars today.[1] It might be quite appropriate to break with this tradition in some cases: for example, in an anthropological study of a local area, to transliterate Moroccan Arabic or the regional Berber dialect using a standard English-language system. However, for this countrywide historical study, which draws heavily on an existing corpus of French-language materials, it is probably best to adhere to tradition to forestall confusion.

The only exception to the general rule of conventional French transliterations for Moroccan place names is the use of the few customary English renditions that exist: for example, Fez instead of the French Fès. With regard to other Arabic terms, I have usually chosen to translate rather than transliterate. In the few exceptions to this strategy, I have used conventional English transliterations; for example, *ḥabūs* instead of the French *habous* for property belonging to a religious foundation. In these cases, I have accompanied transliterations with translations.

[1] A few slight variations persist; for example, one finds both Oued Beth and Oued Beht; Ouerrha, Ouergha, and Ouerrgha; Bine al Ouidane and Bin el Ouidane; and Gharb and Rharb.

Abbreviations

AF   *Afrique Française*: Bulletin du Comité de l'Afrique Française

AG   *Annales de Géographie*

BCAC   *Bulletin de la Chambre d'Agriculture de Casablanca*

BCAR   *Bulletin de la Chambre d'Agriculture de Rabat, du Gharb et d'Ouezzan* (slight periodic variations in title)

BESM   *Bulletin Economique et Social du Maroc* (called *Bulletin Economique du Maroc* until World War II)

BIM   *Bulletin d'Information du Maroc*

BO   *Bulletin Officiel* (Moroccan government publication containing promulgations of laws and decrees)

BONI   *Bulletin de l'Office National des Irrigations* (subtitled *Les Hommes, La Terre, L'Eau*)

CMR   *Cahiers de la Modernisation Rurale*

COM   *Cahiers d'Outre-Mer*

FPAN   *Fruits et Primeurs de l'Afrique du Nord* (slight periodic variations in title)

HTE   *Hommes, Terre et Eaux*

ITOM   *Industries et Travaux d'Outre-Mer*

LMA   *Le Maroc Agricole*

LQA   *La Question agraire au Maroc*, ed. N. Bouderbala et al. (Rabat: BESM, 1974)

LQA 2 *La Question agraire au Maroc*, vol. 2, ed. N. Bouderbala et al. (Rabat: BESM, 1977)

LTM   *La Terre Marocaine*

RC   *Renseignements Coloniaux* (supplement to *Afrique Française, Bulletin du Comité de l'Afrique Française*)

RGM   *Revue de Géographie du Maroc* (from 1963 to present, with hiatus from 1973 to 1977); *Revue de Géographie Marocaine* (from 1925 to 1949)

SAHM   "Spécificités de l'aménagement hydro-agricole au Maroc," unpublished report by the Comité National Marocain de la CIID (Rabat: INAV, 1979)

MOROCCAN MIRAGES
Agrarian Dreams and
Deceptions, 1912–1986

Introduction

This book examines the dreams and deceptions underlying agricultural development in Morocco. Focusing primarily on the policy-making process, it reconstructs the decision-making environments in which major policies were formulated, and explores the rationale behind policy. Its purpose is, first, to help elucidate policy making during the French protectorate period (1912–56) and analyze the continuing impact of colonial policies; second, to explain the failure of agricultural development efforts since independence—failure that is rapidly precipitating political and economic crisis.

Conventional wisdom on European colonization and national development processes in former colonies is a surprisingly rickety construction of premature conclusions. Far too few actual case studies have been conducted. Furthermore, generalizations have been drawn primarily from the British colonial realm. The former French empire has been relatively ignored, despite the fact that British and French colonialism were "as different as chalk from cheese."[1] Unfortunately, several dubious assumptions have evolved into truisms.

For example, it is commonly assumed that the European colonial powers were motivated primarily by hardheaded economic logic in the development of their colonies. As will be shown, this assumption is largely false for French development policies in Morocco. Indeed, to believe that French policy makers were shrewd businessmen completely misses what was perhaps the most striking feature of French colonialism in Africa: "the enormous disparity between the hopelessly unrealistic objectives of French policy-makers and the actual results of their policies."[2]

---

[1] R. E. Robinson, in H. Brunschwig, *French Colonialism, 1871–1914: Myths and Realities* (New York, 1966), p. vii.

[2] A. S. Kanya-Forstner, "French Expansion in Africa: The Mythical Theory," in *Studies in the Theory of Imperialism*, ed. R. Owen and B. Sutcliffe (London, 1972), p. 278. Kanya-Forstner claims that even "the supposedly phlegmatic and calculating British were prey to the same delusions as the French" (ibid., p. 292).

Second, European colonists are commonly considered to have functioned as a monolithic force—as a faceless army of agents implementing imperial schemes devised within Europe's capitals. This homogeneity assumption is not only fallacious with regard to Morocco, it is probably equally fallacious with regard to colonization elsewhere. In the case of Morocco, the interests and influence of France itself, of individual colonial administrators, of different settler groups, of various commercial firms, indeed, of the colonized Moroccans themselves, varied greatly over time. Policies reflected shifting balances of power. To fully understand colonial policies and their legacy in the post-colonial era, it is imperative that research account for the influence of key individuals and power groups, their intentions, and also the elements of time and chance.

Finally, it is commonly but unwisely assumed that there was somehow a clean break between the "before" of the colonial period and the "after" of independence. This is incorrect for Morocco, and is dubious elsewhere.[3] The present study demonstrates that agricultural development in Morocco today is essentially the implementation of obsolete colonial plans—the fulfillment of a colonial vision. A similar pattern may possibly be found in many other developing countries and could greatly help explain contemporary development problems.

Many puzzling questions are posed by the Moroccan case. For example, why, for nearly two decades, did the French administration in Morocco pursue a disastrous agricultural and colonization policy that was based on little more than myth or legend? Why, during the second half of the protectorate period, was official policy ostensibly more concerned to develop irrigation for dispossessed native Moroccans than for colonial farmers? And why, under the guise of national development, are colonial plans favoring large landowners being implemented today when they largely remained on the drafting table during the protectorate period?

The specific answers to these questions will have little relevance elsewhere: Each developing country has its own unique story. Yet in probing beneath the surface of conventional wisdom and challenging commonly held assumptions, this case study should help illuminate general processes that have occurred many other places in the developing world.

Moroccan Mirages focuses on perceptions as well as on actions; on internal processes of policy making as well as on the resulting external

[3] J. L. Miège, "The Colonial Past in the Present," in *Decolonization and After: The British and French Experience*, ed. W. H. Morris-Jones and G. Fisher (London, 1980), pp. 35–49.

forms; and on specific individuals as architects of development as well as on the landscapes actually developed. It views Morocco's agrarian landscapes as the artifacts of past policy decisions. Explanation for these landscapes is sought in the perceptions of the policy makers via reconstruction of the decision-making environments in which policies were formulated.

The main body of the study is divided into three parts, each with two chapters. Part I, covering the 1912–32 period, explores the powerful influence on colonial policy of the "granary of Rome" legend, then examines early efforts to exploit Morocco's water resources. Part II, focusing on the 1930s, examines the major role of the "California image" in reorienting Morocco's export agriculture towards its present form, then analyzes the origins of the "million hectare" irrigation plan. Part III first examines the genesis, during the 1940–56 period, of the basic patterns that characterize present-day agricultural development in Morocco, then analyzes the contemporary fulfillment of the colonial million-hectare plan and its implications for the country.

Historical Prologue

France's North African empire was accidentally conceived following the 1830 invasion of Algeria. France, however, rapidly grew comfortable with the notion of a colony across the Mediterranean. It steadily annexed more and more of the Algerian hinterland. Before long, covetous glances were directed towards neighboring Ottoman Tunisia and the independent kingdom of Morocco. The dream of a French Afrique du Nord was gradually forming.

By 1850, the fledgling Algerian colony was already viewed as "the cradle of an immeasurable future. . . . By unanimous accord, North Africa is the most fertile region in the world. . . . A vast colony at our door offers rich land, a fatherland, for all who have not a stone upon which to rest their head."[4] Morocco during this same period was perceived as a mysterious barbarian stronghold, as the "African China," a land insulated from the world's progress by high mountain barriers and inaccessible shorelines, once rich but now fallen into decay.[5] Colo-

---

[4] P. Christian, *L'Afrique française* (Paris, 1846), p. 315. The belief that Africa would provide an outlet for the proletariat would later characterize Italian colonization in Libya. See C. G. Segrè, *Fourth Shore: The Italian Colonization of Libya* (Chicago, 1974).

[5] E. Reclus, *North-West Africa*, vol. 11 of *The Earth and Its Inhabitants* (New York, 1887), p. 408. A common theme of the period was that Morocco's deteriorated condition was due to despotic mismanagement: "In few other countries are the inhabitants more enslaved. . . . [However] most of the inland Berber tribes have been able to maintain their independence, while in the seaports the Sultan's officials are held in check by

nial propaganda held that "the conquest of Morocco will be, sooner or later, the inevitable corollary of our occupation of Algeria."[6]

In fact, however, l'Afrique française was slow to develop beyond the Algerian frontier. Following a humiliating defeat in the Franco-Prussian war of 1870–71, France became politically introspective. When its prime minister, Jules Ferry, thrust it further down the colonial path with the taking of Tunisia in 1881 and Tonkin in 1884, public outrage led to his downfall. Only a small elite in organizations such as the Société de Géographie de Paris, the Alliance Française, and the Société de Géographie Commerciale actively championed the colonial cause.[7]

A notable shift in public opinion occurred in 1889, however. The colonial exposition in Paris that year generated widespread interest. French pride and patriotism, smarting since the 1870–71 war, sensed a healthy outlet in colonialism. Suddenly, the colonial passion that had been carefully nurtured in certain quarters "burst forth like a spring that had long been compressed."[8]

Within little more than a decade, at least two dozen different colonial interest groups had been founded.[9] Each had its proclaimed region of interest, each its own organ of propaganda. Among the most effective and influential was the Comité de l'Afrique Française. Founded in 1890, its stated objectives were: to organize exploratory missions in those parts of Africa already submitted or capable of being submitted to French influence; to encourage scientific research relative to those regions, particularly research that would subsequently facilitate private commercial ventures; and to keep its members abreast of events in Africa, particularly those concerning France's European competitors.[10] The Comité was most frank in its purpose: "We are witnessing a spectacle unique in history: the actual dividing up of a hardly known continent by a handful of civilized European nations. In this partition, France has the right to the largest portion."[11]

Morocco, however, constituted a particularly difficult colonial problem for France. Not only had Morocco long been resistant to foreign

---

the European consuls. Thus is explained the fact that the Government, although at times aided by drought, locusts, and cholera, has hitherto failed to transform the country to a desert" (ibid.).

[6] Christian, *L'Afrique française*, p. 271.

[7] A. Girault, *Principes de colonisation et de législation coloniale: les colonies françaises avant et depuis 1815* (Paris, 1943), p. 132.

[8] Ibid., p. 133.

[9] See ibid., pp. 133–135, for a complete list.

[10] *AF* 1 (1891): 2.

[11] Ibid., p. 1. Jules Ferry described European imperialism during this period as "an immense steeplechase toward the unknown." Cited in R. Betts, *Tricouleur: The French Overseas Empire* (London, 1978), p. 19.

influence, but many other countries shared France's interest. France was patient. The deftness with which it plotted to acquire Morocco and successfully executed its campaign on financial, political, military, and diplomatic fronts has been well described by several authors.[12]

France's occupation of the Touat oasis in 1900 forced the "Moroccan question" upon the international community. Behind the scenes, French diplomats rapidly contrived to find a solution. In 1901, France signed a secret accord with Italy agreeing to let Italy pursue colonial designs upon Libya in exchange for the same courtesy in Morocco. In 1904, France and Great Britain signed an *entente cordiale*; in its secret provisions, France renounced all claims to Egypt in return for a free hand in Morocco. Another secret pact with Spain in 1904 gave each country free rein within agreed-upon spheres of influence. Finally, the 1906 Algeciras agreement tacitly gave France and Spain approval to partition Morocco. In sum, these accords provided the major answers to the Moroccan question. Germany, the remaining serious contender and potential spoiler, was bought off with a large chunk of French colonial territory in Central Africa. Thus, the Moroccan question became answered in France's favor. The remaining tasks were to prepare the French public and to gather the necessary intelligence for a colonial takeover.

To help accomplish these tasks, the Comité de l'Afrique Française founded a subcommittee in 1904: the Comité du Maroc. In a widely circulated advertisement for membership, the Comité du Maroc openly described its objectives:

> For some time, France's attention has been riveted on Morocco, and rightly so, because the most important task outside our borders at the present hour is assuredly the penetration of Algeria's neighbor. . . . Morocco is, indeed, the land in Barbary that possesses the greatest expanse of fertile land and that receives the most rain. . . . It appears, moreover, more rich in minerals than the other two countries to the east. Unfortunately, this magnificent land . . . is not only unfamiliar to the French public, but is too little known in and of itself. This is the double deficiency that the Comité has resolved to remedy.[13]

The Comité du Maroc was not alone in its endeavor. Competing organizations with similar objectives were established in both France and Algeria. Altogether, they were quite effective. Their reconnais-

---

[12] See, for example, Edmund Burke, III, *Prelude to Protectorate in Morocco: Precolonial Protest and Resistance, 1860–1912* (Chicago, 1976).

[13] From a flyer advertising the Comité du Maroc found in *AF*, 1904.

sance missions to Morocco generated information highly useful in swaying public opinion and assisting the French government in its *oeuvre de pénétration*. On 30 March 1912, Morocco officially became a French protectorate.

The Geographical Setting

Morocco is distinguished among the countries of North Africa by the magnitude of its mountains, the extensiveness of its arable coastal lowlands, and its full exposure to the Atlantic Ocean (Fig. 1). All three geographic features have major significance for agricultural development.[14]

The high, rugged Atlas Mountains, composed of three roughly parallel ranges, extend for more than five hundred miles through the central and eastern portions of the country from south of Agadir to the northeastern border with Algeria. In the hinterland of Fez, the Middle Atlas converges upon the Rif Range, which flanks the Mediterranean. A sizable portion of the Middle and Anti-Atlas exceeds two thousand meters in elevation, and some High Atlas peaks exceed four thousand meters. Morocco's mountains give the country three major environmental zones: the comparatively well-watered coastal lowlands, the mountain highlands, and the eastern deserts.

The Rif and Atlas ranges capture orographic precipitation from moisture-laden storms arriving from the Atlantic and create a significant rain shadow to the east of the mountains. In the western coastal lowlands and mountain highlands, Mediterranean conditions normally predominate. Rainfall is concentrated in the cool months, from October to May, and summers are dry. East of the mountain barrier, desert conditions prevail throughout the year. Generally, precipitation decreases from north to south and from west to east. For example, while the central Rif peaks receive more than 2,000 millimeters of precipitation most years, the High Atlas peaks receive just 800 millimeters. The Gharb Plain normally receives 500–700 millimeters, the Souss Plain about 200 millimeters, and the Middle Draa basin east of the High Atlas only about 25 millimeters.

However, Morocco is located along the southern margin of northern midlatitude frontal storms. Consequently, there are strong irregu-

[14] The sources for this section are D. Noin, "Morocco," in the *World Atlas of Agriculture*, vol. 4; *Africa* (Novara, 1976): 377–387; and J. Martin et al., *Géographie du Maroc* (Paris, 1967). The map of the study area depicts most of Morocco's undisputed national territory; it does not include the still-disputed Western Sahara shown on the inset map of Africa.

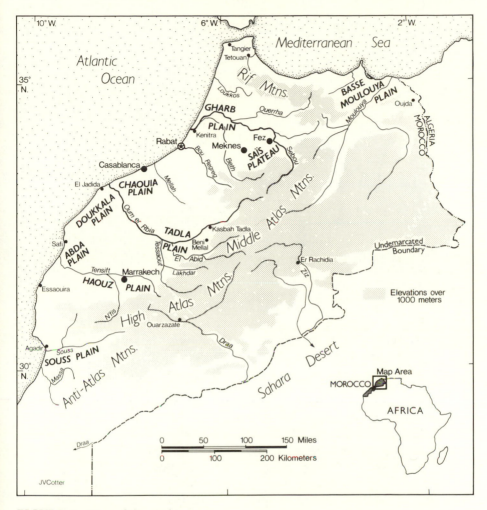

FIGURE 1   Map of the study area

larities in the amount and timing of its precipitation. Droughts are not uncommon in the western coastal lowlands, particularly south of the 400-millimeter isohyet that roughly coincides with the course of the Oum er Rbia River.[15] In fact, agriculture based on rainfall alone is precarious in most regions of Morocco. Fig. 2 demonstrates the enor-

[15] Drought, defined using cereal production figures, has struck Morocco during the following periods covered in this study: 1913, 1919–22, 1926–27, 1930, 1935–38, 1944–45, 1950, 1957, 1959, 1961, 1966, 1973, 1977, 1981, and 1983–84. For a study of drought in pre-1900 Morocco, see C. Bois, "Années de disette, années d'a-

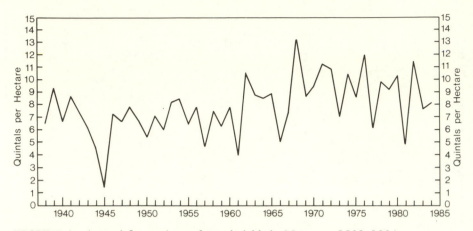

FIGURE 2   Annual fluctuations of cereal yields in Morocco, 1938–1984
SOURCE: A. M. Jouve, "Démographie et céréaliculture," *RGM* 4 (1980): 7; *FAO Monthly Bulletin of Statistics*, 1980–85.

mous variability in annual cereal production that has traditionally plagued Morocco and is a direct consequence of irregularities in precipitation. The figure also documents the overall low cereal yields, even in good years. For the period 1974–84, for example, Morocco's average combined yield for its two principal cereals, barley and wheat, amounted to only 9.2 quintals per hectare.[16] This compares very unfavorably with 55.1 quintals/hectare for the Netherlands during the same period, 44.0 quintals/hectare for France, 18.1 quintals/hectare for Turkey, and 19.3 quintals/hectare for the world as a whole.[17]

Morocco's streams have an obvious potential to help adjust for deficiencies in precipitation through providing water for irrigation. The country is better endowed with water resources than all of its North African neighbors except Egypt. It has numerous perennial watercourses, most of which rise on the western mountain slopes and flow into the Atlantic. Watercourses east of the mountains flowing into the

---

bondance: sécheresses et pluies au Maroc," *Revue pour l'Etude de Calamités* 11–16, nos. 26–35 (1948–57): 33–71. For a more general study of drought in Morocco, with focus on the modern period, see T.M.L. Wigley and S. E. Nicholson, "Drought in Morocco," an unpublished report to the Conseil Supérieur de l'Eau, Morocco (May 1984).

[16] *FAO Monthly Bulletin of Statistics*, 1980–85. Of the roughly 4.5 million hectares annually planted in cereals in Morocco, barley occupies some 2.1 million hectares, wheat some 1.8 million hectares, and maize most of the rest. Hard wheat (durum) from which *cūscūs* is usually made, accounts for approximately 75 percent of the wheat area; soft or bread wheat for the remainder.

[17] Ibid.

Sahara are rare, and the Moulouya is the only major Moroccan stream flowing into the Mediterranean.

However, Morocco's streams are characterized by a marked irregularity that historically limited their utility. For example, while the Sebou had an average flow of some 137 cubic meters per second, its flow during winter floods sometimes exceeded 10,000 cubic meters per second, and during summer dropped to as low as 3 cubic meters per second. Before the arrival of the French at the beginning of this century, the technology to build major storage dams was lacking, and most of the country's surface water was lost to the sea. Summer irrigation in the coastal lowlands was greatly limited both by low streamflow and the rudimentary nature of water diversion technology.[18]

In Morocco's mountain highlands and eastern deserts, agriculture continues today much as it has traditionally.[19] These zones have experienced comparatively little agricultural development; as a result, they lie outside the focus of this study.

The study instead focuses on the coastal lowlands. Modern irrigation and agricultural development in Morocco have taken place almost exclusively in the broad plains and plateaus that border the northern Atlantic and Mediterranean coasts: the Gharb, Chaouia, Saïs, Abda, Doukkala, Haouz, Souss, and Basse Moulouya. Most of Morocco's good soils, level land, and water resources are located in this zone, as are almost all of its urban centers, two-thirds of its agricultural population, and virtually all of its modern commercial agriculture. Most of this zone was the *bilād al-makhzan*, or territory controlled by the central government in preprotectorate times. It was this land that powerfully attracted the French at the turn of the century. They called it "Maroc utile." This was the Morocco they profoundly changed through policies that will be examined in this study, policies that have continued to the present.

---

[18] Qanats, locally called *rhettara*s, were of importance for irrigation in the Marrakech area and in certain oases east of the Atlas Mountains.

[19] See J. A. Miller, *Imlil: A Moroccan Mountain Community in Change* (Boulder, 1984), for an account of the traditional agrarian economy of a High Atlas settlement; and A. Hammoudi, "Substance and Relation: Water Rights and Water Distribution in the Drā Valley," in *Property, Social Structure and Law in the Modern Middle East*, ed. A. E. Mayer (Albany, N.Y., 1985), for insights into the traditional *genre de vie* in Morocco's desert oases.

PART 1

1912–1932

1

In Search of
the Granary of Rome

Acquiring a colony and making a colonial venture profitable are two quite different affairs. Throughout the French protectorate period in Morocco (1912–56), there was a continuous gap between colonial aspirations and actual accomplishments. Later, political and economic factors would be the primary cause. During the first two decades, however, this gap was caused by colonial idealism and ignorance of Morocco's environmental realities. French colonization in Morocco and the protectorate's first agricultural policy were based on legend rather than on solid economic logic. This chapter analyzes France's "wheat policy" in Morocco—the manifestation of a misguided colonial vision. Its purpose is both to help explain French policies in Morocco and to paint the backdrop to modern irrigation development in the country.

Early Economic Appraisal

It is striking how little the French knew about Morocco as late as 1900 when they initiated a series of actions that would lead to the protectorate. Mouliéras, a leading figure in the Société de Géographie et Archéologie d'Oran, probably knew the country as well as any European at the turn of the century. He had periodically explored Morocco from 1872 to 1893. He was able to claim, in *Le Maroc inconnu*, that though Morocco's coastlines had been reasonably well charted, its interior had remained enshrouded in mystery "since the world began" and was an "almost completely unknown land."[1] Ignorance of Algeria's neighbor was viewed as an embarrassing anomaly by French colonialists. It was considered paradoxical that France should have reached remote Timbuktu before it had reached Fez.[2]

In 1900, however, the French government and various colonial interest groups initiated a lively series of study missions to Morocco. Missions sponsored by the Ministry of Commerce, the Comité de l'Afrique Française, the Comité du Maroc, the Société de Géographie de Paris, and others rapidly sketched in a preliminary picture of Moroccan society and its environment. The reports generated had decidedly propagandist overtones. However, they become the foundation upon which both colonial penetration and early protectorate policies were based. By 1907, after the French military had occupied Casablanca and the Chaouia, it was proclaimed that the age of Moroccan exploration was over, that the essential characteristics of *le Maroc utile* were known. What remained to be accomplished was only a methodical inventory.[3]

It rapidly became accepted that "if Morocco is not the Eldorado . . . it is at least the most favored part of North Africa."[4] The extensive Atlantic coastal plains were claimed to be among the richest in the world.[5] Moreover, they were relatively sparsely populated and offered a promising field for French settlement. Finally, Morocco had superlative water resources compared to the rest of Maghreb. Its rainfall appeared to guarantee a prosperous colonial agriculture. And Morocco had real rivers and streams, not just the disappointing, often dry wadis of Algeria and Tunisia.

By 1912, with the start of the French protectorate, Vaffier-Pollet's prediction was common wisdom: "The true fortune of Morocco resides in its agriculture. Through export of the fruit of its soil, Morocco will become rich."[6] There was discouragement in some quarters that Morocco was apparently poorly endowed with mineral resources: Rich coal deposits had been expected. However, the agricultural potential, for most commentators, more than made up for deficiencies in minerals.

[1] A. Mouliéras, *Le Maroc inconnu*, vol. 1: *Exploration du Rif* (Paris, 1895), pp. 17, 3. Mouliéras himself estimated Morocco's population at "at least" 25 million—a level it has only reached after nearly a century of rapid growth (ibid., p. 27).

[2] A. Terrier, *Le Maroc* (Paris, 1931), p. 5.

[3] Dr. Weisgerber, "Les Chaouia," *RC*, 1907, p. 209; "Contribution à l'histoire de la cartographie marocaine," *RGM* 7, no. 1 (1928): 6. See also L. Gentil, "Evolution des connaissances scientifiques sur le Maghreb," *Le Maroc physique* (Paris, 1912), pp. 9–34.

[4] *AF*, 1902, p. 204.

[5] A. Cousin and D. Saurin, *Le Maroc* (Paris, 1905), p. 247.

[6] E. Vaffier-Pollet, "L'Agriculture et l'élevage au Maroc," *RC*, 1906, p. 206.

Morocco appeared to have been predestined for the cultivation of cereals. This perception was encouraged by several factors. First, it was believed that cereal grains had been the specialty of Moroccan agriculture "since the greatest antiquity."[7] Second, barley and hard wheat were the predominant crops in existing native agriculture (Illus. 2). Finally, the black alluvial soils in the Atlantic plains, locally called *tirs*, were believed to correspond to the chernozem soils that had made the Ukraine a major grain-producing region. One geographer, speaking before the Parisian Société de Géographie Commerciale in 1916, confidently predicted that "these rich soils . . . called *tirs* . . . should make Morocco one of the most productive grain-producing regions in the world."[8] (Only later was it discovered that *tirs* soils owed their dark color to iron content rather than to organic matter.)[9]

Besides being "inscribed in the land," cereal crops were also admirably suited to the purposes of colonization. They required a relatively modest capital investment and offered an immediate return—important considerations, since settlers would need to invest large sums in constructing houses and barns, drilling wells, and purchasing farm equipment.

Further, cereal cultivation was entirely harmonious with Lyautey's philosophy of colonization. Lyautey, French Morocco's influential first resident general, had a thinly disguised aristocratic distaste for the "little settler" who had colonized Algeria. He preferred settlers of means. Indeed, there is clear evidence that his ideal for Morocco was a landed gentry.[10] In addition, he had an idealistic resolve to honor the letter and spirit of the protectorate accord. For rural Morocco, this meant there should be none of the wholesale dispossession of native farmers that had characterized French settlement in Algeria—which Lyautey, moreover, considered politically short-sighted.[11] He wanted a circumscribed number of settlers but a strong French presence in the countryside. He was able to accommodate these goals through a colonization policy oriented towards wheat farming on large landholdings.

[7] E. A. de Mazières, *La Culture des céréales dans l'Afrique du Nord* (Casablanca, 1926), p. 3.

[8] M. J. Fourgous, *L'Avenir économique du Maroc* (Paris, 1916), p. 10.

[9] R. Dumont, *Types of Rural Economy* (London, 1957), p. 165. Morocco's *tirs* soils are technically vertisols with an average organic content of about 6 percent.

[10] For example, an official publication of the Résidence Générale to commemorate the tenth anniversary of the protectorate noted, "En somme, la définition du colon idéal est assez exactement fournie par l'expression anglaise de 'gentleman-farmer' " (Résidence Générale de la République Française au Maroc, *La Renaissance du Maroc—dix ans de protectorat, 1912–1922* [Poitiers, 1922], p. 292).

[11] Gen. Catroux, *Lyautey le Marocain* (Paris, 1952), p. 289.

Finally, France suffered from an acute shortage of wheat during World
War I. To French authorities, it seemed natural that Moroccan agriculture should help remedy the mother country's deficit.[12]

The Origin of the Wheat Policy

Official memorandums of the 1915–17 period testify to the protectorate administration's efforts to increase Morocco's cereal production.[13]
Government land was leased for wheat raising, and the Direction de
l'Agriculture provided settlers with loans of soft-wheat seeds.[14] Additionally, throughout this early period of the protectorate, the new network of roads and *pistes* established by the French engineer corps con-
formed to an economic as well as a military strategy. It was designed
to permit delivery of seeds, fertilizer, and agricultural equipment to
settlers as well as to facilitate collection of the harvests. The French
military was the major purchaser of the grain produced.[15]

The "wheat policy" per se began to be formulated in Paris in 1915.
That year, a Comité Consultatif pour le Ravitaillement de la Population Civile was established by the French Minister of Commerce to
develop plans for increasing food production for France. Henri Cosnier, a member of parliament and an agronomist, was the committee
member charged with responsibility for grain production.

In 1916, after several French grain ships had been sunk by torpe-
does, precipitating a food crisis, Cosnier advocated the immediate
planting of cereals "in North Africa in particular, and especially in
Morocco where . . . it appears possible to put into cultivation considerable expanses of land."[16] Several days later, he was appointed head

[12] See, for example, M. Calary de la Mazière, "La Conquête agricole du Maroc,"
Revue de Paris 15 (1923): 688: "The great resource of Morocco is precisely that for
which the metropole has the greatest need, that which will deliver it from its painful
obsession with foreign credits: wheat."

[13] J. Gadille, "L'Agriculture européenne au Maroc—étude humaine et économique,"
AG 66 (1957): 144.

[14] By 1917, this assistance amounted to 10,000 quintals of soft wheat. H. Cosnier,
L'Afrique du Nord—son avenir agricole et économique (Paris, 1922), p. 152. One quintal
equals 220.46 pounds. Soft wheat, also called bread wheat, was not previously cultivated
in Morocco. The French at first imported seeds from Algeria. Soft wheat was favored
by settlers because it received higher market prices than hard (durum) wheat and because it was accorded larger subsidies.

[15] Gadille, "L'Agriculture européenne," p. 145.

[16] Cosnier, *L'Afrique du Nord*, p. xiv. According to Cosnier, military intelligence revealed that important reserves of wheat were being stored in native granaries. This
wheat could be procured by the military—of course at a fair price. It would be interest-

of a study mission to Morocco. The mission's primary purpose was to develop a strategy for increasing Moroccan cereal production for the metropole.[17] Mission members spent three months (April, May, and June 1917) in Morocco. Following their return, Cosnier was appointed Commissaire Générale à l'Agriculture pour l'Afrique du Nord et les Colonies Françaises. He was thus in a position to actualize his mission's recommendations.

Though, as will be seen, there were countervailing views regarding Morocco's development, the recommendations of the Mission Cosnier had an immediate and profound effect. Indeed, they became the blueprint for French Morocco's first agricultural and colonization policy. This policy, the "wheat policy," predominated until the agricultural crisis of the early 1930s. Its impact has remained to the present.

To increase Morocco's cereal production, the Cosnier mission advocated:

1. Wheat production on "new lands" through colonization
2. A higher price for cereal crops
3. Agricultural subsidies and bonuses
4. Agricultural mechanization

All of these recommendations were adopted by the protectorate administration.[18]

With regard to colonization per se, the Cosnier mission advocated large holding sizes. It specifically recommended 400-hectare farms. Large holdings would facilitate mechanization for most efficient wheat production. Furthermore, Morocco could settle immigrants from the war-ravaged grain belt of northern France, who would bring with them "mechanized methods that have succeeded so well" in the mother country.[19]

The mission's advice regarding colonization policy was also followed. An official colonization program was established in 1917 (see Table 1). The program was active until 1931; after 1931, little additional government-sponsored colonization took place.[20] From 1917 to

---

ing to investigate the degree to which protectorate authorities helped to bring about the demise of native granaries, or *agadirs*.

[17] H. Cosnier, "Intensification de la production agricole au Maroc en vue de sa contribution au ravitaillement de la France," unpublished report, 1917, p. 1.

[18] Cosnier, *L'Afrique du Nord*, p. xxxi.

[19] Ibid.

[20] From 1932 until the end of the protectorate in 1956, only about 20,000 additional hectares were distributed by the government, and nearly all of this land went to existing rather than new settlers. See J. Gadille, "La Colonisation officielle au Maroc," *COM* 8 (1955): 322. The government sold official settlers land through obligatory ten- to fif-

TABLE 1   Official Colonization in Morocco, 1917–1931

Years	No. settlers	Total area (hectares)
1917–18	48	7,607
1919	165	12,119
1920	48	10,810
1921	73	17,480
1922	48	9,400
1923	82	14,923
1924	172	22,674
1925	54	27,994
1926	271	34,866
1927	147	30,331
1928	154	17,880
1929	165	11,478
1930	125	22,924
1931	31	4,900
TOTAL	1,583	245,386

SOURCES: Hoffherr, *L'Economie marocaine*, p. 129; Gadille, "La Colonisation officielle du Maroc," p. 315; Faust, *La Colonisation rurale*, p. 45.

1931, the protectorate government settled roughly 1,600 settlers on 250,000 hectares, mainly in the Fez-Meknes, Chaouia, Marrakech, and Gharb regions. As these figures show, the program placed major emphasis on large holdings. Indeed, 97 percent of the land distributed was in holdings larger than 150 hectares; the typical holding was about 250 hectares.[21] The fact that this falls short of the 400 hectares recommended by Cosnier was mainly due to a shortage of available land. Simultaneously, during the same period, an estimated 550,000 hectares were privately settled by some 1,500 Europeans, mostly French.[22] Private colonization was concentrated in the Basse Mou-

teen-year contracts, without interest, at "fair market" prices. Official settlers had to develop this land under the tutelage of government advisors, at their own expense, according to a plan approved by the Comité de Colonisation. By contrast, private settlers purchased their land direct from private Moroccan citizens and could develop their land as they pleased. Both official and private settlers were assisted by the protectorate government through credit facilities; technical advice; agricultural price supports; various bonuses for mechanization, clearing land, planting trees, etc.; and in many other ways.

[21] R. Hoffherr, *L'Economie marocaine* (Paris, 1932), p. 129.

[22] Ibid., pp. 128–129; M. Faust, *La Colonisation rurale au Maroc, 1919–1929* (Algiers, 1931), pp. 44–45.

louya, Gharb, and Chaouia regions. Private settler farms averaged 367 hectares in size—close to the Cosnier ideal.[23]

The Cosnier strategy to convert Morocco into a breadbasket for France dovetailed with a postwar master plan for the development of the French overseas empire. Albert Sarraut, then Minister of Colonies, was the architect of this plan. A central feature of the Plan Sarraut was its conception of a vast division of labor: Each colony should specialize in the production of certain primary materials for the metropole. Thus, for example, Madagascar would produce meat and minerals; the Antilles, sugar and coffee; Indochina, cotton, rubber, and silk; and Equatorial Africa, oil crops and wood.

Owing to the idiosyncrasies of French administrative history, North Africa fell outside the purview of Sarraut's ministry. It was consequently not a part of his specific plan. However, in a speech before the Chamber of Deputies on 12 April 1921, Sarraut emphasized the unhealthy French trade situation with regard to cereals. Of 32 million quintals of grain imported in 1919, only 7 million were produced by France's colonies. As a result, France was losing over 2 billion francs a year. The situation was disastrous; North Africa must develop the remedy.[24] In precisely this way, the Cosnier plan dovetailed with the Plan Sarraut.

While the Cosnier mission presented the blueprint, the details of Morocco's wheat policy were provided by the protectorate administration, charged with its implementation. Major emphasis was placed on *primes*, or the subsidies and bonuses that Cosnier had advocated. The following elaborate system resulted:

1. A special prime of 3 francs for every quintal of soft wheat
2. Primes of 18.5 francs per quintal for soft and hard wheat and 13.5 francs for barley, maize, and sorghum, on condition that these be grown in fields worked by a European steel plow and that the harvest be sold for export to the metropole

[23] The 400-hectare ideal was, in fact, closely matched by reality during the Lyautey period (up to October 1925). In 1924, for example, there were 1,274 settlers, both official and private, on approximately 500,000 hectares, giving an average holding size of 392 hectares. See A. Scham, *Lyautey in Morocco: Protectorate Administration, 1912–1925* (Berkeley and Los Angeles, 1970), p. 137. Besides an increasing shortage of land for colonization, the Steeg administration's (October 1925–January 1929) increased pace of official colonization was a factor resulting in progressively smaller average colonial landholdings.

[24] *Journal Officiel*, Chambre des Députés, Documents Parlementaires (1921), p. 1595.

3. A prime of up to 200 francs per hectare for clearing new land (the exact amount varied according to the density of the dwarf palm or other natural vegetation to be cleared)
4. A prime of 25 francs for each hectare worked with mechanical devices (to allow both for the high cost of gasoline to pull these devices and the expense of repairs due to the shortage of experienced mechanics)
5. A special prime of 50 francs per hectare put into cultivation by tractor beyond the total area that could be cultivated without a tractor.[25]

Clearly, these primes were designed to encourage mechanized cereal production for the metropole and at the same time implant European wheat farmers. The protectorate administration's credit facilities and considerable propaganda efforts also served to implement the wheat policy.

The Wheat Policy in Action

The protectorate administration's efforts succeeded spectacularly—if measured by expansion of acreage in cereal crops. The area planted in cereals increased from approximately 1.9 million hectares in 1918 to nearly 3 million in 1929, an increase of 60 percent.[26] There was a close correlation between the expansion of colonization and the expansion of wheat areas planted by Europeans. Particularly impressive was the spread of soft wheat, a crop new to Morocco. European soft-wheat acreage in Morocco increased from virtually zero in 1912 to 138,090 hectares in 1932.[27] This growth was closely paralleled by the extension of soft-wheat cultivation by native farmers, stimulated by soft wheat's high market price.[28]

The dramatic increase in wheat acreage was proudly touted as a beneficent effect of the French protectorate, as the restoration of an ancient land after centuries of Arab neglect. It was regarded as proof

[25] Cosnier, L'Afrique du Nord, pp. 152–153.
[26] Hoffherr, L'Economie marocaine, p. 145.
[27] BESM 1 (1933): 67.
[28] Beginning in 1923, soft-wheat cultivation by Moroccans matched that by European settlers (see ibid.). One of the significant changes in traditional Moroccan agriculture as a result of the protectorate was the extension of wheat acreages at the expense of barley. With the agricultural methods of the time, the critical rainfall limits for wheat cultivation in Morocco were some 360–400 mm; for barley, they were some 230–300 mm. Thus, an unfortunate result of the wheat policy was an increase in the vulnerability of Moroccan agriculture to deficiencies in precipitation, and an increased chance for poor harvests.

of Morocco's *mise en valeur*, or development. In reality, however, there were steadily increasing danger signs.

Morocco is on the margins of the good earth in terms of wheat cultivation for export. Nearly all of its cereal cultivation (then, as now) is by rainfed or dry farming methods. In short, it is at the mercy of highly capricious fluctuations in precipitation. Climate was the principal reason that Moroccan wheat production could not compete on the world market. It was the primary cause of perennial low yields. In a poor year, such as 1930, soft-wheat production in Morocco averaged only 4.3 quintals per hectare. Even in a good year, such as 1931, it averaged only 9 quintals per hectare. By contrast, France's soft-wheat production during the period 1918–30 averaged 15 quintals per hectare.[29]

Low yields meant relatively high production costs and low net returns. This is because production costs are basically the same regardless of how the harvest turns out. In addition, there was the considerable expense of transport between Moroccan and French ports.[30] The net result, in one economist's estimation, was that in Morocco "The cultivation of cereals for export, particularly wheat, would long ago have been abandoned . . . without the metropole's protection."[31] During the 1920s, despite relatively low costs for land and labor, Moroccan wheat production costs were higher than world wheat prices. By the late 1920s, with a world glut of wheat and concomitant lowering of price, France was supporting wheat cultivation in Morocco with an artificially maintained price three times the world average.

France sustained colonial wheat production in Morocco through a tariff-free quota system and stiff trade barriers. The quota for wheat was established by the French law of 18 March 1923.[32] This law was intended to stimulate wheat production by guaranteeing a lucrative market. It became a vital element of French Morocco's wheat policy.

The law stated simply that each year a certain quota of Moroccan wheat would be admitted into France without tariff, the amount to be determined on the basis of the previous year's production figures. In

[29] M. Amphoux, "Le Maroc et la crise économique," *Revue d'Economie Politique* 47, no. 1 (1933): 118. In certain favored parts of the Gharb and Chaouia plains, however, yields were as high as 20 quintals per hectare in good years (ibid., p. 121).

[30] Six to 8 francs per quintal of wheat in 1923 (P. Garcin, *La Politique des contingents dans les relations franco-marocaines* [Paris, 1937], p. 54).

[31] M. Amphoux, "L'Evolution de l'agriculture européenne au Maroc," *AG* 42 (1933): 176.

[32] See Garcin, *La Politique*, for detailed information on this law and the history of Morocco's *contingents*, or quotas.

practice, this quota was so liberally calculated (at 800,000 quintals) that France absorbed all of Morocco's surplus production.[33]

Once inside France, Moroccan wheat profited from the formidable French trade barriers and commanded the same artificially high price as French wheat.[34] Even on wheat prices within Morocco itself, the 1923 law had a dramatic effect. Before 1923, wheat sold for considerably less in Morocco than in France; after the law (but before the agricultural crisis of the 1930s), the Moroccan price was only 6 to 8 francs less than the French price, the difference being essentially the freight charges to France.[35] In short, "Self-absorbed, indifferent to the problem of markets, Morocco abandoned itself to the collective exaltation of wheat."[36]

The Agricultural Crisis

The wheat policy reflected such a fixed colonial vision of Morocco that rarely, before 1929, was it asked if settlers should be engaged in a more economically viable endeavor. In 1929, however, an agricultural crisis began. In this year, there was a sizable surplus of wheat on international markets. France itself had the "harvest of the century."[37] French overproduction of wheat was estimated at 11 million quintals.[38] This same year, Morocco's wheat exports to France (1,127,000 quintals) for the first time exceeded the annual quota (800,000 quintals). Owing to the domestic glut, Moroccan wheat suddenly encountered hostility on the French grain market.

French producers, through their influential organizations, vociferously began to attack Morocco's wheat quota. Moroccan settler groups and the Moroccan lobby in France, however, were powerful enough to parry stratagems to abolish the quota. The French government organized a conference in Paris on 13–14 March 1929 to settle the conflict.

Arguing that the tariff-free quota was essential to sustain French colonization in Morocco, and dispelling fears that soft-wheat production would continue to grow, Morocco's delegates achieved a compro-

---

[33] After 1928, the law would be interpreted as a limitation rather than an encouragement to Moroccan wheat production.

[34] The French tariff on foreign wheat was 80 francs per quintal by the early 1930s. See Amphoux, "L'Evolution de l'agriculture," p. 176.

[35] C. F. Stewart, *The Economy of Morocco, 1912–1962* (Cambridge, Mass., 1964), pp. 88–89.

[36] Hoffherr, *L'Economie marocaine*, p. 144.

[37] Garcin, *La Politique*, p. 1.

[38] Ibid., p. 73.

mise. The Moroccan wheat quota, it was agreed, would be raised to 1,700,000 quintals. In exchange, however, Morocco would submit to reforms. It would space its exports of wheat so that the entire crop did not arrive at one time and depress the market. It would reduce impurities in its shipments to 1 percent. And to assure metropolitan farmers that France was admitting only the surplus Moroccan harvest and not cheap foreign wheat (also to protect its domestic market), the protectorate administration agreed to ban all imports of foreign wheat.[39] A decree to this effect was passed on 4 June 1929 in clear violation of the open-door provisions of the Algeciras accord.[40]

The higher wheat quotas, unfortunately, did not deliver the settler from the brink of disaster. The agricultural crisis in Morocco was only beginning. No sooner was the settler out of the frying pan through successful arbitration, than he was in the fire of a triple plague of drought, locusts, and the beginning of the world economic crisis.

By the middle of April 1930, trains were being delayed by drifting mounds of locusts, and a severe drought had begun a month earlier.[41] The locust invasion by itself devastated some 860,000 hectares of cropland.[42] Morocco's wheat exports to France in 1930 fell to one-third of their 1929 level.[43] Wheat exports, indeed, should have been prohibited altogether: In Morocco there was a critical shortage of grain for local consumption. The entire 1930 harvest of wheat was only about 85 percent of the amount consumed in Morocco the previous year. Famine was developing. Imports of sugar and tea—staples of the native Moroccan diet—fell sharply. Livestock perished on a massive scale. In all, the native Moroccan loss from locusts and drought was estimated at a half-billion francs.[44]

The protectorate administration implemented an extensive famine and agricultural relief program. Settlers were generally less affected than natives because European colonization was concentrated in the relatively better watered north, and was further from the source region of the locusts. The administration originally intended to aid only set-

[39] For the various other provisions, see ibid., pp. 75–77.

[40] An exception was made for the Spanish Zone of Morocco, which was allowed to export 52,000 quintals annually to French Morocco. However, this was a mere goodwill gesture, because the Spanish Zone was a net importer of wheat. France's justification was that it was necessary for "public order" and thus was sanctioned by a provision in the 1927 convention of the World Economic Conference (Stewart, *Economy of Morocco*, p. 89).

[41] M. M. Knight, *Morocco as a French Economic Venture* (New York, 1937), p. 83.

[42] *BCAR*, 1931, p. 31.

[43] 369,505 quintals in 1930, as against 1,127,000 quintals in 1929 (ibid., p. 143).

[44] Knight, *French Economic Venture*, p. 84.

tlers actually stricken by drought or locusts. Soon, however, it became clear that the agricultural crisis was much more pervasive and deeply entrenched than originally supposed. Merchants began clamoring about impending bankruptcy because settlers were not paying their bills, while settlers raised an aggrieved uproar about impending foreclosures. Both groups demanded that the administration come to their rescue. This was the start of the notorious "debt question" that troubled Morocco throughout the first half of the 1930s and eventually became a massive "feud between most of the Frenchmen in Morocco and the protectorate administration."[45] It was eventually resolved by the administration assuming all debts.[46]

Morocco's 1931 harvest again raised the agonizing question of quotas. Unmindful of its 1929 agreement not to flood the French market, Morocco shipped its entire quota within a short period. This was a grave error. France was just beginning to get rid of its own surplus wheat. There was a violent reaction when the 1931 Moroccan wheat harvest arrived at the French marketplace. One French agricultural organization, in a jammed meeting of 20,000 members, called for a complete ban on all imports of wheat into France.[47] In Algeria (now officially a French province), hard-wheat growers also agitated against Morocco's hard-wheat exports to France. Morocco's wheat quota for the first time was seriously jeopardized.

A final official conference was convened in Paris in February 1932. This time, Algerian settler representatives were also present. The conference was intended to resolve the Moroccan quota question conclusively. After long, often bitter negotiations, an accord was signed. It included the following key provisions:

1. Morocco's wheat quota was fixed through 1937 at 1,800,000 quintals per year (soft wheat not to exceed 1,650,000 quintals, hard wheat not to exceed 150,000 quintals)
2. This quota would be shipped in installments through the year according to a specified formula
3. Morocco would curtail all further expansion of wheat cultivation[48]

The accord was clearly designed to salvage colonial agriculture in Morocco. Though native Moroccan production of soft wheat now

[45] Ibid., p. 87.
[46] See G. Oved, "Contribution a l'étude de l'endettement de la colonisation agricole au Maroc," *Revue Française d'Histoire d'Outre-Mer* 63 (1976): 492–505, for an analysis of the debt question.
[47] *BCAR*, 1932, p. 144.
[48] Garcin, *La Politique*, pp. 83–86.

roughly equaled settler production, this sector would henceforth contribute less than 10 percent of the soft wheat sent to France. The wheat price in Morocco would fall to only half the French price.[49]

Morocco's wheat problem, however, did not disappear. Instead, it only grew more nightmarish. In 1932, there was a surplus of between 200,000 and 250,000 quintals of soft wheat that could neither be exported nor sold domestically.[50] Settler groups began to demand a ban on imports of secondary cereals (principally maize and rye), which were replacing the more expensive wheat in native Moroccan diets, hurting domestic wheat sales.[51] This was accomplished in 1933— again, in clear contravention of the Algeciras Treaty.[52] By 1933, the "excédent sans emploi" amounted to 950,000 quintals; there was now grave concern that growing stockpiles would cause the 1934 domestic wheat market to collapse completely.[53] World wheat prices were now far below wheat production costs in Morocco. In fact, world prices would fall to one-sixth of the French price.[54]

In the gloom of this hour, the president of the Casablanca Chambre d'Agriculture undertook a special mission to Paris. His purpose: "to attempt the impossible" in seeking an augmentation of the Moroccan wheat quota.[55] He encountered only hostility. Defeated, he reported back to Morocco that not an additional quintal of wheat could be admitted into France.[56]

It was now abundantly clear that the wheat policy was a failure. To summarize, it failed for two main reasons: (1) Morocco's generally marginal environment for wheat cultivation meant high production costs, periodic crop failures, and the perennial need for costly price supports; and (2) Moroccan colonial wheat production competed directly with French production because Moroccan wheat was too expensively produced to be sold on the world market and had to be absorbed by the metropole.

Official colonization in Morocco, which was intimately linked to the

---

[49] *BESM* 1 (1933): 67; Stewart, *Economy of Morocco*, p. 90. Quotas would henceforth be filled from the grain silos of the government-sponsored cooperatives, from which Moroccans were effectively excluded. For a time, protectorate authorities even considered prohibiting soft-wheat cultivation by native Moroccans (Garcin, *La Politique*, p. 193).

[50] *BCAC* 29 (1932): 13.

[51] Ibid.

[52] Stewart, *Economy of Morocco*, p. 89.

[53] *BESM* 2 (1933): 65.

[54] Knight, *French Economic Venture*, pp. 119–120.

[55] *BCAC* 36 (1933): 9.

[56] Ibid.

wheat policy, ground to a nearly complete halt in 1931. Despite the protectorate administration's rescue efforts, a great many European settlers were in desperate straits. Approximately one-fourth of all official settlers failed, some even before the 1930s agricultural crisis, most during it.[57] These failures can primarily be attributed to the poor wisdom of the wheat policy.[58]

The question thus arises: Why, despite steadily mounting evidence that the wheat policy was "economic heresy,"[59] did the protectorate administration continue to pursue this policy up to the moment of crisis? Further, how did the policy happen to become established in the first place? Both questions were bitterly posed by settlers during the early 1930s.

The following factors have been noted: (1) France's shortage of grain during World War I and the immediate postwar period; (2) the belief that cereal crops were ordained by nature as the agricultural specialty of the new protectorate; (3) the comparatively low investment demands and rapid returns of wheat cultivation, which made it particularly suitable for beginning settlers; (4) Lyautey's desire to avoid mass colonization, which suggested large landholdings for which wheat raising was appropriate; and (5) the highly influential recommendations of the Cosnier mission. Each of these factors played a definite role in the formulation of the wheat policy. They do not, however, explain why it was stubbornly maintained.

The "Granary of Rome" Factor

The wheat policy represented such a rigid French vision of rural Morocco, such an idée fixe, that some deeper animating force can be suspected. In this regard, the pervasive "granary of Rome" ideal seems to have considerable explanatory power. In the French mind of the period, Morocco was considered to have been part of the bountiful granary of ancient Rome. This image stemmed from rudimentary, if not fallacious, historical and geographical knowledge of Morocco. Beyond doubt, the image exerted a powerful influence on early protectorate policy. It was perhaps the major factor behind the formulation of the wheat policy.

French colonial literature of the period 1900–30 is suffused with the evidence for this interpretation. The image of France as the true

[57] Gadille, "L'Agriculture européenne," p. 151.
[58] R. Gallissot, "Le Maroc et la crise," *Revue Française d'Histoire d'Outre-Mer* 63 (1976): 485.
[59] Amphoux, "Le Maroc et la crise économique," p. 121.

heir of the Roman empire was widely promoted, and can be considered a key element of an important colonial faith. To simplify, according to this faith North Africa under the beneficent influence of Roman civilization was a peaceful, fertile, prosperous land. However, after the coming of the Arabs, all fell into anarchy and decay. As France was the torchbearer of Roman civilization, the reconquest of Roman Africa devolved upon her. France would restore these lands to their former peace and productivity, and they would again supply grain and other foodstuffs to the metropole as they had in Roman times.

Of course, this faith betrays an unconscious colonial rationale: It converts the base realities of colonialism into a work of loftier purpose. Thus, in the conversion process, colonial conquest becomes an irredentist issue of recapturing a former empire; and "restoring to former productivity" becomes the mask for colonial exploitation.[60]

This faith surfaces in outbursts of self-congratulatory gallic chauvinism in the colonial literature of the early protectorate period. The following passage is representative.

> Following the prosperous days of the Roman era, Algeria, Tunisia and Morocco . . . vegetated, barely surviving, cultivating piracy . . . One by one, the former riches disappeared . . . all fell into ruin. Of the splendid golden age of Roman Mauretania only a sun-baked rocky desert remained, where the beneficent river had become a devastating torrent, where agriculture had atrophied, where livestock subsisted or perished according to the vagaries of rainfall, and where the native sought to secure by force or ruse what his neighbor had produced instead of producing himself.
>
> Suddenly, a new breeze; and France . . . combating as little as possible, arrived to conquer so that Roman civilization could be saved.[61]

[60] A very similar version of this colonial faith animated Italian colonization in Libya. See C. G. Segrè, *Fourth Shore: The Italian Colonization of Libya* (Chicago, 1974). This faith also shares many characteristics with the "Moroccan Vulgate" that Edmund Burke, III identified as the image of the Moroccan state shaping early protectorate "Berber policy." Both were rigidly stereotyped visions of Morocco, both were based on rudimentary data, both were employed to serve specific colonial ends, and both led to crises around 1930. Edmund Burke, III, "The Image of the Moroccan State in French Ethnological Literature: A New Look at the Origin of Lyautey's Berber Policy," in E. Gellner and C. Micaud, eds., *Arabs and Berbers* (Lexington, Mass., 1972), pp. 175–199.

[61] J. Germain and S. Faye, *Le Nouveau Monde français—Maroc, Algérie, Tunisie* (Paris, 1924), pp. II–III. Other representative specimens are in A. Fribourg, *L'Afrique latine—Maroc, Algérie, Tunisie* (Paris, 1922), pp. 14-17; J. Célérier, "La Ruine de la civilisation

Often, tenets of this colonial faith assume a quaintly humorous form. Jean Colin, for example, addressing a group of Native Affairs officers in Morocco in 1925, urged them to let the *indigènes* know, "We Romans were here before the Arabs."[62] Archeology was employed to support this claim. Excavations and restorations were intended to reveal the former splendor of Roman civilization in Morocco. (Important Arab sites, on the other hand, were virtually ignored by French archeologists.) Illus. 1 portrays the Roman ruins at Volubilis, excavated during World War I with the help of German prisoners of war.

Morocco, as the "granary of Rome," was the key environmental component of the faith. Indeed, this environmental ideal was applied to all of French North Africa. As early as 1896, when the Moroccan protectorate was still only a gleam in the French colonial eye, one authority was berating Algerian settlers for being hypnotized by the granary-of-Rome legend. This pernicious legend, he argued, was based on nothing more than a few tenuous citations from the classical period; it was preventing settlers from discovering Algeria's true agricultural vocation.[63]

A probe into the myth of Morocco as a Roman breadbasket confirms that it was based on little more than hearsay. One finds only a few classical references such as Pomponius Mela's comment that for cereals Mauretania Tingitana (northern Morocco) was "more favored yet than the Caesarian province" (northwestern Algeria).[64] Gsell, the great authority on the classical period in North Africa, notes that Mauretania could hardly have developed commerce with Italy and western Europe without a flourishing agriculture. However, he emphasizes that the only hard evidence is depictions of cornucopias and spikes of wheat on coinage found in Morocco.[65] In Carcopino's frank estimation, "For the Roman period . . . documentation is still too poor to permit a study that would only assemble, overhastily, incoherent details for premature conclusions."[66]

---

romaine," *RGM* 2, nos. 7–8 (1921): 427–428; O. Reclus, *L'Atlantide—pays de l'Atlas— Algérie, Maroc, Tunisie* (Paris, 1918), pp. VII–VIII.

[62] Cited in P. L. MacKendrick, *The North African Stones Speak* (Chapel Hill, 1980), p. 319.

[63] J. Saurin, *L'Avenir de l'Afrique du Nord* (Paris, 1896), pp. 31–34. Saurin believed that Algeria's "true agricultural vocation" lay in mixed farming involving stock raising and cultivation of forage crops.

[64] R. Thouvenot, *Une Colonie romaine de Maurétanie tingitanie: Valenta Banasa* (Paris, 1941), p. 53.

[65] S. Gsell, *Histoire ancienne de l'Afrique du Nord*, vol. 8 (Paris, 1928), p. 235.

[66] J. Carcopino, *Le Maroc antique* (Paris, 1943), p. 9.

However, despite the poverty of evidence for a lush breadbasket twenty centuries before, and despite cautioning by experts on North African agriculture that settlers should not overestimate North Africa's grain-producing past; the granary-of-Rome legend became well established.[67]

There is clear evidence that Cosnier was under the spell of this legend. For example, in a 1918 speech he bluntly stated, "North Africa was formerly the granary of Rome."[68] And in a 1920 letter to the French president introducing an official report on North African agriculture, he invoked the major tenets of the colonial faith: "North Africa is completely covered with monuments which attest to the importance of Roman colonization in this land. Sons of this same civilization, we . . . must have the courage to restore this empire in all its power and splendor."[69] Elsewhere in the same letter, he concluded: "Thus must we employ all our means to settle and solidly organize this New France where, as did ancient Rome, we will find the foodstuffs and raw materials necessary to nourish our old France."[70]

As noted, the Cosnier plan dovetailed with France's postwar colonial master plan, the Plan Sarraut. Sarraut, the Minister of Colonies, was also influenced by the granary-of-Rome legend. Speaking in 1921 of the burdensome French foreign imports of cereals, he railed against those responsible for North Africa's development: "This situation is disastrous, and yet we possess the granary of Rome and of the ancient world."[71] He insisted that it was up to North Africa, not his colonies, to fill this critical deficit.

Thus, the strong image of North Africa as a former imperial granary became manifested and perpetuated in Morocco's influential wheat policy. This policy dominated colonization and agricultural development efforts up to the crisis of the early 1930s. One can conclude that the wheat policy was a case of historical determinism. One can agree with the conclusion of a French economist who, writing from the vantage point of 1933 when the colonial wheat venture had already been exposed as economic folly, claimed that "Morocco was launched into cereals for historical reasons—the memory of ancient Rome."[72]

The idealistic image of Morocco as a former lush granary was obviously grounded in environmental misperception. Agricultural efforts

[67] P. Berthault, *La Production des céréales en Afrique du Nord* (Paris, 1928).
[68] Cosnier, *L'Afrique du Nord*, p. 336.
[69] Ibid., p. LI.
[70] Ibid., p. XXXV.
[71] *Journal Officiel*, p. 1595.
[72] Amphoux, "L'Evolution de l'agriculture," p. 183.

in Algeria, France's oldest North African colony, had already demonstrated how completely French settlers were capable of misreading the North African environment, of glossing over its harsh realities. In the second half of the nineteenth century, for example, there had been numerous attempts to establish tropical agriculture in Algeria. Coffee, mangoes, black pepper, cacao, tea, and coca were but a few of the tropical crops the French had hoped would flourish on Algerian soil. All such experiments were resounding failures.[73]

Early French images of Morocco also erred on the side of fertility and lushness. Owing probably to explorers' reports of its perennial watercourses and exaggerations concerning the regularity and abundance of rainfall, one preprotectorate sobriquet for Morocco was "la Normandie africaine."[74] The distinctly aridic aspect that French settlers instead commonly encountered was explained as due to Arab deforestation and neglect. It was certainly no reflection of Morocco's potential. France would restore Morocco to the state of productivity it had enjoyed during Roman times.

The granary-of-Rome legend, however, was so flagrantly challenged by repeated poor harvests that it began to be reinterpreted. Perhaps the bountiful wheat lands had only been possible through irrigation. One author, indeed, had already posited this interpretation for Algeria and Tunisia in 1891. The numerous scattered remains of Roman irrigation works, he felt, were compelling proof that North Africa had been just as arid during classical times. The Romans would not have expended such time and effort if ample rain fell from the heavens; their irrigation works were intended to supply what nature denied. Their ruined irrigation works, he concluded, "show us clearly what we must do."[75]

Cosnier also noted that North Africa was littered with Roman irrigation ruins. "It behooves us," he urged, "to rebuild these works as soon as possible so that the land that was once the granary of Rome can become the granary of France."[76] For du Taillis, the Roman irrigation ruins in Morocco were a "lesson inscribed in the land" which the "new conquerors" should heed.[77]

Irrigation development in Morocco, however, did not really begin until the arrival of Théodore Steeg, Lyautey's successor. Steeg, while

[73] C. Rivière and H. Lecq, *Cultures du Midi, de l'Algérie, de la Tunisie et du Maroc* (Paris, 1917).

[74] Cousin and Saurin, *Le Maroc*, p. 18.

[75] G. Boissier, *L'Afrique romaine* (Paris, 1895), p. 139.

[76] Cosnier, *L'Afrique du Nord*, p. 336.

[77] J. du Taillis, *Le Nouveau Maroc* (Paris, 1923), p. 305.

serving as Algeria's governor general (1921–25), had launched a major program of irrigation. Consequently, settlers' hopes ran high following the news of his appointment as Morocco's resident general. Greeting Steeg at a public ceremony in Rabat in October 1925, Obert, the powerful president of the Rabat Chambre d'Agriculture, claimed:

> The agricultural community rejoices . . . at your appointment because it is aware of your great efforts to increase agricultural production in Algeria. Mindful of the prosperity of the Proconsulate, the famous ruins of the massive irrigation systems left by the Romans, you have devoted yourself to reconstituting this wealth by inaugurating . . . the water policy, which you will surely continue to pursue in Morocco.[78]

Before the agricultural crisis, irrigation was regarded as a means of improving colonial wheat production.[79] However, constructing expensive irrigation works for relatively low-value crops like wheat is normally not economically feasible. A major irrigation program in Morocco did not emerge until a more prosperous agricultural specialty was found.

Beginning with French overproduction of wheat in 1929, the Roman breadbasket image became a relic.[80] With France no longer needing wheat, with Moroccan wheat threatening French farmers, the tariff-free quota that alone permitted most settlers to survive was suddenly placed in jeopardy. The policy had been successful in settling French wheat growers in the Moroccan countryside, but it had established them in a vocation with a precarious future.

For the first time, the question was asked: "What can be the value of a crop cultivated only by the grace of . . . tariff-free quotas?"[81] It was natural that France would continue to sustain colonial rubber producers in Indochina or peanut growers in Senegal. Neither crop was grown in the metropole, and both were normally quite profitable. But wheat production in Moroccan had never proven to be a viable colonial enterprise. Worse, it did compete with agriculture in France.

---

[78] Cited in Dr. Lucien-Graux, *Le Maroc économique—rapport à Monsieur le Ministre du Commerce et de l'Industrie* (Paris, 1928), pp. 38–39.

[79] See, for example, J. Célérier and A. Charton, "Les Grands Travaux d'hydraulique agricole au Maroc," *AG* 34 (1925): 76–80.

[80] The granary-of-Rome image, however, still survives in Morocco today. The Moroccan minister of the Secretariat for Planning reminded a visiting reporter in 1977 that in ancient times Morocco "supplied half the bread needed by Rome." See J. Dingle, "Moroccan Agriculture: Which Way Forward?" *Middle East International* 71 (1977): 15.

[81] Amphoux, "Le Maroc et la crise économique," p. 121.

A more somber question was posed. Was export-oriented colonial agriculture even possible in Morocco?[82] In France, and among settler leaders and protectorate officials in Morocco, the answer was solemnly but clearly perceived: No . . . unless there was a radically new orientation.

Towards a New Future

The solution to the predicament of Morocco's heavily indebted settlers, and the salvation of its colonial agriculture, was now sought in a new emphasis on economically viable "rich crops." But which crop, or crops, could form the basis of a profitable agricultural economy, as did wine grapes in Algeria or olives in Tunisia?

Experiments initiated soon after the start of the protectorate had examined the potential of cotton, sugar beets, hemp, ramie, flaxseed, sisal, peanuts, sesame, castor beans, mustard, and sunflowers.[83] But none of these crops, interesting as some might prove for individual farmers, was capable of becoming the new backbone of Moroccan colonial agriculture.[84] Instead, as will be demonstrated, Morocco's salvation was found in citrus fruits and market vegetables.

As early as 1931, Paul Guillemet, one of Morocco's foremost advocates of irrigated agriculture, could proclaim that all who examined the plight of French colonization in Morocco were persuaded that "the future lies in the development of fruit and early vegetable crops."[85]

Early vegetables, indeed, had already proven themselves. Crops such as tomatoes, new potatoes, and string beans reached maturity in Morocco at least two weeks earlier than in Algeria and a month earlier than in France. They could therefore arrive on the French market when prices were highest. Since 1920, market gardeners in the immediate hinterland of Casablanca had quietly begun to export their produce to France, where it had met with good reception. These exports had steadily grown.

For political reasons, however, cultivation of early vegetables could only be further developed on a limited scale; it remained only a partial solution to colonial agriculture's predicament.[86] Instead, fruit crops, particularly oranges, captured the imagination of settlers.

---

[82] Ibid.

[83] E. Miège, "Les Cultures complémentaires au Maroc," *BESM* 14 (1936): 293–297.

[84] J. Célérier, "Le Maroc, est-il un pays neuf?" *RGM* 8, nos. 3–4 (1929): 75.

[85] *FPAN* 1 (1931): 7.

[86] Célérier, "Le Maroc, est-il?" p. 76. The potential for large-scale colonial market garden production was limited by the fact that it competed with French agriculture.

From the ashes of Morocco's wheat policy, a new agricultural policy gradually emerged during the 1930s. Based on irrigation, it was oriented toward the export of citrus and early vegetables. This policy has essentially continued intact to the present.

The granary-of-Rome image—so solid a point of orientation during the first two decades of the protectorate—proved to be a mirage that had vanished in the reality of the Moroccan natural environment. A major government commitment to irrigation agriculture would follow.[87]

[87] With the new orientation in Moroccan colonial agriculture, there was an interesting groping for a new classical image: Morocco as the Garden of Hesperides. Canal, a French Algerian geographer, had noted in a popular 1902 work that classical authors placed the famous Jardin des Hespérides in Morocco, and that, in fact, beautiful orange orchards still remained. With intelligent management, they could provide "immense sources of wealth" (J. Canal, *Géographie générale du Maroc* [Paris, 1902], p. 62). This image had lain dormant until 1931. Guillemet revived it during the dark period of the agricultural crisis. He insisted that all legends were rooted in reality. Scholars were agreed that the site of the famous garden was in western Morocco. Centuries of anarchy and the devastation of war had left of the former splendors only forgotten vestiges in a few remote valleys. Yet they should have been sufficient to inform the protectorate government of Morocco's true vocation. Instead, it had directed settlers towards "des productions misérables" (*FPAN* 1 [1931]: 7). The Hesperides image was soon put to work in the protectorate administration's effort to encourage fruit production. However, this image did not become established as a new point of orientation; instead, it merely served as a counterpoise to the granary-of-Rome image. The "classical era" in Moroccan colonization was over.

2

Not a Drop of Water
to the Sea

Many nineteenth-century European explorers noted Morocco's comparatively abundant water resources. Dr. Gerhardt Rohlfs's comments following an 1861 visit were typical: "There are many rivers in Morocco—all rising from the Atlas. . . . Nothing is positively known respecting the height of the loftiest points . . . but the natives say that the summits of those mountains are covered with perpetual snows."[1] Most explorers' reports were similarly sketchy. However, the Englishmen Hooker and Ball were both remarkably explicit and amazingly accurate in their appraisal of the country's potential:

> Of the material resources of Marocco it is difficult to say too much. Even under existing conditions, a great portion of the territory is extremely fertile. . . . The two natural disadvantages with which it has to contend are, occasional deficient rainfall and the ravages of locusts. For the first, the remedy is to be sought in irrigation. The unfailing streams from the Atlas already serve to a limited extent; but the area of productive land might by intelligent management be very largely increased. We have seen an estimate of the quantity of water discharged by the five principal streams that fall into the Atlantic north of the Atlas, which fixes

[1] *Adventures in Morocco and Journeys through the Oases of Draa and Tafilet* (London, 1874), pp. 32, 31. Rohlfs's comment on the perpetual snows of the Atlas echoes a much earlier statement by the Roman general Suetonius Paulinus. See E. Reclus, *North-West Africa*, vol. 11 of *The Earth and Its Inhabitants* (New York, 1887), p. 348.

that amount at 9,000 cubic feet per second; and if to these were added the Moulouya, which falls into the Mediterranean, and the Siss, the Draha, the Asakka, and the Sous, which drain the southern slopes of the main chain, we should probably double the above estimate, and find an aggregate amount sufficient to irrigate three millions of acres.[2]

This estimate is uncannily close to the current government estimate of Morocco's perennially irrigable area: 1,150,000 hectares, or 2,840,000 acres.[3]

Hooker and Ball's estimate was circulated in the French literature on Morocco. It was cited to support the argument that Morocco's future prosperity would come from its rivers.[4] Important French investigators like Vaffier-Pollet, in the lively 1900–12 inventory period, emphasized the virtually unexploited nature of the major Moroccan streams: Nowhere had "serious irrigation works" been constructed; dams would enable the vast coastal plains to be enriched by water flowing into the Atlantic.[5]

It is clear that the drive to bring Morocco into the French empire preceded any coherent idea of how this country should be developed. Some Frenchmen even considered Morocco to have rich potential for

[2] J. D. Hooker and J. Ball, *Journey of a Tour in Marocco and the Great Atlas* (London, 1878), pp. 348–349.

[3] SAHM, p. 21.

[4] See, for example, Reclus, *North-West Africa*, p. 356; J. Canal, *Géographie générale du Maroc* (Paris, 1902), p. 33; A. Cousin and D. Saurin, *Le Maroc* (Paris 1905), p. 18. Cousin and Saurin referred to Hooker and Ball as "Hell et Hooker." Observers enthusiastically emphasized that Morocco's problem was not so much a dearth of water as its unequal distribution. Certain regions had too much water—for instance, the extensive Gharb marshlands that a French hydraulic engineer had to inventory using a native reed raft (J. Célérier, "Les 'Merjas' de la plaine du Sebou," *Hespéris* 2 [1922]: 109). According to Henri Catherine in 1919:

Nature has been generous in endowing Morocco with a respectable quantity of water, but it did not complete the gesture by assuring a good distribution of this precious gift. Here, the Sebou creates marshes that perennially flood and are detrimental to the health of the surrounding region; there, immense plains are arid while large volumes of water meander through them to be lost to the sea; elsewhere a lake serves only to reflect the azure overhead or to permit flocks of teal to frolic on its surface, while expanses of rich land downslope remain parched. It belongs to our genius to drain, to irrigate, to distribute parsimoniously. (H. Catherine, "L'Hydraulique au Maroc," *Bulletin de la Société de Géographie du Maroc* 8 [1919]: 15).

[5] Vaffier-Pollet, "L'Agriculture et l'élevage au Maroc," *RC*, 1906, p. 206.

irrigated cotton production. Indeed, the nascent granary-of-Rome image was initially challenged by an "Egyptian image."[6] Several writers compared the Sebou or the Oum er Rbia to the Nile. Others noted that a native cotton industry formerly had flourished. One early authority claimed that wise harnessing of Morocco's rivers would convert Morocco into "a little Egypt."[7] And another described the Sebou Plain as a "vast delta" where cotton could generate untold wealth as it had in the Nile Delta.[8]

Intrigued by such speculation, the French Minister of Commerce appointed a special representative to accompany the 1917 Cosnier mission. His specific task was to determine to what extent Morocco could supply France with cotton.[9] The Cosnier report treated the question as follows: Approximately 60,000 hectares in Morocco were suitable for cotton. However, envisaging a triennial rotation cycle, only 20,000 hectares could be planted each year. Moroccan production could therefore not surpass 8,000 metric tons per annum—a mere 2 percent of France's cotton import needs. In conclusion, French cotton growers should look to more promising colonies like Senegal or Niger.[10]

This unfavorable finding effectively aborted the early movement to establish colonial cotton production in Morocco. It also helped nullify the immediate need to develop irrigation and gave the green light to a nearly exclusive dryland development policy.

Following the Cosnier mission, official efforts to harness Morocco's rivers were slow to develop, then were initially for hydroelectric purposes. Nonetheless, large-scale irrigation development remained a widely shared colonial vision. This vision, in fact, evolved into an administrative imperative.

Paul Penet, a hydraulic engineer and head of the Bureau des Contrôles Civiles in Tunisia, was summoned to Morocco in 1917 to evaluate the new protectorate's water resources. His advice was that "The ideal in Morocco . . . would be to allow not a single drop of fresh

[6] Leading Lyautey to warn in 1923, "Le Maroc n'est pas la vallée du Nil" (*BESM* [1935], p. 267).

[7] De Campon, cited in Canal, *Géographie générale*, p. 33.

[8] Y. [anon.] "L'Hydraulique agricole au Maroc," *Revue Générale des Sciences Pures et Appliquées* (1914), pp. 354–355. To evaluate commercial cotton's performance in Morocco, test plots were established in 1913 in the Ouerrha Valley and at Sidi Kacem and Azemmour. See M. Widiez, "La Culture du cotonnier en Afrique du Nord," *Agriculture Pratique des Pays Chauds* 10 (1931): 284–285.

[9] H. Cosnier, "Intensification de la production agricole au Maroc en vue de sa contribution au ravitaillement de la France," unpublished report, 1917, p. 1.

[10] H. Cosnier, *L'Afrique du Nord—son avenir agricole et économique* (Paris, 1922), pp. 42–43.

water to flow into the sea."[11] Not a drop of water to the sea! The expression soon became a catch phrase that echoed throughout the protectorate period, and still reverberates in Morocco today. It precisely articulates a major idealistic goal: full development of the country's watercourses. Originally the task was regarded as an "imperious necessity" both for Morocco's colonial economy and to extend France's "good works" overseas.[12] Today, in independent Morocco, it is a central pillar of national development efforts.

The protectorate's development history, then, presents a paradox: Given the widespread early awareness of Morocco's irrigation potential, why did large-scale irrigated agriculture not actually begin until the mid-1930s? The principal reason was the administration's preoccupation with dryland cereal production. However, the wheat policy by itself does not fully explain the two-decade delay. Further investigation reveals a combination of secondary factors deeply embedded in the protectorate's decision-making matrix. This chapter will: (1) explore these secondary factors to help provide an understanding of how colonial policy was formulated in Morocco; and (2) examine the protectorate administration's efforts to develop Morocco's water resources prior to the 1930s crisis, when irrigation finally became the central thrust of agricultural development policy.

Factors Delaying Irrigation

Most authorities who examined the question of irrigation in the early protectorate period emphasized the need for careful preliminary studies. For example, Paul Penet, the hydraulic expert brought in to appraise Morocco's water resources, concluded that "the only urgent matter at present is to conduct studies."[13] Cosnier made a similar recommendation.[14] Following their advice, the protectorate government created a Service de l'Hydraulique in 1917. Its charge was to conduct a complete inventory of Morocco's surface waters, then to identify and investigate potential development projects. The inventory proceeded rapidly. By 1927, a Public Works memorandum would confidently claim: "Morocco has now determined its water resources; it is formulating water projects."[15]

---

[11] *Les Richesses hydrauliques du Maroc occidental* (Grenoble, 1918), p. 12.

[12] Dr. Russo, "Les Eaux souterraines au Maroc central," *Bulletin de la Société de Géographie du Maroc* 10 (1919): 49.

[13] *Richesses hydrauliques*, p. 40.

[14] "Intensification," p. 20.

[15] Anon. "Note sur l'hydraulique au Maroc" (1927), found in a dossier labeled "Hy-

Preliminary studies naturally delayed actual projects. Increasingly strident voices, however, would claim that the administration had developed a pathological obsession with conducting studies of water projects as an end in itself—to avoid taking action. Such criticism became increasingly common after 1 August 1925; on that day, a decree was issued that effectively removed irrigation development from the hands of private initiative and made it the responsibility of the government. The decree, according to one Marrakech settler, substituted the "massive incompetence" of the central administration for the "modest effectiveness" of private individuals.[16] In a letter to the editor of *Le Petit Marocain*, this settler described how, when the decree was issued, he had been drilling for water with neighboring settlers. This work had had to be suspended. However, Public Works had announced it would begin a vast irrigation project to regenerate the entire Haouz region. This project was supposed to be completed in only eighteen months. Five years had already passed, however, and the settler still had not received any water. What conclusion could be drawn? he asked. Perhaps that the government was trying to teach settlers patience. Meanwhile, for lack of water, "One plants promises, one harvests only the wind!"[17]

This is but one case. The minutes of Chamber of Agriculture meetings are liberally sprinkled with charges of procrastination, ineptness, and subterfuge concerning the administration's handling of water development. The charges often seem to be justified. However, several comments can be made in partial defense of the administration.

First, while the inventory of Morocco's surface waters was largely accomplished by the mid-1920s, the inventory of preexisting water rights proved to be a much more time-consuming and politically sensitive task.[18] (Indeed, this task continues today.) A few Arab or Arab-

---

draulique 1925–1930" in the unclassified archives of the Travaux Publics at the Bibliothèque Générale in Rabat, p. 9.

[16] Anon. "La voix d'un colon," in *Le Maroc à la croisée des chemins*, ed. L. Delau (Casablanca, 1931), p. 50.

[17] Ibid., p. 54.

[18] Water legislation passed on 1 July 1914 (somewhat modified by legislation passed on 8 November 1919) incorporated all of Morocco's waters into the public domain; however, existing water rights were to be legally recognized if they were based either on a concession from the *makhzan* or ten years' customary usage prior to 1 July 1914 (or prior to 8 November 1919 for subsurface waters and marshlands). See A. Sonnier, *Le Régime juridique des eaux au Maroc* (Paris, 1933). Until August 1925, determination of existing water rights was one of the many responsibilities of the civil controllers in "civil regions" and of Native Affairs officers in "military regions." Beginning in August 1925, however, with the appearance of a decree designed to expedite water registration,

ized tribes possessed notarized documents that testified to "peaceable public possession" of water rights, and certain notable families held actual legal titles. In cases where the sultan's government, or *makhzan*, had become involved in water litigation, records of water rights also existed.[19] All these cases were the exception, however. In the vast majority of cases, proof of water rights existed only in oral tradition. It was impossible for the central administration to determine prior ownership without lengthy field surveys.

Making matters more difficult, in no case did water rights refer to a fixed quantity of water. Traditional rights were usually based on a "turn" of water. All of the water in a *seguia* (irrigation canal) was diverted onto a water proprietor's land for a given period—for example, a twelve-hour period once a week. Less commonly, water was distributed in continuous fashion from a seguia, with sluice gate sizes reflecting percentage of ownership. Either way, the cultivated area fluctuated annually with availability of water. The traditional system was a good example of cultural adaptation, given the highly variable regimes of Morocco's watercourses. Unfortunately, it was in conflict with the European conception of water rights.

The absence of written proof of water rights, the complexity of Moroccan traditions of water management, the constantly fluctuating size of water shares, the need to proceed cautiously to avoid political conflict, all these factors inevitably delayed colonial irrigation development.[20]

Additionally, however, the protectorate administration was caught in a quandary. On the one hand, its charge was to assist colonization. On the other hand, it was also responsible for "protecting" Moroccan interests. This dual mission was always a difficult balancing act. It was further complicated with regard to irrigation development: By the late 1920s, European colonization had generally dispossessed Moroccans of the best rainfed agricultural lands; however, much of the land best suited for large irrigation projects remained in Moroccan hands. This situation created a major stumbling block. Before the mid-1930s, few

---

water rights began to be ascertained by commission hearing following a month-long waiting period during which claimants were supposed to assemble their cases.

[19] A. Sonnier, "Contribution à l'étude du régime juridique des eaux au Maroc," *RGM*, 1931, pp. 321–323. In the unclassified French archives of the Bibliothèque Générale in Rabat, there are numerous dossiers containing copies of the Arabic-language records pertaining to water rights.

[20] For a detailed survey of traditional water use in Morocco, see P. Roché, "L'Irrigation et le statut juridique des eaux au Maroc," *Revue Juridique et Politique d'Outre Mer* 19 (1965): 55–120, 255–284, 537–561.

Frenchmen envisaged developing irrigation for Moroccans. For example, Chabert, director of the Service de l'Hydraulique, speaking to
a group of Native Affairs officers in 1922, described the Tadla Plain
as "superb" for irrigation and of a "remarkable fertility."[21] However,
he continued, because of the relatively dense indigenous population in
the area, it would be "almost impossible to create large holdings . . .
deliverable to colonization. A large-scale irrigation project . . . could
only be developed for natives. It would appear that other tasks are
more pressing."[22]

Another conflict for the administration was between agricultural and
hydroelectric interests within the colonial community itself. One notable early example of how this conflict affected water development
involved the hydroelectric dam on the Oum er Rbia at Sidi Maachou.
This dam, Morocco's first modern dam, was finally begun in 1926.
However, blueprints for the project had collected dust for many years
beforehand owing to competing demands for irrigation development.
The decision to construct the dam—primarily to provide Casablanca
with electricity and water—cancelled plans for a large irrigation project
upstream. According to an editorial in *La Vigie Marocaine*, this was a
clear-cut example of distant bathtubs taking priority over fertile agricultural land surrounding the river: "What one would do for the city
that consumes, one would not dream of doing for the hinterland that
produces."[23] The tug-of-war between diverse colonial interests inevitably hampered water development.

Another conflict operated on a purely petty bureaucratic level within
the administration itself. Through a quirk of administrative history,
irrigation development in all of French North Africa had been placed
under the dual authority of the Public Works and Agriculture departments. There was a certain simplistic logic in this: Irrigation required
major public works but involved agriculture. In practice, however, the
arrangement was one of the single most important causes of delays in
Morocco's water development.[24]

[21] M. Chabert, *L'Hydraulique au Maroc* (Rabat, 1922), p. 21.

[22] Ibid. Lebault, president of the Casablanca Chambre d'Agriculture, argued in a
1933 policy statement that irrigation water absolutely must not be permitted to enrich
native lands, for these lands would then be too expensive for colons to purchase. The
administration should proceed by creating irrigable "perimeters of colonization"—buy-
ing up native land at low prices before developing irrigation for these areas (*BCAR* 7
[1933]: 53).

[23] "Aux Bords de l'oued qui monte et de la mère du printemps," *La Vigie Marocaine*,
24 April 1931, p. 1.

[24] See, for example, G. Duval, *L'Hydraulique au Maroc* (Paris, 1933), p. 148. Cosnier,
in his 1920 report on North Africa's development, had urged reform of the dual au-

The Direction de l'Agriculture proposed irrigation projects, determined their order of priority, and ultimately governed the use of irrigation water. However, Public Works decided whether or not to implement the proposed projects and had full control over their construction. The inefficiency inherent in the arrangement, and rivalry between the two departments, worked to delay irrigation projects. A bad situation was made worse by two additional facts. First, the director of Public Works was also the legal manager of Morocco's public domain waters—virtually all water resources to which preexisting rights did not exist. Second, throughout the protectorate period, the directors of Public Works had a clear tendency to favor hydroelectric development over irrigation.

Several attempts were made to break the administrative deadlock and expedite irrigation projects. These attempts were only partly successful, mainly because they involved the granting of even greater authority to Public Works. By 1937, water development had become completely centralized under the Public Works Department.[25]

Gaston Lebault, president of the Casablanca Chamber of Agriculture, was the most prominent of many settlers who blamed the Direction de l'Agriculture's progressive loss of authority over water development on timid, ineffective leadership. His charge resonates with truth, at least during the first half of the protectorate period. Not only was water development captured from Agriculture by the more aggressive Public Works, but control over agricultural funding was gradually appropriated by Finance, and forest management was relegated to a new autonomous agency, Eaux et Forêts. Pointing to this unfortunate trend, Lebault scornfully predicted that agricultural experimentation would soon be conducted by the PTT (Postes, Télégraphes et Téléphones), and stock raising would become the concern of the Education Department.[26]

Lebault, on many occasions, indicted the protectorate government for its longstanding failure to make colonial agriculture viable through irrigation works and other major investments. He claimed that the government had continuously squandered its funds on unproductive

---

thority arrangement for water development. Interdepartmental quibbling, he claimed, was the cause of "endless suspension of all water projects." See Cosnier, *L'Afrique du Nord*, p. 207. In this case, his advice was not heeded.

[25] "Dahir du 12 novembre 1937 relatif aux attributions respectives de la direction générale des travaux publics et de la direction des affaires économiques en matière d'hydraulique," *BO* 1317 (1938): 86.

[26] G. Lebault, "Un Budget de mendicité," in *Le Maroc à la croisée des chemins*, ed. L. Delau (Casablanca, 1931), p. 95.

infrastructure, and that agriculture's share of the budget had never amounted to more than "a few crumbs at the budgetary banquet."[27] Budget figures confirm the latter claim. Up to 1927, "agriculture and colonization" received less than 1 percent of the protectorate's development funds, and "major water projects" received only slightly over 2 percent, while "ports, railroads, roads, and administrative buildings" received over 90 percent.[28] However, this prioritization reflected a certain sound logic. Most dam sites were in remote areas that were the last to be reached by road, just as they were the last to be pacified.[29] Dam construction was out of the question before access routes had been established. The director of the Service de l'Hydraulique estimated in 1922, for example, that to transport a sack of cement overland to a promising dam site on the upper Oum er Rbia not yet accessible by road would cost ten times the original price of the cement.[30]

Additionally, when the first large irrigation projects finally got underway in the late 1920s, unforeseen technical problems created major delays as well as huge cost overruns that drained funds. The Beth Dam was a notorious example (Illus. 7). Begun in 1927, it was supposed to be completed by 1930 and to cost only 12 million francs.[31] However, the dam's foundation began to sag in mid-1928. Massive amounts of cement had to be injected more than a hundred meters underground in order to stabilize the foundation. This caused an outraged newspaper editor to speak of "a sponge . . . made of millions."[32] When finally completed in 1935, five years behind schedule, the dam's total price was 110 million francs for a cost overrun of more than 800 percent.[33]

In summary, preliminary studies, existing water rights, early government policy, the early pattern of colonization, the long pacification

[27] Ibid., p. 100.

[28] J. Maréchal, "Les Dépenses du protectorat pour la mise en valeur du Maroc entre 1928 et 1936," *BESM*, 1936, p. 91.

[29] A major motive behind the pacification of the Middle Atlas was France's desire to control the water resources in these mountains and to provide security for the neighboring irrigable plains. See A. Bernard, *Afrique septentrionale et occidentale*, vol. 11 of *Géographie universelle*, ed. P. Vidal de la Blache and L. Gallois (Paris, 1937), p. 157.

[30] Chabert, *L'Hydraulique*, p. 20.

[31] Anon., "Hydraulique agricole" (1928), found in a dossier labeled "Hydraulique 1925–1930" in the unclassified archives of the Travaux Publics at the Bibliothèque Générale in Rabat, p. 3.

[32] Editorial of 27 November 1930 in the *Journal du Maroc*, cited in Duval, *L'Hydraulique au Maroc*, p. 82.

[33] *BCAR* 1936, p. 725.

campaign, hydroelectric interests, bureaucratic inefficiency and inertia, technical problems, and finally the dearth of funds during the early 1930s economic crisis, all these factors formed an operational matrix that delayed irrigation development. Nonetheless, the colonial administration from the beginning took steps that would ultimately culminate in an irrigation program.

The Preliminary Steps toward Water Development

Soon after the beginning of the protectorate, on 1 July 1914, the government issued a decree that placed all of Morocco's surface waters in the public domain.[34] This legislation was intended to prevent private settlers from usurping water resources regarded as vital for France's colonial effort.[35] Five years later, on 8 November 1919, it issued another decree extending the public domain to subsurface waters and marshlands.[36] The 1919 decree's intent was first, to obviate political and legal complications that had previously occurred in Algeria; and second (as will be discussed in detail later) to bring the extensive Gharb marshlands under government control so that they could be drained for French settlement.

France rationalized its incorporation of Morocco's waters into the public domain with two principal arguments: (1) that all waters were traditionally owned by Morocco's sultans, who merely ceded usufruct rights; thus, all water rightly belonged to the state;[37] and (2) that the concept of public domain was more in accord with the true precepts of Islam than the complex tangle of existing water-use customs.[38] The clear intent of the legislation, however, was to protect Morocco's water resources until they could be developed by the protectorate administration.[39]

Besides laying the legal foundation for eventual large-scale water development, the protectorate administration became involved with modest water projects. Just as it had taken over the makhzan or central government's land with the signing of the protectorate accords, so had it assumed control over makhzan water. Most of this water was already

[34] This decree closely followed existing water law in Algeria and Tunisia (Sonnier, *Le Régime juridique*, p. 5).

[35] Duval, *L'Hydraulique au Maroc*, p. 15.

[36] Ibid., p. 16; Sonnier, *Le Régime juridique*, pp. 6–7.

[37] Duval, *L'Hydraulique au Maroc*, p. 12.

[38] Ibid.; Sonnier, *Le Régime juridique*, pp. 35–36.

[39] A similar motive was behind the 1919 decree on collective lands: to preserve them for future colonization. See discussion on p. 49.

harnessed in traditional systems. It was immediately delivered to colonization. In the Marrakech region, where agriculture was generally not possible without irrigation, official colonization was based on the existing system of makhzan canals.[40] Makhzan water was also delivered to colonization in the Fez, Meknes, and Gharb regions.[41] As might be expected, the makhzan systems were already some of the best endowed of the traditional water systems in Morocco. However, the protectorate administration used several tactics to "improve" them: (1) moving their intakes further upstream to usurp water from intervening seguias and gain priority in the overall system; (2) regulating the amount of water that upstream native seguias could withdraw to ensure the viability of the settlers' seguias; (3) employing outright legal chicanery, whereby it robbed tribal groups, such as the Ourikas, of traditional water rights; and (4) improving systems belonging to Moroccans through technical means, such as cement-lining canals, to free up extra water for settlers.[42] Elsewhere, the administration embarked upon an ambitious though relatively inexpensive program to provide watering points for man and beast. It drilled wells and constructed troughs, cisterns, windmills, and pumping stations. Its efforts, temporally and geographically, had a high correlation to the expansion of colonization.

When a drought in 1919–20 caused numerous wells to go dry, angry settlers demanded that the administration conduct research on Morocco's aquifers. Responding to this pressure, the Direction de l'Agriculture developed a program late in 1920; after delays, the program was initiated in 1923.[43] Sixty-seven deep exploratory wells were drilled in six different regions. The results were not encouraging. There were numerous dry holes, much of the ground water was found to be excessively saline, and many of the aquifers were too deep to be exploited economically.[44] The failure of this exploration program led

[40] Martin, "La Question hydraulique dans la région de Marrakech," *RGM* 6 (1927): 56; P. Durand, "La Région de Marrakech et du sud marocain," *RGM* 6 (1927): 127.

[41] M. Faust, *La Colonisation rurale au Maroc, 1919–1929* Algiers, 1931), pp. 63–64; anon., "Hydraulique agricole," p. 4.

[42] P. Pascon, *Le Haouz de Marrakech* vol. 2 (Rabat, 1977), pp. 496–501; Sonnier, "Contribution," p. 312; J. Pilleboue, "Aspects de l'irrigation dans le Haouz de Marrakech," unpublished thesis, University of Paris, 1962.

[43] R. Faure-Dère, *L'Hydraulique agricole au Maroc* (Tunis, 1936), pp. 23–29.

[44] Ibid. Critics charged that the exploratory wells were drilled without adequate preliminary studies and with the naive assumption that groundwater was to be found everywhere. This assumption, in point of fact, had originally led the administration to estab-

to extensive use of "water witches" during the late 1920s and early 1930s. Indeed, the administration itself now regularly employed these *sourciers*.[45] More important, the program's failure served to concentrate the administration's focus almost exclusively on surface water resources.

On a modest scale, early settlers privately developed irrigation for their farms. They pumped water from wells in the Marrakech region, and from streams in the Gharb. However, most of the groundwater in the Marrakech area was already exploited by traditional rhettara or qanat systems. Very little new water could be pumped without decreasing the outflow of existing rhettaras and triggering political conflict—an occurrence that local authorities were careful to guard against. In the Gharb, the summer stream flow was already so meager that it was soon drained nearly dry by pumping.[46] Also, during the early period, pumps and fuel were expensive and mechanics and spare parts were scarce.[47]

The year 1925 marked a major turning point for irrigation in Morocco. On 1 August 1925, the protectorate administration passed legislation that effectively put a stranglehold on private water development. The immediate effect of this legislation was noted in the earlier account of a disgruntled Marrakech settler. It made authorization for any water use exceeding 40 cubic meters per day mandatory, and permitted the administration to revoke this authorization at any time, without indemnity.[48] The legislation also expedited the registration process for existing water rights. Why was the 1925 legislation passed? Because the protectorate administration was poised to launch a major water development program. A number of different forces were im-

---

lish settlers in arid regions where well water subsequently could not be found. See A. Arnaud, "Note sur l'hydraulique marocaine," *Echo du Bled*, 5 July 1931, p. 1.

[45] In a dossier labeled "Hydraulique 1931" in the unclassified archives of the Travaux Publics at the Bibliothèque Générale in Rabat, there are numerous references to the administration's use of water witches.

[46] A. Sonnier, "Les Merjas de la plaine du Gharb," *BCAR*, 1935, p. 488; J. Le Coz, "Les Agrumes marocaines," *Notes Marocaines* 13 (1960): 54.

[47] J. Le Coz, *Le Rharb, fellahs et colons* vol. 2 (Rabat, 1964), p. 503.

[48] A campaign led by Guillemet upon his return from California, where, he claimed, the concept of public domain was unknown (see Sonnier, *Le Régime juridique*, p. 9), was successful in bringing about an important revision in the 1925 legislation, with a subsequent decree issued in 1932. The objectionable clauses—prior authorization for any use exceeding 40 cubic meters per day and lack of indemnity in the case of revoked authorization—were amended. However, by 1932 the government had firmly seized the initiative; private enterprise would henceforth play comparatively little part in the development of Morocco's water resources.

pelling it in this direction. The 1925 legislation completed the legal foundation for water development by giving the administration total control over Morocco's public domain waters.

Push and Pull Factors

The first large-scale water project in Morocco developed out of energy needs. Early hopes that Morocco would be endowed with important coal deposits had been disappointed. With the new protectorate's economy booming after World War I, energy demands of the new railroads and urban areas steadily increased. The concession for Morocco's first hydroelectric facility, to supply Fez, was granted in 1914. In 1923, when imported English coal started to soar in price, the administration resolutely decided to expedite hydroelectric development. It gave a semiprivate company called Energie Electrique du Maroc (EEM), in which the powerful Banque de Paris et des Pays-Bas held a controlling interest, the exclusive concession for Morocco's electricity development. The company's first hydroelectric project— and Morocco's first modern dam—was the Barrage Sidi Maachou on the Oum er Rbia. This project was begun in 1926 and completed in 1929.

By far the strongest push factor for water development in the 1920s, however, was the pressing need to provide new land for colonization. Suitable makhzan land, appropriated by the administration when it signed the protectorate accords, had been quickly absorbed by the large influx of settlers after World War I.[49] As early as 1922 the geographer Célérier would write, "Among the problems confronting the Protectorate Administration, there is perhaps none more important than the search for available land."[50]

Two promising new sources of land, however, had been identified: first, the collective or tribal lands covering the greater part of the country, land traditionally used for stock raising and extensive agriculture to which no legal titles existed; and second, the Gharb marshlands, regarded as vastly underutilized, which had a nebulous legal status, the

[49] Immigration to Morocco jumped from an average annual figure of 3,414 for the period 1915 to 1918 to 10,705 for the period 1919 to 1922. The peak was in 1921, with 13,598 immigrants. See *RC*, 1926, p. 493.

[50] Célérier, "Les 'Merjas,'" 223. Estimates of land that could eventually be made available for colonization varied greatly. For example, Obert, one of the most influential settler leaders, claimed in 1922 that 1 million hectares could be distributed over a twenty-year period. However, Malet, director general of Agriculture, estimated that only 153,000 hectares could be distributed. See *AG*, 1924, p. 311.

administration could manipulate. In both cases, water management was the key to creating viable new land. Storage dams would enable the tribal lands to be irrigated and the marshlands to be drained. Cosnier specifically pointed to these lands as the "solution" to the land shortage in his influential report on Morocco's development.[51] Again, his recommendations had a strong impact. In 1919, the protectorate administration passed legislation to preserve both types of land for official colonization.

First, on 27 April 1919, a decree was passed to "protect" collective land from the improvidence of the tribal councils (*jma'as*) by placing this land under the management of an advisory council of French officials and Moroccan notables. Though ostensibly for the good of the *indigènes*, the motive behind this legislation was thinly disguised. As Captain Bondis explained to a group of Native Affairs officers:

> In bringing peace to Morocco, France vanquished the feeling of insecurity that formerly dominated the mentality of the native and prevented him from legally acquiring land. Had we not intervened in time [through issuing the 1919 decree] we would little by little have seen the collective domain transformed into private holdings. . . . In a word, we would have been largely deprived of the land necessary for colonization.[52]

The decree deftly preserved tribal lands for official colonization by preventing private sales. It established a procedure by which the advisory council, or Conseil de Tutelle, could expropriate "superfluous" land for colonization. Native Affairs officers were given extensive instructions on how to carve out "perimeters" of colonization. The general rule of thumb was that 12 hectares of good land, 15 of average land, and 20 of poor land should be left for each Moroccan family.[53] After an officer had determined how much land was "surplus," he was to collaborate with technical advisors to determine the "best possible areas" with regard to land value, water resources, and lines of communication.[54] Clearly, potential for irrigation was one of the major factors affecting which tribal land was distributed to settlers. By this process, to cite one example from the Gharb, 13,200 hectares "of the

[51] *L'Afrique du Nord*, pp. 154–155.
[52] A. Bondis, *La Colonisation au Maroc* (Rabat, 1932), p. 14.
[53] Ibid., p. 17.
[54] Ibid., p. 18.

best land" of the Cherarda tribe was expropriated.[55] Nearly all was within the future Gharb irrigation area.

A second decree, issued on 8 November 1919, incorporated marsh-lands into the public domain (as earlier noted). According to the geographer Célérier:

> These vast marshlands could not have failed to attract the attention of both settlers and an Administration in quest of land. Here were thousands of hectares, little used, whose ownership was quite vague . . . land located in a peaceful region, easily accessible, right along the most important river in North Africa, and in the proximity of future railroad lines. The marshlands belong to the most sought-after category in this warm and arid region: land capable of being irrigated.[56]

The marshlands—called *merdja*s, meaning "pastureland"—were not true marshes. Rather, they were large expanses northeast of Rabat that flooded during winter and spring and largely dried up during the rest of the year. Their reeds and rushes were traditionally used for weaving mats and constructing conical huts called *noula*s. Fishing and hunting locally provided important sources of protein. However, the paramount economic significance of the merdjas was as summer grazing land. Receding waters left in their wake lush natural pasture for livestock from throughout the Sebou basin and surrounding highlands.[57]

The 1919 legislation incorporating merdjas into the public domain nominally respected traditional rights. However, in practice, only the land "least interesting" for colonization was preserved for Moroccans. The remainder was delivered to colonization. This was legally accomplished through a provident clause that permitted land within the public domain to be declassified and returned to the state's "private domain" if it was deemed to be without public utility. From the private domain, this land could subsequently be sold for colonization. The procedure was a brilliant example of colonial legal chicanery. As Sonnier, one of the protectorate administration's main legal experts, wryly explained, "It is because merdjas can be declassified from the public domain that it is worthwhile first to classify them into it."[58]

At first, the protectorate administration hoped to have the merdjas

---

[55] Letter from the director of Public Affairs on 29 April 1939 to Priou, president of the Rabat Chambre d'Agriculture. See *BCAR*, 1939, p. 263.

[56] "Les 'Merjas'," pp. 223–224.

[57] W. Fogg, "The Sebou Basin," *Scottish Geographical Magazine* 47 (1931): 80–97.

[58] A. Sonnier, "Considérations sur la condition juridique des merdjas du Gharb," *RGM*, 1931, p. 33.

drained by private firms. In November 1919, it gave the Compagnie du Sebou a concession to drain two of the merdjas. This consortium represented a merger of powerful financial interests: on the one hand, a group backed by the Banque d'Indochine and represented by the Marquis de Segonzac, the well-known early explorer of Morocco; on the other hand, a group backed by the ubiquitous Banque de Paris et des Pays-Bas. The Compagnie du Sebou was obligated to implement a rapid drainage scheme devised by Public Works. For this, it received title to 9,800 hectares of drained land in September 1924. Unfortunately, the Public Works scheme soon failed. In 1927, one of the merdjas, now in cultivation, flooded and could not be drained for forty days. The whole plan thus proved to be a costly fiasco and the Compagnie du Sebou was subsequently liquidated.[59] The experience, however, had a major impact: It convinced the protectorate administration that the Gharb marshes could not be successfully drained without large storage dams, strengthening the resolve of Resident General Steeg to commit major government resources for their construction.

The Steeg Administration, 1925–29

While French colonization in North Africa always pursued the twin goals of *mise en valeur* (development) and *peuplement* (settlement), there were shifting degrees of emphasis, depending on the administration.[60] Throughout the long period of his residency in Morocco (1912–25), Lyautey emphasized *mise en valeur*, and preferred leaving this task to well-financed private firms and an elite group of colonists.[61] The opposite was true of Théodore Steeg, whose views on North Africa were molded while he served as governor general of Algeria (1921–25), and whose political leanings were decidedly left. Steeg willingly opened Morocco to an increased movement of colonization after his arrival in 1925, settling nearly as many colonists in just over three years as Lyautey had in thirteen (see Table 1).[62] French settlement in Morocco became the major goal of the Steeg administration. However, Steeg viewed irrigation development as the primary

[59] Le Coz, *Le Rharb*, pp. 423–427.

[60] A. Bernard, "Rural Colonization in North Africa," in W.L.G. Joerg, ed., *Pioneer Settlement: Cooperative Studies* (New York, 1932), pp. 221–235.

[61] See R. Bidwell, *Morocco under Colonial Rule: French Administration of Tribal Areas, 1912–1956* (London, 1973), pp. 201–202.

[62] From 1912 to 1925, 690 official colons were settled. All but the last few months of this period were during Lyautey's residency. From 1926 to 1928, the major part of Steeg's residency, 572 official colons were settled (R. Hoffherr, *L'Economie marocaine* [Paris, 1932], p. 129).

means to this end. Irrigation would not only "create" new land for colonization, but irrigated plots could be smaller, enabling more settlers to be established in a given area.

Steeg's initiatives would represent an important new thrust. Previous government efforts had focused primarily on "improving" existing irrigation; that is, on trying to liberate water from traditional systems for the benefit of settlers. This strategy had become stalled by the mid-1920s: The amount of water previously controlled by the central government was relatively limited; technical improvements of existing systems had reached a barrier of diminishing returns; and legal manipulations were becoming no longer possible without intolerable political repercussions. Beginning with Steeg, emphasis would be on "creating" new water resources through constructing storage dams.

When Steeg became Morocco's new resident general in October 1925, the protectorate administration had already taken most of the background steps necessary for water development. Indeed, two major dam projects were already near the point of implementation: the previously noted storage dam on the Beth, to create a perimeter of colonization in the Gharb; and a storage dam on the N'fis to create a similar perimeter in the Haouz (refer to Fig. 8). Other projects had also been formulated. Steeg provided the impetus. As he announced in 1926, with regard to Morocco's water development, "In a word, after studies that have been long and delicate . . . the hour of action has arrived."[63]

The site on the Beth had inspired visions of dams since the earliest years of the protectorate. Located at El Kansera, it consisted of a deep, narrow gorge cut through resistant limestone on the edge of the fertile lowlands. French engineers had determined that the Beth's winter floods were the principal cause of the extensive merdjas on the left bank of the Sebou. These merdjas would be ideal for large-scale official colonization when drained. In winter, the El Kansera Dam would protect the plain against flood waters; in summer, the stored water would enable some 30,000 hectares of drained marshland to be irrigated and delivered to colonization.[64]

In the Marrakech, or Haouz, region, the administration's desire to create viable new land for colonization had been channeled into a top-

[63] *RC*, 1926, p. 562. While governor general of Algeria, Steeg had launched a major irrigation program that had earned him the sobriquet "le Gouverneur de l'eau." See T. Steeg, *La Paix française en Afrique du Nord* (Paris, 1926), p. 121.

[64] J. Célérier and A. Charton, "Les Grands Travaux d'hydraulique agricole au Maroc," *AG* 34 (1925): 78–79.

priority dam project on the N'fis.[65] The N'fis site was similar to the El Kansera site: a deep gorge on the edge of the lowlands. It is noteworthy that, on strictly technical grounds, taking into consideration only potential dam sites and the estimated costs of dam construction, the N'fis itself would have been third choice in the Marrakech region as the stream to be dammed. Both the Lakhdar and the Tessaout were better choices.[66] However, the N'fis was the most irregular of all the region's streams, with a winter flow of up to 800 cubic meters per second and a summer flow as low as one-third of a cubic meter per second.[67] It therefore possessed the greatest volume of unused water— "ressources nouvelles" or "ressources à créer" in the French lexicon. Damming the N'fis would create the largest volume of new water, which could all be delivered to European settlers.

To expedite the Beth, N'fis, and other existing projects, Steeg issued a decree on 4 January 1927 creating a centralized fund for major irrigation projects.[68] Formerly, funds had been dispersed in several different annual budgets. Thus, financing had been difficult to coordinate and was continually subject to interruptions—a state of affairs that had discouraged major undertakings. Steeg's legislation centralized these funds in the Caisse de l'Hydraulique Agricole et de la Colonisation, and also provided for the generation of new funds for irrigation projects.[69] To give added impetus, Steeg also obtained a loan from France of 400 million francs for water development.[70] What resulted was termed "la politique des grands barrages"—Morocco's first real irrigation development program.[71]

The Beth and N'fis dams were both begun in 1927. The following year, construction was also begun on two other dams: a storage dam on the Mellah to provide water for Casablanca's market gardens and the rapidly growing city itself; and a diversion dam on the Oum er Rbia at Kasbah Tadla to provide water for some 45,000 hectares of future colonization in the rich Tadla Plain (see Table 9 and Fig. 8).

[65] Ibid.

[66] Pascon, Le Haouz, vol. 2, p. 501.

[67] Martin, "La Question hydraulique," p. 52.

[68] "Dahir du 4 janvier 1927 portant institution d'une caisse de l'hydraulique agricole et de la colonisation," BO 746 (1927): 282.

[69] New funds were purportedly to come from the sale of phosphates, from water use fees, and from a "windfall profits" tax levied on private lands receiving government-supplied irrigation water. In fact, however, new funds came mostly from loans from France.

[70] Faure-Dère, L'Hydraulique agricole, pp. 102–104. Funds from this loan became available in 1928.

[71] Duval, L'Hydraulique au Maroc, p. 81.

In addition, the administration engaged in planning for two dams on the Moulouya to irrigate 20,000 hectares of new colonization land in the lower Moulouya Plain: a storage dam at Mechra Klila, and a diversion dam downstream at Mechra Sfa. Construction was to begin as soon as studies had been completed. Steeg also initiated planning for dam projects on the Lakhdar, the Tessaout, the el Abid, and other major streams. In all, the Steeg administration's "grands barrages" program visualized the development of perennial irrigation for nearly a quarter-million hectares.

Unfortunately, by the early 1930s, owing to economic crisis, "la politique des grands barrages" had been brought to a near standstill. Indeed, the protectorate administration could barely sustain construction on the Beth and N'fis dams alone. (The Kasbah Tadla Dam was completed in 1930, the Mellah Dam in 1931.) This was particularly true given the huge cost overruns on the Beth Dam. The administration's expensive fumbling with this dam project, and the resultant delays in irrigation, generated widespread criticism.

The difficulties experienced with the Beth Dam, however, generated criticism of a more general nature regarding the administration's handling of water development. Critics were alarmed that the administration was taking no measures to ensure that only high-value exportable crops were grown with the new irrigation water. As Lebault, president of the Casablanca Chambre d'Agriculture, laconically noted, "It is not helpful to build enormous dams to grow low-value crops."[72]

Lebault and other settler leaders organized a lobbying campaign that secured the following vow from the Government Council in 1934: "The Government should require irrigated land to be developed as rapidly as possible, and in such a manner as to pay for the dams and diminish our budget deficits."[73] By 1935, when water from the Beth and N'fis dams first became available, settlers were required to grow only citrus and other high-value crops in the irrigation perimeters. The conscious model for Morocco's new irrigation agriculture was California, as Chapter 3 will show.

Settler leaders similarly criticized the administration because its dam projects were not integrated elements of an overall development program. Projects seemingly were being implemented on an ad hoc basis. There was no attempt to prioritize projects, or to coordinate construction of canal networks with dam construction. Lebault and other lead-

[72] G. Lebault, "La Politique de l'hydraulique au Maroc," in Proceedings: *Congrès international d'Arboriculture fruitière et de Pomologie, 20 janvier–1 février, 1934* (Casablanca, 1934), p. 132.
[73] *BCAC* 49 (1934): 8.

ers mounted a vigorous lobbying campaign during the early 1930s for the kind of comprehensive irrigation plan that had been developed in California.[74] Their efforts proved to be influential. However, stronger forces ultimately swayed the administration. Chapter 4 will demonstrate how a powerful combination of unforeseen forces led to the adoption of a master irrigation plan in 1938, a plan that has served as the basis for all subsequent irrigation development.

[74] The Count de La Revelière, who was charged with an economic study mission to Morocco in 1917, had strongly advocated a comprehensive water development plan "such as has been formulated in Egypt and California." See La Revelière, *Les Energies françaises au Maroc* (Paris, 1917), p. 274.

PART II

THE 1930s

3

The California Dream

There are many interesting parallels between California and Morocco. Located at approximately the same latitude on the west coasts of their respective continents, with similar prevailing winds and cool ocean currents offshore, they are roughly equivalent in size and shape (Fig. 3). Each has a distinct backbone of high mountains in the east. Both have predominantly Mediterranean climates and sizable desert areas. Los Angeles and Casablanca, at nearly the same latitude, have almost identical statistics for average annual temperature, temperature range, and precipitation.[1] Similar correspondence exists between Sacramento and Meknes, Fresno and Settat, Bakersfield and Chichaoua, Riverside and Marrakech, and Indio and Dar Ould Zidouh, to give a few examples.[2] Morocco is one of California's closest natural analogues.[3]

These parallels are significant because they hypnotized French settlers, entrepreneurs, and protectorate administrators during the crisis of the 1930s in Moroccan colonial agriculture. In probably no other country did California come to exert such an influence on foreign agriculture.

Why California? The answer lies in the brilliant example that the state had set through development of its agricultural resources. By

[1] Los Angeles: lat. 34° N, 63° F average annual temperature, 17° average annual temperature range, 381 mm average annual precipitation; Casablanca: lat. 33° 36′ N, 63° F average annual temperature, 18° average annual temperature range, 406 mm average annual precipitation (*Great International Atlas* [Milwaukie, 1981], pp. x–xi, Index 24, 72).

[2] *LTM* 28 (1933): 14–15.

[3] R. W. Durrenberger and R. B. Johnson, *California: Patterns on the Land* (Palo Alto, 1976), p. 26; R. W. Hodgson, "L'Industrie et les possibilités de l'arboriculture fruitière en Afrique du Nord française," *FPAN* 118 (1941): 167.

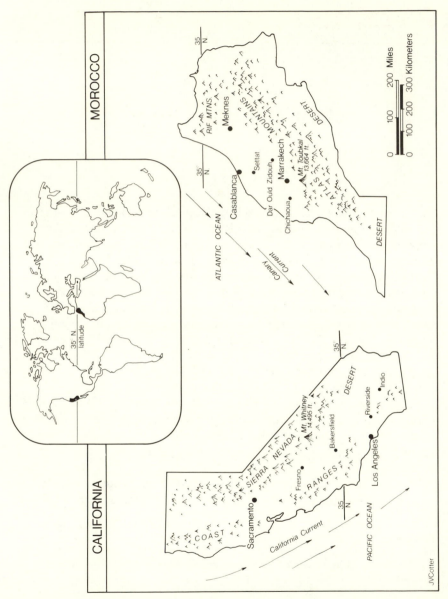

FIGURE 3 The California–Morocco analogy

1930, California accounted for 90 percent or more of all U.S. production in almonds, apricots, avocados, dates, dried prunes, figs, grapes, lemons, olives, and walnuts, and for well over half of its cantaloupe, orange, peach, fresh plum, and prune production.[4] Moreover, thanks to its fruit industry's formidable technical and commercial organization, the Golden State was rapidly penetrating world markets.

As one Casablanca reporter proclaimed in 1931:

> The reputation of California's wealth through irrigated agriculture is worldwide and is so striking . . . because the majority of these crops have been developed on formerly worthless land, indeed on desert wastelands. . . . Throughout the entire world the California example . . . symbolizes the modern miracle of irrigation.[5]

To be sure, Morocco was not the only country to be influenced by California. Spain, South Africa, Argentina, Brazil, Italy, Palestine, Russia, New Zealand, Canada, even neighboring Algeria, were among the countries that carefully studied California's innovative fruit industry and adopted certain of its highly successful methods.[6] However, the California example was probably most faithfully replicated in Morocco. Only in Morocco did certain policymakers aspire to create "une nouvelle Californie."

The California example was introduced in 1928. During a subsequent "implantation period," from 1929 to 1933, a major new orientation towards California-style irrigation agriculture emerged. Finally, after 1933 there was a broad-based effort "to convert the Morocco first conceived as a granary of wheat into a vast orchard" following techniques pioneered in California.[7]

This chapter's primary purpose is to explain how during the 1930s a modern, highly capitalistic, agribusiness approach—representing a clean break with past French tradition—became tightly woven into agricultural policy in Morocco. Its secondary purpose is to show how, after the collapse of the colonial wheat venture, policy in Morocco began to be formulated by a broad spectrum of actors, including settler leaders, private businessmen, commercial agents, foreign legation staff, journalists, and local colonial officials.

---

[4] U.S. Department of Agriculture, *Yearbook of Agriculture 1933* (Washington, D.C.: GPO, 1933), pp. 508–562.

[5] G. Louis, *Sources d'eau, sources d'or, sources d'hommes (un reportage de la "Vigie Marocaine" en Californie, juin 1931)* (Casablanca, 1932), p. 5.

[6] *LTM* 26 (1933): 27; *RC* 1931, p. 107; *FPAN* 51 (1935): 143.

[7] R. Hoffherr, *L'Economie marocaine* (Paris, 1932), p. 152.

Introduction of the California Example

In 1928, M. Laguerre, the French commercial attaché in San Francisco, traveled to Morocco to address an agricultural conference. His topic was California's fruit industry and its implications for Morocco. Portraying the "grandes analogies" between California and Morocco, Laguerre detailed what California had accomplished.[8] Beginning with a desert, it had created over a million hectares of admirably maintained fruit orchards through irrigation. The California fruit industry generated an unbelievable 16 to 18 billion francs a year. Fruit was shipped throughout the United States, to Europe; indeed, throughout the world. California agriculture had achieved phenomenal success.

What lesson could Morocco derive? Laguerre emphasized that Morocco not only had California's mild climate, water resources, and rich earth, but certain additional advantages. California was forty days by boat from Europe, and its fruit often spoiled in transit. By contrast, Morocco was admirably situated near the large European markets. Second, labor costs in California were comparatively high. Here Morocco, with cheap native labor, had a clear economic advantage. In short, Morocco could prosper through developing a fruit industry.

Laguerre was convinced that Morocco could produce all the major fruit crops. Oranges and almonds, he claimed, would find their true home in Morocco; the apricot and plum would also succeed admirably. As for varieties to adopt, he cautioned against looking to nurseries in France. Instead, settlers should go directly to sources in California. California had already adapted its fruit varieties to a land "which very much resembles Morocco."[9] For oranges, for example, he recommended the major California varieties: the Valencia late and the Washington and Thompson navels. By specializing in California citrus, Morocco could also profit from the intensive advertising campaigns that the California fruit industry had waged. California growers, for example, had already established a market in Paris for navel oranges.

Marketing, Laguerre emphasized, was the secret of California's success story; it was the key that would also unlock Morocco's agricultural fortune. He described in great detail how California had revolutionized agriculture. Growers had joined together into powerful cooperatives, had established rigorously controlled standards for each crop, had standardized packaging, had created popular brands such as

[8] Direction Générale de l'Agriculture, *Journée de l'arbre fruitier, 15 avril 1928* (Casablanca, 1929), p. 12.
[9] Ibid., p. 14.

"Sunkist," and had hired marketing experts to analyze and penetrate markets. In marketing, above all, Laguerre urged Morocco to follow California's example "blindly."[10]

Laguerre's speech made a deep impression on the settlers and administrators in his audience. Indeed, from the present vantage point, it reads like an uncannily accurate vision of Morocco's future fruit industry. Laguerre's sketch of California's powerful growers' cooperatives could be mistaken for a blueprint of the official Office Chérifien de Contrôle et d'Exportation established in 1932. His description of California's procedures of standardization and marketing could within a few years be accurately applied to Morocco. And even his recommendations regarding the California orange varieties to adopt seemingly were followed. These varieties became the backbone of Morocco's citrus industry.

The "Implantation Period," 1929–33

California was immediately perceived as a beacon that could guide colonial Morocco out of its dark agricultural crisis. Between 1929 and 1933, at least a half-dozen French agricultural study missions visited California. Influential colonists went to study horticulture at the University of California. French commercial attachés and agents in California actively engaged in agricultural "espionage." Agricultural methods, irrigation techniques, and select crop varieties were transferred en masse from California to Morocco. Private and governmental propaganda energetically promoted the new orientation; new journals were founded to instruct growers. In addition, the protectorate government created an agency to organize and regulate the new industry. By 1933, five years after Laguerre's speech, a major new colonial agriculture had emerged in Morocco, based on irrigation and the export of citrus fruits and early vegetables on the California pattern. Events during this brief period greatly influence Moroccan agriculture today. To understand the origins of Morocco's present agricultural policy, it is necessary to examine key phenomena of this period.

[10] Ibid., p. 15. Laguerre claimed that future world demand for fresh fruit was practically unlimited. Through clever advertising, the Californians were outstripping supply with demand: Growers simply could not keep up. The California Fruit Growers Exchange began advertising oranges in a trial newspaper campaign in Iowa in 1907. This campaign rapidly succeded in doubling orange sales in the target area and was gradually extended to other areas.

GUILLEMET'S MISSION

Paul Guillemet, president of the Casablanca Chamber of Agriculture during the late 1920s, was well known throughout Morocco for his indefatigable advocacy of irrigation development (Illus. 4). In October 1929, Guillemet traveled at his own expense to witness California's irrigation miracle.[11] He probably hoped this mission would provide convincing propaganda for his campaign for a new agricultural policy in Morocco.

Upon his return, Guillemet held numerous conferences to popularize the California model. He became, according to one newspaper reporter, "the great initiator of California methods in Morocco."[12] His basic message was that California was indeed one of the wonders of the modern world. Western Morocco was remarkably like California. Irrigated agriculture based on the California example was the remedy for Morocco's moribund colonial agriculture.[13]

Guillemet was a skillful promoter. For example, he translated and published extracts from the annual financial report of the California Fruit Growers Exchange, which represented approximately three-fourths of California's citrus growers. In his words, "My goal is . . . to let readers remark the incredible wealth generated by California's growers, particularly orange growers. May this financial report . . . be an encouragement to all who would like to see Morocco covered with fruit plantations."[14] Guillemet also had taken numerous photos depicting California's lush orchards, which he had published (see Illus. 5). They suggested the prosperous future open to Morocco through adoption of the California model.

MISSION OFFICIELLE

As a result of Guillemet's efforts, the Casablanca Chamber of Agriculture demanded that an official mission be sent to California to study "the procedures of irrigation, cultivation, and market preparation that have been pushed to such a high degree of perfection in this land."[15]

[11] P. Guillemet, "Regards sur l'hydraulique agricole au Maroc," *LTM* 54 (1934): 14. Guillemet was probably the organizing force behind the 1928 conference at which Laguerre spoke.

[12] *La Vigie Marocaine*, 7 May 1931, p.1.

[13] P. Guillemet, "La Colonisation nord-africaine, l'exemple de la Californie," *RC*, 1931, pp. 475–476.

[14] P. Guillemet, "Un Bel Exemple de coopération agricole," *BCAC* 9 (1930): 3–4.

[15] *BCAC* 18 (1931): 34.

As in many other instances, when the powerful colonial chambers proposed, the protectorate administration soon disposed.

Lucien Saint, Morocco's resident general, announced on 24 June
1930, "We have been attempting to identify crops that would fare well
on world markets. Fruit cultivation is of the greatest interest from this
point of view and justifies sending a study mission to California."[16]

A week later, at the sixth North African Conference in Algiers, Saint
met with his Algerian and Tunisian counterparts. The three leaders
agreed to send an official mission to gather precise information on
California's irrigation development and fruit industry. For agriculture,
specifically, the mission was:

1. To seek out the fruit varieties that were prolific bearers, were in
   high demand on world markets, and would prosper in North Africa
2. To determine the most appropriate root stocks
3. To identify the most advanced horticultural methods
4. To take comprehensive notes on the techniques of selection, clas-
   sification, preservation, and packaging used in California
5. To carefully study how the producer organizations functioned.[17]

It is unclear why the plan for this Mission Nord-africaine broke
down. Instead, Morocco and Algeria each sent separate official missions.[18] By contrast, Tunisia hired a California horticultural expert to
recommend how it might develop its own fruit industry. Interestingly,
this expert, Professor William Hodgson of the University of California, reportedly came to North Africa as a "double agent," hired by the
U.S. government to evaluate the potential of French North Africa's
fruit industry[19] (see Illus. 4). This amused, flattered, and encouraged
Morocco's settlers. "California cannot be indifferent to our hopes and
plans, and nothing is more normal than that she should come here to
see the degree to which we might present a threat, and how, in consequence, she should defend herself."[20]

[16] RC, 1930, p. 460.

[17] Ibid., p. 443.

[18] For the reports of the Algerian mission to California, see M. J. Brichet, *Mission
algérienne agricole et commerciale aux Etats-Unis (mai–juin 1932): rapport technique sur les
cultures fruitières* (Algiers, 1932); and M. R. Martin, *Mission algérienne agricole et commerciale aux Etats-Unis (mai–juin 1932): rapport sur les irrigations aux Etats-Unis* (Algiers,
1932).

[19] LTM 6 (1931): 35; 7 (1931): 23.

[20] LTM 6 (1931): 35. While in Morocco during summer 1931, Hodgson visited
orange orchards near Marrakech, Oulad Said, and Larache, and in the Gharb and
Chaouia plains. His pronouncement following this tour—at least, according to one
colonial editor—was that "Morocco possesses a unique synthesis of agrologic, hydro-

Morocco's official mission visited California during autumn 1930. It consisted of Trintignac, from Rural Engineering; Brayard, the director of the government's experimental farm at Marrakech; Picard, a hydraulic engineer and adjunct director of Public Works; and Durand, a pioneer orange grower at Moghrane.[21]

After the group's return, and while an official report was being drafted, Trintignac and Brayard gave a series of preliminary reports to settler groups that received wide press attention. What most impressed Morocco's settlers was the vastness of California's irrigation development, the minimal number of fruit varieties that were cultivated, and the high profit margin that accrued to California's growers as a result of their participation in powerful cooperatives like the Fruit Growers Exchange.[22]

It is clear from statements of the period that the protectorate administration intended to place heavy emphasis on the official report when it was completed. The report was to be the primary source of the new agricultural policy.[23] Meanwhile, there were three influential private missions to California. They clearly demonstrate that the establishment of California agricultural methods in Morocco resulted from the efforts of a broad spectrum of different interest groups. Each mission will be briefly described to show its specific character and impact.

THE PLM MISSION

At a colonial agricultural conference in Morocco in spring 1931, Monsieur Loubet, a representative of one of France's largest transport firms, announced his company's intention to promote production of fruit and early vegetables in Morocco. He candidly noted that because agricultural freight was a major portion of his company's business, development of a fruit and vegetable industry in Morocco would have a major positive influence on its profits. His company, the Compagnie de Chemins de Fer PLM, believed that fruits and vegetables could have

graphical, climatic, and geographical elements. They uncontestably constitute a potential Empire whose fruit-producing perspectives, particularly for oranges, are unlimited" (*LTM* 7 [1931]: 23).

[21] *BCAR*, 1931, p. 298.

[22] *FPAN* 3 (1931): 88; *BCAC* 18 (1931): 35. Trintignac reported that navel oranges and Valencia lates made up 98 percent of California's total orange production.

[23] See, for example, Resident General Saint's comments before the Government Council on 27 December 1930 (*RC*, 1931, p. 62); the comments of E. Miège, director of Agricultural Experimentation, on 30 January 1931 (*BCAR* 1931, p. 41); or the comments of Lefevre, director general of Agriculture, before the Rabat Chambre d'Agriculture on 23 December 1931 (ibid., p. 164).

an "unlimited future" in Morocco.[24] However, marketing would first need to be organized on a sound, rational basis. Loubet informed Morocco's settlers that with their country's nascent fruit and early vegetable industry in mind, he had visited California (also Florida and southern Texas) in June 1930 to study American methods of marketing agricultural products. The trip had convinced him that the keys to the American success were producer cooperatives, brand names to inspire consumer confidence, a limited number of select varieties, rigorous sorting and inspecting, and skillful advertising.

The fruit industry worldwide, he noted, was characterized by increasingly aggressive competition. Italy and other major exporters had already adopted American methods. But here Morocco had an advantage: It was a new country. American methods could more easily be established. He urged settlers to demand that the protectorate government put American agricultural marketing methods in place.

Loubet's mission to California demonstrates that powerful private commercial interests were involved in promoting California-style agriculture in Morocco. Specifically, the PLM Company's behind-the-scenes lobbying in Paris and Rabat probably helped bring about the establishment of the Office Chérifien de Contrôle et d'Exportation.

DUCROCQ'S MISSION

Pierre Ducrocq's was perhaps the stealthiest mission sent to California. Ducrocq was the son of Georges Ducrocq, the pioneer of horticultural experimentation in Morocco and the owner of a large nursery near Casablanca.[25] In 1930, the elder Ducrocq sent his son Pierre to study horticulture for two years at the University of California. This mission had ulterior motives: "not only to study California methods, but also to gather information on all fruit varieties cultivated on a large scale for export."[26] The younger Ducrocq was obviously busy. During

[24] *BCAC* 17 (1931): 9.

[25] Georges Ducrocq introduced and acclimatized more than five hundred fruit and ornamental tree varieties to Morocco between 1915 and 1931. See *LTM* 4 (1931): 1. With a Monsieur Sanchez, he was the first European citrus planter in Morocco: Ducrocq and Sanchez shared a 1921 shipment of orange trees from Misserghine, Algeria, with which Ducrocq established an experimental orchard at Tit-Mellil. See R. Lauriac, *Le Maroc, terre d'agrumes* (Casablanca, 1938), pp. 37–38. Brayard, director of the government's experimental farm at Marrakech, who went on the 1930 official mission to California, had been director of experimentation at Ducrocq's Tit-Mellil orchard. Georges Ducrocq was also one of the seventeen members of the Casablanca Chambre d'Agriculture—a fellow member with Guillemet.

[26] *LTM* 4 (1931): 1.

his stay in California, his father once wrote, "Each post brings us grafts, seeds, cuttings, and pieces of information gathered through great effort in various California orchards."[27] During this period, and largely through the Ducrocqs' efforts, pure California varieties of oranges, principally navels and Valencia lates, were introduced into Morocco.[28] The Ducrocqs' private experimentation, far more than any governmental experimentation, established Moroccan fruit cultivation on a secure foundation. From their nursery, a large portion of Morocco's future citrus orchards derived.

In the mid-1930s, Pierre Ducrocq replaced his father as director of the Ducrocq nursery operation. He was thus in an influential position to continue disseminating California-style agriculture in Morocco. His mission to California had an impact in another way. At least two other French settlers followed his example and went to study horticulture at the University of California: George Decoux, who afterwards became director of the principal journal of the French citrus industry, the influential *Fruits et Primeurs de l'Afrique du Nord*, published in Morocco; and M. Gérard, who later managed a large orange plantation near Marrakech.[29]

MISSION OF *La Vigie Marocaine*

The final mission during the crucial implantation period was undertaken by Georges Louis. Louis was a well-known journalist for *La Vigie Marocaine*, the leading French newspaper in Morocco. His mission was by far the most highly publicized of all the California missions, and was possibly the most influential of all.

Why was another mission sent to California, after the previous missions had thoroughly documented the essentials of the California success story? The answer lies in this mission's different motive. It was undertaken expressly to sell the general public on the California example. Louis's employer, Pierre Mas, owner of *La Vigie Marocaine*, was convinced that irrigation was the key to Morocco's future. He conceived the idea of a major *reportage* on California as an effective means to promote Moroccan irrigation development.[30]

[27] Ibid.

[28] Lauriac, *Le Maroc*, pp. 37–38.

[29] Hodgson, "L'Industrie," p. 168.

[30] G. Louis, "D'une enquête marocaine à un reportage en Californie," *La Vigie Marocaine* (7 May 1931), p. 1; Louis, *Sources d'eau*, p. 6. Another colonial newspaper launched a related campaign during the same period. From February to July 1931, seemingly in orchestration with Louis, *Le Petit Marocain* conducted a sustained attack

The Vigie mission took place during June 1931. Louis drafted a total of forty-six articles, and these appeared in *La Vigie Marocaine* upon his return. In 1932, they were published together with the clever title *Sources d'eau, sources d'or, sources d'hommes*. The title accurately summarizes Louis's message. California, through irrigation, had caused the desert to blossom, creating immense wealth that had become a magnet for men, creating more wealth. Morocco could do the same.

Specific case histories formed bright examples in Louis's account. For example, the Imperial Valley in California's far south—a desert Louis claimed was more barren than any in Morocco—had become the "winter garden" of the United States through irrigation. In 1900, no inhabitants lived in the region; in 1928, there were 60,000. That same year, 56,000 railway cars of agricultural produce left the valley— about one per inhabitant.[31] In the lush Merced irrigation district further north in the Central Valley, deserted placer mine tailings were now all that remained from Gold Rush days. Mining wealth had been ephemeral. Irrigated agriculture created wealth in perpetuity.[32]

California had already converted some 40 percent of its cultivated acreage to irrigation.[33] Yet it was characteristic of the California spirit, Louis emphasized, that the state was optimistically and enthusiastically planning for the future. A master plan for water development had been formulated. Louis analyzed this master plan in detail. He described, for example, how the state planned to conquer the desert expanses of its "far south." By the damming of the Colorado River, 7.5 million new inhabitants were to be settled in this desert region.[34] The concept of a comprehensive water plan grew rapidly in the Moroccan colonial imagination. Half a decade later, Morocco developed its own master plan, as will be discussed in Chapter 4.

---

on the protectorate administration's handling of water development. Its major theme was that it would be useless to become entranced by Californian agriculture if one did not allow for the practical means: irrigation. With irrigation, France could make Morocco "an Egypt multiplied by a California" (L. Delau, ed., *Le Maroc à la croisée des chemins* [Casablanca, 1931], p. 229. Delau's work is a compilation of the *Petit Marocain* articles).

[31] Louis, *Sources d'eau*, p. 45.

[32] Ibid., p. 17. Louis was quite eloquent in his enthusiasm for California. For example, in contrast to the arid ruins of the Merced gold mines were "the beauty of the irrigated landscapes, their sweetness and poetry, the joy and sense of repose they inspire, the life they fecundate and perpetuate."

[33] Ibid., p. 134.

[34] Ibid., p. 24.

In sum, Louis sought to seek out and portray "all in California that could inspire a Moroccan."[35] Morocco, assaulted by economic crisis and poised at a dark crossroads, would not hesitate if it could see California's accomplishment. In arid lands such as Morocco and California, water was the measure of development and wealth. He concluded that the California example "dictates to our leaders their duty."[36]

Louis's newspaper campaign was a tour de force. In selling the California dream, it was remarkably successful. As might be expected, its impact was particularly significant within the agricultural community. In an investigation of Morocco's citrus industry conducted in 1938, many prominent growers credited Louis with inspiring their decisions to begin fruit cultivation and to adopt California's production techniques.[37]

NEW SPECIALIZED JOURNALS

In the campaign to foster irrigated agriculture *à la Californie* in Morocco, special mention must be made of two journals: *Fruits et Primeurs de l'Afrique du Nord* and *La Terre Marocaine*. L. Cornice, a citrus grower and prominent settler, founded the former in January 1931 to disseminate technical and commercial information and to create an organ for Morocco's new growers and associated industries. *Fruits et Primeurs* soon became the principal journal for the entire North African fruit industry. Its impact on Moroccan agriculture was particularly important during the early and mid-1930s. Almost every issue contained detailed reports on aspects of California's irrigated agriculture. Translations of reports by University of California agricultural experiment stations and similar agencies also figured prominently.

The second journal, *La Terre Marocaine*, was established in June 1931 as an official publication of the Direction de l'Agriculture. It was sent free of charge to every settler in Morocco, and therefore served as an instrument of government agricultural policy. *La Terre Marocaine* conducted a campaign during the early 1930s to promote irrigated agriculture and diversification toward "rich" crops following the California example. Like *Fruits et Primeurs*, it also disseminated information on American agricultural and irrigation techniques gleaned from legation reports or its own translation efforts. The amount of technical information transferred to Morocco within a short period of time was

---

[35] Ibid., p. 133.
[36] Ibid., p. 123.
[37] Lauriac, *Le Maroc*, passim.

remarkable. The new Moroccan industry thus became established on a solid foundation.

OFFICIAL MISSION REPORT

The official report, oddly entitled *De Los Angeles à Rabat*, was published in biweekly installments in *La Terre Marocaine* beginning 15 October 1932.[38] Because it arrived in regular installments in each settler's home, it can be presumed that it was seen by virtually all of the colonial agricultural community. It was *the* official report, and had the force of official policy. *La Terre Marocaine* referred to it as "a charter" of the new fruit industry in Morocco.[39]

Replete with tables and graphs, this report was the longest and most comprehensive analysis of the California-Morocco analogy and of California's irrigation agriculture. It convincingly established the similarity between California and Morocco and projected a prosperous future for Morocco if it followed the Golden State's example. The report was organized into two major sections: one written by Trintignac on Californian irrigation and how it could be applied in Morocco; the other by Brayard on the California fruit industry.

From the diagrams and precise detail Trintignac presented on California's irrigation techniques, it is clear he intended his report to serve as a practical manual for Morocco's colonial farmers. Indirect evidence suggests that Trintignac's report had some direct impact. For example, the 1938 survey of Morocco's citrus industry noted that leading settlers were employing Californian irrigation techniques, though it did not specify which techniques.[40] Advertisements in Moroccan settler magazines and journals indicate that the specific term "l'irrigation californienne" then referred primarily to buried irrigation pipes (Illus. 6). This technology was probably adopted only by the wealthiest fruit growers because of its expense.

Trintignac revealed that he had personally attempted to apply the "lesson received" in California within his own area of authority.[41] He claimed he had had the principal canals of the Marrakech region lined with concrete, and had formulated a preliminary plan for the irrigation of the Haouz plain based on the principles of the Reclamation Service.[42] As will be seen, Trintignac later was responsible for irrigation

[38] *De Los Angeles à Rabat, LTM*, 18 (1932) to 33 (1933).
[39] Ibid., 18 (1932): 26.
[40] Lauriac, *Le Maroc*, passim.
[41] *LTM* 33 (1933): 25.
[42] Ibid.

development in all of Morocco, and was thus in a position to apply the California lesson to the country as a whole.

In general, it is apparent that the official mission was highly impressed with the scientific, rational, and extensive nature of California's irrigation. The mission's favorable response cleared the way for the protectorate government's major commitment to irrigation development.

Brayard's section of the official report presented a complete history of the California fruit industry. Its most important part, however, was its analysis of cultivation methods for each principal California fruit crop. For citrus, it offered comprehensive recommendations on varieties, selection of grafts and trees, propagation, appropriate soils, spacing of trees, pruning, fertilizing, irrigation, harvesting techniques, packaging, and shipping. Similar information was provided in less detail for the other major subtropical fruits. The report, in essence, put a complete California fruit growers' manual at the disposal of the nascent Moroccan fruit industry.

The official report specifically advanced one major policy recommendation, the creation of a government agency to organize Morocco's new fruit and vegetable industry: "Only by strict cooperation between all producers, and the establishment of a technical and commercial agency by the protectorate administration, an agency capable of guiding growers, will Morocco be able to achieve the place it deserves on the world market."[43] From this recommendation came the California-inspired Office Chérifien de Contrôle et d'Exportation.

THE OCE

The Office Chérifien de Contrôle et d'Exportation (OCE) officially came into being on 1 April 1932. It was patterned closely after the California Fruit Growers Exchange, to which some 75 percent of California's citrus growers belonged.[44] Following the lead of the California cooperative, which marketed products under the "Sunkist" label, the OCE immediately created a "Maroc" label (Fig. 4).

The OCE's role was basically identical to the California Fruit Growers Exchange: to establish standards for each Moroccan fruit or vegetable to be exported; to confer the "Maroc" label only on shipments of highest quality; to reject produce of inferior quality; to oversee research on new varieties; to disseminate information to the agricul-

---

[43] Ibid., 26 (1933): 29.
[44] BCAR (1931), pp. 164–165.

LA QUALITÉ

sauvegarde du contingent:

La marque qui garantit la qualité

FIGURE 4 The OCE's "Maroc" label for select agricultural exports, 1932

tural community; to analyze markets; and to conduct advertising for Morocco's fruits and vegetables. Essentially the same institution has continued to the present.[45] The success of the Moroccan fruit industry can to a significant degree be attributed to the OCE's implementation of agricultural marketing techniques pioneered in California.

[45] See *LTM* 12 (1932): 3 and *BCAR* 1935, p. 273, for the role of the OCE. The OCE was in 1986 in the process of being transformed, if not dismantled, because it had become more of a hindrance than a help to Morocco's export agriculture.

Realizations: The Maturation
of the California Dream

The 1929–33 implantation period, in sum, was a crucial turning point for modern commercial agriculture in Morocco. The various study missions to California, "espionage" efforts of French attachés and agents in California, the great publicity given to the California example, the zeal and effectiveness of the individuals who aspired to sell this example to Morocco, all combined to create a new direction for colonial agriculture in Morocco.

While many different varieties of fruits and vegetables were introduced from California to Morocco during the early 1930s, and are still grown there today, citrus (particularly oranges) quickly became the dominant specialty of Morocco's new agriculture. The explanation for this is simple. By 1934, production of market vegetables in Morocco had reached a quota ceiling established by France to protect its own domestic growers.[46] Beyond this ceiling, tariffs were applied. This put a damper on vegetable production in Morocco, which lasted until after independence. On the other hand, from 1933, the citrus quota ceiling was set so high that it guaranteed a lucrative market in France for Morocco's citrus growers.[47] In addition, Morocco's settlers were warned that the Parisian government and agricultural groups in France looked favorably on citrus production, but were indisposed toward cultivation of other fruit varieties that might compete with agriculture in France itself.[48]

The strong influence of the California example is clearly reflected in statistics on the expansion of citrus cultivation in Morocco. Table 2 demonstrates that only 265 hectares of citrus were planted by European settlers in Morocco from 1912 to 1928, when the wheat policy was in full force.[49] During the subsequent implantation period, 1929–33, Europeans planted over 2,000 hectares of citrus. Finally, after 1934, colonial citrus cultivation in Morocco rapidly expanded.[50] Plant-

---

[46] *BCAR* 21 (1934): 25.

[47] J. Le Coz, "Les Agrumes marocains," *Notes Marocaines* 13 (1960): 54.

[48] *BCAR* 21 (1934): 26. See p. 84 below for more on this theme.

[49] Sources for Table 2 include: Le Coz, "Les Agrumes marocains," p. 52; *Annuaire Statistique, 1940–1945* 56 (Paris, 1946), p. 353; FAO, *Yearbook of Food and Agricultural Statistics* (Rome, 1948–1959).

[50] Besides the large tariff-free quota on Moroccan citrus granted by France in 1933, which guaranteed a profitable market, two additional factors helped to stimulate the expansion of citrus in Morocco: (1) the Spanish Civil War (1936–39), which diminished Spain's citrus exports and created an extra demand for citrus from Morocco; and

TABLE 2   Expansion of Citrus and Comparison of Citrus Exports with
Wheat Exports in French Morocco, 1912–1956

Period	Hectares planted		Total hectares	Average annual exports (1,000s of metric tons)	
	Europeans	Moroccans		Citrus	Wheat
1912–28	265	1,205	1,470	—	N.A.
1929–33	2,020	400	3,890	—	N.A.
1934–38	5,745	1,215	10,850	5.5	117.8
1939–43	5,240	1,420	17,510	11.3	99.9
1944–48	4,335	1,940	23,785	27.8	10.1
1949–53	11,216	2,774	37,775	104.8	41.3
1954–56	7,069	1,436	46,280	127.5	207.7

SOURCES: See note 49.

ing of citrus by wealthy native Moroccans was a parallel phenomenon.
By the end of the protectorate in 1956, citrus orchards in Morocco
covered nearly 50,000 hectares.

The table also compares citrus exports with exports of wheat, the
earlier colonial specialty crop, in order to document the growing importance of citrus in the protectorate economy. After 1942, annual
citrus exports from Morocco generally exceeded wheat exports in total
tonnage, and nearly always greatly exceeded them in value.[51]

Expansion of citrus growing in Morocco during the protectorate
period would have been even more dramatic had it not been dependent on government irrigation development, which was stymied by various political and economic factors. Nonetheless, by the late 1930s, a
French journalist proclaimed, "The miracle of irrigation, which made
California's fortune, is occurring again on Moroccan soil."[52] And in
1951, an American analyst noted, "French Morocco has the most rapidly growing citrus industry . . . perhaps in the world."[53]

The comparative success of the California policy contrasts sharply
with the failure of the earlier wheat policy. Both policies were significantly influenced by idealistic environmental visions. What differed

(2) the flight of capital from France during World War II and its investment in citrus
production in Morocco. See Le Coz, "Les Agrumes marocains," p. 54.

[51] Only in 1944 and 1955 did wheat exports from Morocco exceed citrus exports in
value during the 1942–56 period. Morocan citrus usually commanded double the price
of Moroccan wheat for equal weight.

[52] Lauriac, Le Maroc, p. 83.

[53] J. H. Burke, The Citrus Industries of North Africa, Foreign Agriculture Report 66,
(Washington, D.C., January 1952), p. 70.

was the degree of fit between environmental vision and Morocco's environmental reality.

The California connection continued up to the end of the protectorate, as translation efforts of the Direction de l'Agriculture, continuing reports from the French legation in San Francisco,[54] and agricultural study missions to California in 1948, 1950, 1951, and 1953 attest.[55] The 1938 survey of Morocco's citrus industry revealed that many settlers were employing Californian agricultural techniques and had planted primarily Californian varieties.[56] Confirming this point, the Syndicat Général Marocain des Producteurs d'Agrumes found in 1948 that 80 percent of all Moroccan orange production consisted of California varieties: Washington navels and Valencia lates.[57]

The California connection is today an almost completely forgotten chapter in Moroccan agricultural history. The same California-inspired policy, however, forged during the early 1930s in the crucible of a colonial agricultural crisis, founded on large-scale irrigation development, and oriented toward export production of citrus fruits and early vegetables, has continued intact. Exports of fruits and vegetables accounted for over four-fifths of all Morocco's agricultural exports in 1986.[58] For oranges alone, Morocco is currently the world's second largest exporter, accounting for 13 percent of the international trade in 1984.[59]

The following 1933 account provides a fitting summation:

> Their dream was to create a new California in Morocco. Struck
> by analogies of climate and natural conditions—as well as by the

---

[54] Agricultural reports from California began in 1926. In the uncatalogued French archives at the Bibliothèque Générale in Rabat, there are several dossiers of legation reports.

[55] For the Garnier mission of 1948, see *BCAR*, 1948, pp. 1374–1379; 1949, pp. 1746–1750, 1773–1784, 1870–1875. For the 1950-51 mission, see L. Blanc, H. Chapot, and G. Cuenot, *La Culture et la sélection des agrumes subtropicaux aux U.S.A. (Notes de Mission, novembre 1950–janvier 1951)*, mimeographed report (Rabat, 1951). For the Darlot-Monzies mission of 1951, see M. Darlot, "Considérations sur l'organisation des zones irriguées . . . aux Etats-Unis," *Bulletin de la Société des Agriculteurs du Maroc* 37 (1951): 6–21; Monzies, "Compte rendu d'une mission aux Etats-Unis: 'les irrigations,'" ibid. 34 (1951): 4–24. Darlot and Monzies were supported by Marshall Plan funds. For Mussard's 1953 mission, see *FPAN*, 1953, pp. 435–442; *BCAR* 1954, pp. 4387–4396.

[56] Lauriac, *Terre d'agrumes*, passim.

[57] Burke, *Citrus Industries*, p. 69. The clementine, of Algerian origin, which according to the same survey accounted for nearly 17 percent of Morocco's citrus production, was the most important non-California variety established in Morocco.

[58] *FAO Monthly Bulletin of Statistics* 1986, various issues.

[59] Ibid., 1985.

results of a dynamic irrigation policy that had succeeded in transforming a near-desert into a magnificent orchard, furnishing the entire world with choice fruits—settlers wanted to achieve the same miracle in Morocco.[60]

The present Moroccan landscape testifies that they were at least partly successful. This very success, however, would later lead to agricultural crisis.

[60] G. Duval, *L'Hydraulique au Maroc* (Paris, 1933), p. 94.

4

One Million Hectares
by the Year 2000

The primary motive of government irrigation policy in the early 1930s was to rescue colonial agriculture. However, a comprehensive irrigation plan had emerged by the late 1930s that envisioned irrigation development for Moroccan peasants on a vast scale. This surprising turn of events will be analyzed in the present chapter. Its purpose is to explain the genesis of the plan to put a million hectares under perennial irrigation—a plan that has served as the foundation of all subsequent irrigation development in Morocco.

Water for Colons: The Doldrum Period

Henri Cosnier, in his 1920 report on colonial agriculture, estimated that "at least 50,000 hectares" in Morocco could be put into perennial irrigation.[1] This figure must have seemed embarrassingly modest even as his report appeared. Official estimates of Morocco's irrigation potential rapidly expanded as pacification annexed the fiercely independent highlands, French engineers methodically inventoried the country's

[1] H. Cosnier, L'Afrique du Nord—son avenir agricole et économique (Paris, 1922), p. 17. The protectorate administration had conducted studies from 1915 to 1918 on the three major rivers of the western French zone: the Oum er Rbia, the Sebou, and the Tensift. It had found that, although nearly all of the Tensift was diverted during summer for native irrigation, summer flows of 40 cubic meters/second for the Oum er Rbia and 12 cubic meters/second for the Sebou flowed unused out to sea. Cosnier's 50,000-hectare figure was arrived at via a calculation that used 50 cubic meters/second as the combined flow for the two rivers and that allowed 1 liter/second per hectare for irrigation.

water resources, attractive dam sites became identified, colonial agriculture suffered the curse of Morocco's arid climate, and the colonization program exhausted its reserves of viable land. By 1928, the Steeg administration's ambitious "grands barrages" program embraced a goal of nearly a quarter-million hectares.

This same year, however, Picard, adjunct director of Public Works, estimated Morocco's irrigable area as "at least 1 million hectares."[2] This echoed the estimate of the British explorers Hooker and Ball sixty years earlier. Hooker and Ball's promising appraisal of Morocco's irrigation potential had been widely circulated in the French colonial literature. Now, the million-hectare vision gradually resurfaced, resurrected by the desperate need to improve colonial agriculture, lured forth by California's golden example.

Unfortunately, the irrigation dream was expanding to full form just when funds to fulfill it were receding to their lowest ebb. During the first half of the 1930s, the protectorate government could barely sustain construction on the few dam projects already initiated. Other dam projects gathered dust in ministry drawers for lack of funds. New funds would not be forthcoming until 1936.[3] The wide gap between irrigation dream and Morocco's arid reality, between rising expectations and declining possibilities, generated a high level of discontent among settlers.

The plight of settlers during the agricultural crisis motivated them first to seek comfort from the government, then to demand it. The government gradually responded with an extension of protective care over the whole settler community, not just the official, or government-supported, settlers. It now assumed an almost condescending attitude: "Given the natural and human conditions of North Africa . . . the settler there is like a delicate and valuable plant that has been transplanted at great cost and that cannot be left without constant attention lest it be choked by the natural vegetation."[4] Unfortunately, owing to lack of funds, the government could merely attempt to appease the agricultural community with inexpensive gestures like the official mission to California. While the Moroccan colonial ship was stalled by lack of funds, its idle crew used its energies to complain.

An example will serve to illuminate this difficult and penurious pe-

[2] *BCAR*, 1946, p. 379.

[3] J. Maréchal, "Les Dépenses du protectorat pour la mise en valeur du Maroc entre 1928 et 1936," *BESM* 12 (1936): 91. The last previous funding for irrigation development had been provided by the 1928 loan from France.

[4] A. Bernard, "Rural Colonization in North Africa," in W.L.G. Joerg, ed., *Pioneer Settlement: Cooperative Studies* (New York, 1932), p. 230.

riod. During December 1933, the Sebou overflowed its banks and flooded a major portion of the Gharb, eliciting angry demands for flood control. Responding to the demands of one Gharb group, the General Secretariat reminded settlers that "these floods are unfortunately periodic and inevitable."[5] The administration, of course, was not uninterested. Public Works would study the matter "very attentively." However, "the only real solution is eventual dams on the Sebou and Ouerrha."

Gharb settler groups instead demanded measures to evacuate flood waters to the ocean, claiming that the Sebou and Ouerrha dams "are seductive solutions, but unrealizable before the distant future for lack of capital."[6] They complained bitterly to friends in the administration that the Public Works department was only interested in "Jules Verne" projects. However, "We claim that, in awaiting the distant realization of these grandiose schemes, certain minor projects could very considerably ameliorate the situation in the region."[7]

Settler demands focused on a canal to link the Gharb marshlands to the Atlantic. The estimated total cost of this project was only 3 million francs, as opposed to 600 million for the Ouerrha and Sebou dams.[8] Gharb settlers campaigned energetically for two years for the canal. The stock reply from the government was that no funds were available. Then, in late December 1935, the director general of Public Works agreed to implement the project—when funds became available. He subsequently reneged on this promise, then agreed to a compromise late in 1936: Public Works would "trace" a canal in the sand in the hope that future flood waters would bore it out and make it useful. The expense was to be a mere 1.5 million francs.[9] Such a lengthy delay for a relatively minor expenditure demonstrates the near-total paralysis in government water development due to lack of funds during the 1930s crisis.

Ironically, at the same time that settlers clamored for ever greater government assistance, they increasingly struggled against government interference. One of the main points of contention concerned the government's residency obligation. Government-sponsored settlers were required to live on allotted parcels as long as mortgage payments remained outstanding. The requirement, of course, was essential to the *peuplement* vision. It was the government's attempt to establish a

[5] Letter of 14 March 1934, printed in *BCAR* 16 (1934): 11–12.

[6] *BCAR* 18 (1934): 58.

[7] *BCAR* 21 (1934): 56.

[8] *BCAR* 18 (1934): 57.

[9] *BCAR*, 1936, pp. 730–731.

strong French presence in the countryside. However, as the colonization policy of the first two decades ended in disaster, as the administration grudgingly admitted its error, settlers seized the opportunity
to exact new freedoms.

They marshaled ingenious arguments against the residency obligation. Guillemet, for example, argued that the administration, in reserv-
ing lots for retired bureaucrats, former army officers, and such had as
much as admitted that its "family farming" vision was of little consequence. It was ridiculous to hope to successfully transplant such ex-
otics to the Moroccan *bled*. The residency requirement was therefore
ill conceived if not meaningless.[10] Lebault, the Casablanca Chamber
president, cannily reasoned that settlers willing to make the larger ex-
penditures necessary to hire managers (while they, themselves, lived in
the cities) would be demonstrating even greater attachment to the
land.[11] Settlers even argued that mandatory residence on their farms,
once these lands became irrigated, would expose them unduly to risk
of malaria.[12] Settler lobbying was effective. As the new colonization
program in the Beth (or Sidi Slimane) perimeter became established
in 1934, residency was not required.

In most other ways, however, the administration's handling of the
new Beth perimeter drew strong criticism. Some of this was bound up
with the history of the perimeter itself. Beginning in 1920, settlers and
would-be settlers in the Petitjean region had demanded that the
administration extend the perimeter of colonization, which then comprised only 5,000 hectares. The perimeter's small size was due, in part,
to the fact that the extensive holdings of the Cherarda tribe had effectively deadlocked the expansion of colonization by private initiative:
The 1919 decree on collective or tribal lands effectively barred private
sales of these lands. The Lyautey administration rebuffed settler demands, claiming that the land remaining to the Cherardas (approximately 50,000 hectares) was already too small for their estimated
20,000 members.[13]

In 1928, however, the Steeg administration suddenly created a new
5,000-hectare perimeter of colonization between Petitjean and Sidi
Slimane. This perimeter was situated so it would eventually benefit

[10] *BCAC* 29 (1932): 8.

[11] Ibid.

[12] *BCAC* 50 (1934): 6.

[13] In fact, however, De Mazières, the Petitjean civil controller, was able to deliver an
additional 1,000 hectares to colonization in the Bou Maiz frontier area between the
Cherarda tribe and the neighboring Beni Ahsen through skillful manipulations. See
BCAR 2 (1933): 32.

from irrigation water from the El Kansera Dam. The perimeter was created primarily by crowding the Cherardas onto less desirable portions of their collective holdings.

News of Steeg's new perimeter was received by settlers with distrust. Their misgivings soon proved to be justified. They learned from natives leaving the area that the administration had already mysteriously allotted "la plus belle partie."[14] The administration subsequently confirmed this: It had allotted 1,350 hectares to the Société Agricole Marocaine, 175 hectares to the Société Continental, 265 hectares to M. Etienne of Casablanca, and 187 hectares to a M. Solal.[15] The administration's action drew the following acrimonious response from a colon:

> If this land had been covered with jujube trees, dwarf palm and stone, the administration would have reserved it for settlers; however, a promising plain with such rich land in the most important irrigation district in Morocco was automatically reserved for professional speculators and land investment companies . . . experts in the art of buying cheap who, while waiting for the land to escalate in value before selling, devote themselves to ruining unfortunate settlers obliged by dearth of land to fall into their grasp.[16]

The administration incensed settlers in many other ways. For example, settlers charged that the Public Works department, in its placement of irrigation canals, had been guided "much more by technical considerations" than by concern to irrigate the most suitable soils.[17] Settlers also perennially complained about being left in the dark concerning the administration's agricultural experimentation. In 1930 and 1931, special experiment stations had been established at Fez, Sidi Slimane, and Dar Ould Zidouh.[18] These stations were intended to explore the potential of new high-value irrigated crops. They seem, however, to have had little effect on colonial agriculture. Indeed, as late as 23 March 1936, Gharb settlers complained in a letter to the director general of Agriculture that the Sidi Slimane station "persists in operating in total mystery . . . it has never furnished any documentation on its activities nor the findings of its experiments."[19]

[14] *BCAR* 3 (1933): 4.
[15] Ibid.
[16] Ibid.
[17] *BCAR*, 1937, p. 5.
[18] The Fez station was equipped with the latest California irrigation technology.
[19] *BCAR*, 1936, p. 362. In the Marrakech region, settler disgruntlement assumed yet

Such complaints were serious enough in themselves. However, they constitute only some of the charges of a much more damning overall indictment: The government, despite its efforts since 1926 to develop irrigation, had never bothered to formulate a coherent irrigation plan.

This governmental lack of vision beyond dam building became acutely apparent as the El Kansera Dam neared completion in 1933:

> Only several months away from the anticipated completion date of the project . . . one has as yet no definite ideas on how the water will be used. This clearly seems to be the gravest indictment one can bring against the administration . . . this absence of a general plan.[20]

Settlers took the initiative in lobbying for a comprehensive irrigation plan. Gaston Lebault, president of the Casablanca Chamber of Agriculture throughout the 1930s (and of the Federation of Moroccan Chambers of Agriculture during the second half of this decade), and Henri-Bernard Priou, a wealthy Gharb farmer, a member of the Rabat Chamber (and its president beginning in 1938), assumed the leadership roles.

Lebault became concerned as the El Kansera Dam neared completion that the government had taken no steps to ensure that the irrigation water would be used responsibly. The government had apparently not learned the lesson of the agricultural crisis. The previous error, according to Lebault—the error that had fatally led to crisis— was putting social ahead of economic considerations. The government had been more concerned to establish settlers than to see that colonization was viable. It should henceforth emphasize economic viability. Irrigation development was the remedy for the crisis. However, there was critical need for a "rational" irrigation program to ensure that only high-value crops such as oranges were grown.[21]

Lebault was alarmed that the government's preliminary formula for

---

other forms. Colons claimed that the infamous "settler debt question" was intimately linked to the government's paralysis in irrigation development. If the government had provided settlers the water they had been promised, settlers would not be in debt. This was a particularly sensitive issue. In the Steeg administration's energetic pursuit of its *peuplement* vision, numerous lots had been distributed that were too small or of too poor quality to be viable by dryland methods. Thus, in 1935, Marrakech settlers would complain in a Chamber meeting that the Attaouia-Chaibia subdivision "is at the point of death, as a result of the very poor soils . . . that it cannot irrigate for lack of water" (minutes of the 9 January 1935 meeting of the Marrakech Chamber of Agriculture, found in the unclassified archives of the Bibliothèque Générale in Rabat).
[20] G. Duval, *L'Hydraulique au Maroc* (Paris, 1933), p. 96.
[21] *BCAC* 40 (1933): 7.

the new Beth perimeter called for relatively large (40-hectare) lots, little or no capital up front, only minimal charges for water, and no stipulations governing what was to be grown. This situation, he believed, would lead either to cultivation of low-value crops such as wheat or to completely idle land held for speculation.[22] He campaigned energetically against both possibilities.

Priou was simultaneously defining the policy of the influential Rabat Chamber of Agriculture, which represented nearly 45 percent of Morocco's colons. He had been given the task of developing recommendations for the new Beth irrigation perimeter, which fell entirely within the Rabat Chamber's region. Priou presented his recommendations to the Chamber on 4 August 1934. He emphasized that, above all, the "development of the perimeter . . . must take into consideration our market possibilities."[23] He discussed the various options. Industrial crops such as cotton and linen, while they grew well in Morocco, would not be feasible without price supports; these were not apt to be forthcoming. Production of early vegetables and market vegetables for export had already reached the limits of the quota that France had established. His conclusion: "The rational development of the perimeter . . . can only be achieved with fruit plantations."[24]

As for specific types of fruit, Priou noted that

> to give a very large extension to noncitrus species would not appear to be very prudent: The metropole has warned us in this regard, and the Assembly of the Chambers of Agriculture in France has clearly specified that it would be favorable to citrus production, but indisposed toward any other fruit production that might compete with metropolitan agriculture.[25]

Fruit crops, Priou noted, required at least 20,000 francs per hectare initial investment. If one allowed a portion of each irrigated lot to be planted with other crops, this sum could probably be halved for the lot as a whole. The government should therefore require prospective settlers to demonstrate capital amounting to at least 10,000 francs per hectare. Each contract should also require "in draconian terms" that the required capital be expended in productive ways.[26]

In order to take into account the diverse spectrum of candidates, the government should sell 10-hectare lots. Those who could demon-

[22] *BCAC* 43 (1934): 19; 49 (1934): 8.
[23] *BCAR* 21 (1934): 25.
[24] Ibid., p. 26.
[25] Ibid.
[26] Ibid., pp. 26–27.

strate sufficient capital should be allowed to purchase several lots. However, a ceiling of 50 hectares should be set to ward off excessive concentration.

Priou's recommendations were unanimously adopted by the Rabat Chamber. A copy of his report was sent to the director general of Agriculture, and Priou himself was appointed to represent the Chamber at the government's next Comité de Colonisation meeting.

The lobbying efforts of Lebault, Priou, and their respective chambers of agriculture were highly influential. Their desiderata were nearly fully met in the actual colonization program in the Beth perimeter. The fifty-one lots sold from 1935 to 1937 varied in size from 14 to 21 hectares.[27] They were reserved exclusively for citrus and other high-value irrigated crops. Candidates, who had to demonstrate solid financial and agricultural qualifications, were permitted to purchase no more than three lots (at 2,500 francs per hectare, payable over ten years). They were required to consign 100,000 francs per lot to the General Treasury as security. Finally, they were required to conform fully to the program of development they had submitted with their applications. Water charges by the government were to reflect the estimated true costs.

Securing a sound economic foundation for official colonization in the new irrigation perimeters was a major accomplishment for the settler leaders. Still missing, however, was a government plan to bind the various dam projects together into a coherent irrigation program oriented towards long-term economic goals. Lebault would note in 1936: "The water from the Beth Dam has flowed for the past two years; next year water will flow into the Beni Amir plain. We need an overriding idea, a program."[28] This would become his next campaign.

By 1936, Public Works engineers had identified nearly all of the potential dam sites in Morocco. Projects for these sites already existed in varying stages of development. It was true, as settler critics charged, that many of these projects had been formulated on the basis of their technical merits alone; that the needs of colonial agriculture and the

---

[27] BCAR, 1936: pp. 341–342, 811–812. Many of these lots were sold to wealthy private settlers. Nearly all were sold to existing settlers in Morocco. For its first sale of twenty-four lots, totaling 440 hectares, the administration had trouble finding buyers. Indeed, in the minutes of the 27 October 1934 meeting of the Federation of Moroccan Chambers of Agriculture, it was noted that only one candidate had applied for a lot and that the administration was planning to spend 15,000 francs for advertising. See BCAC 55 (1935): 17–18. The principal reason given by Aucouturier, president of the Meknes Chamber, for the poor response was "lack of confidence in . . . la terre marocaine."

[28] BCAC 71 (1936): 9–10.

constraints of funds available for their implementation had not been prime considerations. However, Morocco was in urgent need of economic reform. These projects, altogether, would accomplish the nearly complete harnessing of Morocco's streams and create a major source of national wealth.

Lebault developed a concrete set of proposals for a national irrigation plan that he subsequently persuaded the Government Council to adopt as part of its economic reform program. This program was submitted to Resident General Ponsot in December 1935. Ponsot rejected the Government Council's program. However, within two years the irrigation plan that Lebault visualized would come into being. This plan would be precipitated by a census and a famine. "Natives," however, would be the critical new element. Previously, large-scale irrigation development had been envisioned exclusively for settlers. After 1936, irrigation development would be oriented equally towards small native farmers.

The shift of focus was striking. To be fully comprehensible, it is necessary to examine a cul-de-sac in which French colonization had become stalled. From this cul-de-sac, an unexpected new pattern had emerged.

Water for Moroccans: The Other Strand of Development

According to an ingenious twist of logic in the early protectorate period, Moroccans were to be assisted through being neglected. Indeed, official wisdom held that

> the only way to guide the [Moroccan] peasant towards progress is to place before his eyes the example of success through less primitive means than his own. For this, he must see land cultivated by Europeans. Thus, colonization will make Morocco prosper, first in augmenting the production of its soil, then in serving as an example to the native, perfecting him little by little through contact.[29]

Theoretically, colonization was merely to fill in the empty interstices of agrarian Morocco. Because these were so few, however, it quickly was discovered that Moroccan peasants could not entirely be neglected. Their lands were vital for the "superior needs" of colonization.

[29] R. Kann, *Le Protectorat marocain* (Nancy, 1921), p. 174.

Colonial logic therefore cut deeper: "In taking land from the natives, we are assisting them."[30]

Prior to the mid-1930s, major irrigation projects were formulated exclusively with European settlers in mind. For example, the Beni Amir Plain in the Tadla region—an arid but potentially fertile expanse that abutted the well-watered Middle Atlas Mountains—struck both French hydraulic engineers and casual observers as an ideal region for irrigation development.[31] In this plain, irrigation "was virtually inscribed in the nature of the land."[32] However, as the director of the Service de l'Hydraulique noted in 1922, the indigenous population in the plain was too dense; there was not sufficient land to create a perimeter of colonization, and thus an irrigation project was out of the question.[33]

By 1925, however, the acute shortage of land, Resident General Steeg's determination to extend colonization, and the successful conquest of the neighboring highlands prompted the administration to begin planning to develop the Beni Amir Plain.[34] Now the plain was seen as asleep on its riches: "The day when French plows trace their furrows in the plain and French farmhouses enliven the landscape . . . the region will become one of the most prosperous and fertile in Morocco."[35] Because of the strength and bellicosity of the tribes, however, sensitive political manipulations first were needed to lay the foundation for this new development.[36] Not until 1928 was a project initiated to create three "perimeters" of official colonization in the plain, covering some 45,000 hectares "deducted from the native lands" and based on the building of the dam at Kasbah Tadla.[37]

[30] A. Bondis, *La Colonisation au Maroc* (Rabat, 1932), p. 9. It became a related article of colonial faith that the Moroccans were "insufficient in numbers and in degree of civilization . . . to exploit the greater part of the resources of their country without the intervention of Europeans" (Bernard, "Rural Colonization," p. 221).

[31] "L'Hydraulique marocaine dans le Tadla," *La Vigie Marocaine*, 17 April 1931, p. 1.

[32] C. Tallec, "L'Equipement hydraulique de la plaine des Beni Amir et ses incidences politiques," unpublished confidential report, *Mémoire* no. 556, red series (1941), CHEAM, Paris, p. 5.

[33] M. Chabert, *L'Hydraulique au Maroc* (Rabat, 1922), p. 21.

[34] Tallec, "L'Equipement hydraulique," p. 1. Military authorities had been scouting the region since 1921 to determine what portion could ultimately be delivered to colonization. See P. Durand, "La Colonisation au Tadla," *RC*, 1930, p. 5.

[35] Dr. Miègeville, "La Situation économique de la région de Beni-Mellal," *RGM* 6 (1927), p. 49.

[36] J. Célérier and A. Charton, "Les Grands Travaux d'hydraulique agricole au Maroc," *AG* 34 (1925): 79.

[37] Tallec, "L'Equipement hydraulique," p. 6.

Ironically, a key element of the "sensitive manipulations" involved the political use of water. The "hearts and mind" approach to conquest, which had been pioneered by Gallieni and brought to Morocco by Lyautey, was skillfully employed in a major campaign of *petite hydraulique*. The basic principle had already been used in the pacification effort: As soon as an area had been conquered militarily, wells were established, or existing water systems improved, to convince the native of the kind intentions of the new European master. However, in the Tadla region, the political use of water became a major stratagem.

French authorities devised the stratagem to counter raids into the now-pacified Tadla plains by unconquered mountain tribal groups during late 1928 and early 1929. In one sensational incident on 20 October 1928, a civil controller named Rozier and his chauffeur Sanz were slain at Kouif. On other occasions, Frenchmen were kidnapped and ransomed. These raids were viewed as a constant menace that hindered all development and threatened to "contaminate" tribes that had already submitted.[38] Specifically, the protectorate's node of colonization to the north at Oued Zem was jeopardized, as were its plans for the three colonization perimeters to the south (Fig. 5).

The formula used to counter these raids was termed "wells of security." It was recognized that no military strategy could efficiently prevent infiltration along so extensive a front. Instead, recourse was made to the classic strategy of establishing a friendly tribe as a buffer. But how to establish a "human barrage" on the arid plateau bordering the plains? Through drilling wells! "By the miracle of water," the French would "fix to the soil" the nomads who merely wandered through the region.[39] Nomads leading their flocks to a dependable supply of water would serve as a screen through which unruly mountain brigands could not easily penetrate. Each well would provide automatic security for many miles in each direction; what was presently a *zone dangereuse* would be transformed into a *cordon sanitaire*. As one newspaper editor paraphrased a Lyautey maxim, "A well is worth a battalion!"[40]

Five wells were drilled in 1929: at El Gzaouna, Sedret Cheraga, Bled Hlassa, Ain Kaicher, and Kouif (Fig. 5). Three additional wells were planned: at Hartita, Melget Chaab, and Koudiet Degig. Altogether, these wells would provide a defensive wall along the entire southern boundary of the circonscription of Oued Zem.

The well at Kouif was particularly symbolic because it was near the

[38] P. Durand, "La Sécurité du Maroc central par l'eau," *RC*, 1929, p. 655.
[39] Ibid., p. 656.
[40] "L'Hydraulique marocaine," *La Vigie Marocaine*, p. 1.

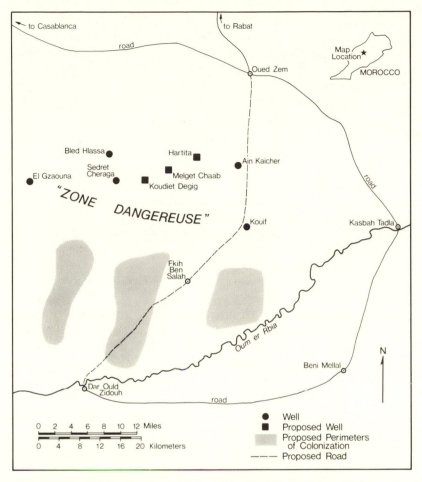

FIGURE 5 The "wells of security" and proposed perimeters of colonization in the Beni Amir Plain, 1929
SOURCE: Durand, "La Sécurité du Maroc central," *RC*, 1929, p. 655.

site of the Rozier-Sanz assassination. On 24 September 1929 at Kouif, the pasha of Beni Mellal orchestrated a massive demonstration of tribes "enthusiastic about the coming of water," to which French notables were invited.[41] A colorful *fantasia* and "the inevitable sacrifice" of a sheep took place against a background of joyful ululations.[42] In the speeches on the occasion, the Kouif well was heralded as the dawn of a bright new day for the region.

[41] Durand, "La Sécurité du Maroc central," p. 655.
[42] Ibid.

However, only a year and a half later, three of the original wells were broken down, with no plans to fix them, owing to an ostensible "lack of funds."[43] Furthermore, the wells at Hartita, Melget Chaab, and Koudiet Degig had never been drilled and were no longer envisioned. The rapidly expanding pacification of the neighboring highlands had made the well strategy obsolete.

Construction on the dam at Kasbah Tadla had begun in 1928. When completed, the dam would divert enough water from the Oum er Rbia to irrigate some 45,000 hectares of new colonization land in the Beni Amir Plain. However, the official colonization program found its stumbling block in the slow procedure for expropriating native lands. Before land could be delivered to colonization, it needed to be surveyed and registered, its boundaries delimited and established by decree, and the native residents settled elsewhere. As these steps were taking place, "clever adventurers" swept in, attracted by the promise of government-supplied irrigation water, anxious to acquire large holdings before the government could conduct land registration.[44]

Lively land speculation occurred throughout the irrigable portion of the Beni Amir Plain. The collective, unsurveyed status of the land made it easy for abuses to take place. Speculators were able to obtain titles, for small sums, from Moroccans willing to sell land out from underneath their fellow tribal members or land of which they did not even share possession.[45] As described by one French administrator,

> A veritable field day of land-grabbing, which the public powers could only oppose with feeble means due to the confused legal status of the land, soon ended with a few individuals—most agents of powerful land investment companies—amassing an important part of the Beni Amir's patrimony.[46]

Suddenly, the protectorate administration was confronted with a dilemma. So much of the land in the plain had passed into private European hands that to continue with official colonization would be to dispossess the Beni Amir tribe almost completely. It was decided that private colonization would now establish a French presence in the region—one of the motives behind the official program. In consequence, the administration renounced its original plan in 1932, and

[43] "L'Hydraulique marocaine," *La Vigie Marocaine*, p. 1.
[44] Tallec, "L'Equipement hydraulique," p. 6.
[45] Ibid.
[46] Ibid., p. 7.

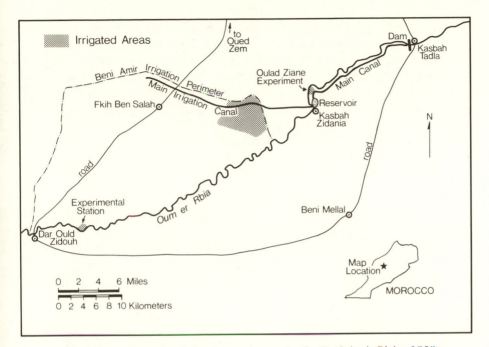

FIGURE 6   The native irrigation perimeter in the Beni Amir Plain, 1939
SOURCE: *RC*, 1939, p. 163.

became preoccupied with safeguarding native lands from further expropriation.[47]

In this same year, the administration began construction on a 24-
kilometer main canal between the Kasbah Tadla Dam and Kasbah Zidania (see Fig. 6). Now, however, the administration's plans for the
water passed out of focus. Indeed, the irrigation scheme entered a state
of limbo that lasted until 1936. Cancellation of the official colonization plan had removed the major motive for the irrigation project.

It is probable that planning for colonization was back on the drafting board. The administration had already estimated that 3 hectares of
irrigated land could support a native family. Through multiplying the
estimated 2,500 families in the Beni Amir Plain by a factor of three,
it was clear that the administration could "canton" the entire population on approximately 7,500 hectares. This meant that a sizable
amount of irrigable land could still be freed for colonization.[48]

[47] Ibid.; F. Giscard d'Estaing, "L'Office de l'Irrigation au Beni Amir–Beni Moussa et
la mise en valeur de la plaine du Tadla," unpublished *Mémoire de stage* (1949), ENA,
Paris, p. 3.
[48] Reports on the progress of the Kasbah Tadla project kept alive the prospect of

However, the administration announced it would table the issue while experimentation was conducted with the Oum er Rbia's water. For several years, a question had lingered as to whether the natural salinity in the middle course of the river would be detrimental to agriculture. In 1930, the administration had decided to establish an experimental station at Dar Ould Zidouh (Fig. 6). The 50-hectare farm and laboratory were to monitor the fluctuating salt content of the river water, test its effect on various crops, and experiment with new crops and irrigation techniques.

Did the administration use the salinity issue as a stalling ploy? It seems that it did. No reputable agronomist claimed that the river's salinity would pose a serious problem. However, the administration was both divided by dissension over whether a colonization program could still be implemented and buffeted by demands that the Kasbah Tadla water be used for hydroelectric generation.[49] These demands were based on the water's reputed unsuitability for irrigation. Testing could settle this issue and also give the administration time to resolve the issue of colonization.

The outcome of the affair cannot be understood without a brief introduction to the individual who played the leading role: Corentin Tallec, the *chef du territoire* of the Tadla region. Tallec was described as "a gigantic man, of herculean force,"[50] with a personality as "solid as the granite of his native Brittany."[51] He was reviled by Moroccan nationalists for representing the worst in authoritarian tendencies within the protectorate administration. However, he was clearly one of a handful of protectorate administrators who dedicated their careers to helping dispossessed Moroccan peasants. And of this handful, he was probably the most effective.

Unfortunately, only Tallec's own confidential reports and the following overly idealistic account record the hidden events of the period:

> At this moment, a man intervened whose undertaking would be one of the noblest in Moroccan history. . . . He was to launch

---

large-scale colonization. See, for example: Y. Le Moigne and J. Bourcart, "Un Projet d'utilisation d'un fleuve marocain: l'Oum er Rbia," *Revue de Géographie Physique et de Géologie Dynamique* 6 (1933): 31; P. Guillemet, "Regards sur l'hydraulique agricole au Maroc," *LTM* 54 (1934): 17; *BESM* 12 (1936): 87.

[49] Le Moigne and Bourcart, "Un Projet d'utilisation," pp. 30–32.

[50] J. LeGray, "Une Oeuvre franco-marocaine," *Revue Politique et Parlementaire* 631 (1953): 172.

[51] F. Brassac, "Réflexions sur le développement par l'irrigation dans le Sud-Marocain," *Maghreb* 52 (1972): 42.

an idea with immense future significance for the entire Moroccan economy, one that could only have been born in an inspired soul.

From his hilltop eyrie, he had often contemplated his domain. He knew each village, each family. He knew how much misery it contained, yet what a blessed land it could become. . . .

Framed in the arcaded entrance to the Beni Mellal headquarters is a marvelous landscape . . . of olive, almond, mulberry, and orange trees, with lines of white poplars marking the watercourses that flow from pure, gushing springs. Under the shade of these trees . . . flowers thrive; and gardens border the numerous filaments of irrigation water, all supported on the slopes by terraces. [However] little by little in descending to the plain, this oasis vanishes into dusty desolation.

Since 1932, the *chef du territoire* had contemplated this scene; of it he divined the symbolic significance. Save in certain rare spots . . . the entire plain could offer, in fifteen or twenty years, the same tableau of prosperity.

He decided forthwith to dedicate his career to fulfilling this vision.[52]

Under Tallec's leadership, the original colonization plan was scrapped in 1932. He subsequently devoted his energies to protecting remaining collective lands and pushing through the cadastral survey of the Beni Amir Plain. This survey was largely complete by the end of 1934. Once collective land had been surveyed, it could not legally pass into private hands except through official colonization procedures. Tallec additionally began to lobby for legislation to protect privately owned Moroccan holdings from land speculation. He also enlisted local notables in a campaign against speculators. This campaign was temporarily successful; between 1933 and 1936, very little land changed hands.[53] It is apparent from one of Tallec's confidential reports that, from 1932, he envisaged the Kasbah Tadla Dam's water as the due of the disinherited Beni Amir tribe.[54] In this regard, however, Tallec faced an uphill battle.

In 1933, the experiment station at Dar Ould Zidouh tentatively concluded that most crops would not be negatively affected by the Oum er Rbia's salinity. It also had discovered that the permeable soils in the Beni Amir Plain would permit removal of accumulated salts by off-season flushing. Further, hydraulic engineers had determined that

[52] LeGray, "Une Oeuvre franco-marocaine," pp. 169–170.
[53] Tallec, "L'Equipement hydraulique," p. 9.
[54] Ibid.

the heaviest concentration of salts came from a single tributary, the Serrou; if need arose, a modest dam on this stream could completely cure the problem. Or, alternatively, a diversion dam could be constructed on the Oued el Abid to channel its purer waters into the Oum er Rbia's.[55] In short, the administration decided that irrigation should receive priority, though a turbine would be constructed at Kasbah Zidania to utilize the Oum er Rbia's water during the off season. Settler hopes for new irrigated lands were strongly rekindled.

By 1936, the test was over: The Dar Ould Zidouh station had officially concluded that the Oum er Rbia's salinity would present no obstacle whatsoever to agriculture.[56] Soil analysis showed that there had been no accumulation of salts even after five years of irrigation.[57] Both the main canal and the small reservoir at Kasbah Zidania had now been completed. Furthermore, construction on the siphon under the Oum er Rbia, which would lead water into the rich Beni Amir Plain, was actively in progress. Land speculation again broke out in the plain.[58]

There were two principal reasons for the new rash of land speculation. First, the prospect of the Beni Amir Plain blossoming through irrigation in the near future was virtually certain. Second, and more important, the administration had decided to allocate nearly all of the irrigation water to the Beni Amir tribe's land. From originally visualizing the Kasbah Tadla project as a way to establish colonization in the Beni Amir Plain, the protectorate administration had come to regard it as an expeditious means of improving the condition of the Moroccan peasant. The decision to orient irrigation towards native agriculture was seized upon in 1936. Why had this decision suddenly been made?

The effectiveness of Tallec's lobbying efforts cannot be discounted. With the creation of the Office de l'Irrigation aux Beni Amir–Beni Moussa in 1941—Morocco's first irrigation office, of which Tallec was director—he would fully demonstrate his ability to transform personal designs into government actions. Also, by 1936, settler leaders such as Lebault were convinced that full harnessing of Morocco's waters was the answer to Morocco's troubled economy; in Lebault's vision,

---

[55] Le Moigne and Bourcart, "Un Projet d'utilisation," pp. 27–31.

[56] P. Surugue, "La Renaissance du paysannat marocain," *RC*, 1939, p. 163.

[57] "Une Tournée résidentielle dans le territoire de l'Atlas central," *BIM*, 1938, p. 150.

[58] This time, speculation focused on privately owned Moroccan land (*melk*), not collective land, because collective land was inalienable except by the state according to the 1919 legislation, and all collective land in the plain had now been registered (Tallec, "L'Equipement hydraulique," p. 9).

the native population was to play a major role, cultivating strategic, labor-intensive crops. However, stronger forces were at work.

By 1936, the new nationalist movement was a firmly established threat. Second, the first real census of the Moroccan population was conducted in 1936. This census focused attention on the rapid rate of population increase and revealed the magnitude of the *bidonvilles* or shantytowns mushrooming around the major cities, populated mostly from rural exodus. In short, the census underscored both the plight of traditional agrarian Morocco and its alarming implications for the protectorate. Third, a major drought, which began in 1935, had by 1936 turned into a famine affecting one-fourth of Morocco's population. For all these problems, irrigation development appeared as a possible bright solution.

The arrival of General Noguès as resident general in September 1936 was a final decisive factor. Noguès was a spiritual heir of Lyautey. During his residency, Noguès consistently made decisions favorable to the native Moroccan population. He noted, for example, in a speech before the Government Council a year after his arrival, "It would not be exaggerating to state that my principal preoccupation has been to remedy the consequences of the drought . . . to fight against famine, disease and death."[59] Irrigation development would prove to be the applied remedy.

Census of 1936

Prior to 1934, complete and accurate enumeration of the Moroccan population in the French zone was impossible because much of the territory had not yet been brought under effective French control: Pacification was completed only in 1934. Nevertheless, censuses in 1921, 1926, and 1931 had followed in the wake of the pacification campaign. Augmented by population estimates for the as-yet-unsubmitted tribes, these gave some idea of Morocco's demographic growth. The estimate of the "Muslim population" in the French zone in 1926 was 4,682,000. In 1931, French authorities estimated that this population had increased to 5,068.000.[60] While it was recognized that these estimates were only rough approximations, still it could be stated:

[59] *BCAR*, 1937, p. 528. For an excellent study of the Noguès administration in Morocco, see W. A. Hoisington, Jr., *The Casablanca Connection: French Colonial Policy, 1936–1943* (Chapel Hill, N.C., 1984).

[60] D. Noin, *La Population rurale du Maroc*, vol. 1 (Paris, 1970), p. 30.

[The] native population increases rapidly. . . . This increase is only a source of congratulation, first, because it proves that French rule has been beneficial to the natives by freeing them from internecine wars, famines, and epidemics and, second, because this native population provides the necessary labor for the European settlers.[61]

The 1936 census, however, was different from previous censuses. Indeed, it was by far the best census conducted during the protectorate period.[62] Earlier censuses had estimated the native population in many regions simply by counting houses and tents and multiplying by five. Now a well-organized army of census-takers, assisted by local officials, carefully combed the countryside. Later surveys verified that the count was accurate to within 2 percent.[63] The total Muslim population was found to be 5,904,000—effectively 6 million, or 18 percent more than was estimated five years earlier. The census was an eye-opener. According to Montagne, "The 1936 census suddenly and for the first time made apparent the full magnitude of a previously overlooked phenomenon: the compact formation in the cities of the Maghreb of a proletariat of rural origin."[64]

The 1936 census, unlike its predecessors, also gave rise to detailed analysis. It focused attention on the extreme population density in many parts of Morocco and stimulated follow-up studies. Bois, for example, conducted a study of the Doukkala region south of Casablanca, where the 1936 census had found population densities averaging 48 per square kilometer. According to Bois,

> Progressively as the mouths to feed have increased, the fellah has intensified his efforts, appropriating and cultivating all of the arable pasture land, clearing any clump of land that might be capable of supporting a crop, extending progressively onto more and more barren land, and reducing the fallow by a very strong percentage.[65]

Bois drew attention to the fact that, although the cultivated areas had more than doubled during the preceding twenty years, total agricul-

---

[61] Bernard, "Rural Colonization," p. 224.

[62] Noin, La Population rurale, p. 31.

[63] Ibid.; A. Bernard, "La Recensement de 1936 dans l'Afrique du Nord," AG, 1937, pp. 84–88.

[64] R. Montagne, "Naissance et développement du prolétariat marocain," in C. Celier et al., Industrialisation de l'Afrique du Nord (Paris, 1952), p. 199.

[65] J. Bois, "La Surpopulation rurale des Doukkalas," unpublished Mémoire no. 300 (1938), CHEAM, Paris, p. 10.

tural production had remained nearly the same as a result of soil exhaustion. Given this vicious cycle, the already dense population, and
the alarming rate of population growth, how, Bois asked, could the
Doukkalis continue to sustain themselves? "The French authorities,"
he concluded, "must immediately attend to the problem; the solution
cannot be deferred for long without unleashing disastrous, wide-rang-
ing consequences."[66] From being a source of congratulation for the
protectorate authorities, rapid population increase in Morocco became
regarded as a dangerous problem after the 1936 census.

The 1936–37 Famine

The rural exodus signaled by the census became a mass migration by
late 1936. Its major cause was the drought that had begun in 1935.
For over two years, there was very little rain in southern Morocco,
with the result that several hundred thousand Moroccans were deprived of all food resources.[67] Wells dried up, and streams that normally sustained oasis agriculture were entirely absorbed by irrigation
in the mountains. According to one contemporary account:

> The search for water and food has unleashed towards the north a
> vast exodus of animals and men, first slow and sporadic, then as
> massive as an avalanche. Heartrending scenes shock the sensibili-
> ties of Europeans, powerless witnesses: human beings emaciated
> to the final degree of misery, resorting, in an attempt to stave off
> famine, to all the practices one reads about in ancient descrip-
> tions.[68]

The rural exodus became so ominous for cities of the north that the
protectorate authorities established roadblocks to turn it back, or channeled it into concentration camps where the uprooted population
could be fed, deloused, and vaccinated against typhoid.[69]

Though southern Morocco was the worst hit, the drought also affected portions of the north. Regions that normally had 200–250 mm
of annual precipitation received only 30–50 mm.[70] In all, it was estimated that 800,000 native Moroccans in the south (the pre-Saharan
and Souss regions), 400,000 Moroccans northwest of the mountains
(in the Beni Amir Plain and the broad region south of the Oum er

---

[66] Ibid., p. 46.
[67] J. Célérier, "La Disette dans le Maroc du Sud," *AG* 46 (1937): 544.
[68] Ibid.
[69] Ibid.
[70] *AF*, 1937, p. 291.

Rbia), and 200,000 Moroccans in the Moulouya were touched by famine. Of these, a half million became entirely dependent on government food distributions for survival.[71]

The drought highlighted the dangerously vulnerable condition of much of rural Morocco. It awakened a sense of responsibility both among the colonial community and in France. For example, the geographer Célérier, speaking of the south in 1937, noted:

> The total absence of a crop during two consecutive years underscores the fact that, on the basis of its traditional technology, the pre-Saharan zone of Morocco is overpopulated. Its normal economic state is one of deficiency; a very large part of the population is undernourished, its level of life being just that which prevents death.
>
> With such a fragile margin, the slightest accident becomes a catastrophe. The establishment of our protectorate, instead of remedying the situation, has tended rather to aggravate it.[72]

The Beni Amir Native Irrigation Perimeter

The Beni Amir Plain was a major source region of rural emigrants, both before and during the 1936–37 famine. Its vulnerability to drought—Tallec estimated that crops failed six times out of seven—and its unfavorable man/land ratio, made it a "region of mirages, a land of misery, not capable . . . of nourishing its overly dense population."[73] In this, it was like most of the southern half of Morocco and the Moulouya. What distinguished the Beni Amir Plain, however, was that at the beginning of the famine, a cure for its proneness to drought was at hand. The Kasbah Tadla Dam, which could provide irrigation water for up to 45,000 hectares, had been completed since 1930. The 24-kilometer main canal had also been finished. And the siphon to lead water directly into the Beni Amir Plain was nearing completion. Irrigation could forthwith improve the lot of the native population on a massive scale.

Furthermore, Tallec had conducted an experiment in 1935 that demonstrated the feasibility of "native irrigation perimeters."[74] A plot

---

[71] Ibid.

[72] "La Disette," p. 545.

[73] Tallec, "L'Equipement hydraulique," p. 1; Surugue, "La Renaissance," p. 164.

[74] Both "Une Tournée résidentielle," *BIM*, p. 151, and J. Sermaye, "L'Irrigation de la plaine des Béni-Amir fait naître un paysannat marocain," *Annales Coloniales*, 11 July 1938, p. 2, incorrectly have Tallec's experiment beginning in 1933.

of land owned by the Oulad Ziane clan near Kasbah Zidania was divided checkerboard-fashion into thirty lots of 1.33 hectares each (see Fig. 6 for site of experiment). While the number of lots was determined by the number of families, the structure of the new plot was dictated by the network of irrigation canals. Each irrigated lot was redistributed to one of the Oulad Ziane families. Under the watchful eye of a team of French monitors from the experimental farm at Dar Ould Zidouh, native Moroccans were guided through the agricultural season, planting, irrigating, and harvesting wheat, barley, maize, and alfalfa—the last a crop not previously known in the region. Despite the complete inexperience of these seminomads in irrigated agriculture, and certain technical problems, the experiment reportedly gave "results greatly above average and particularly appreciated because the crop was nil . . . for tens of kilometers in any direction."[75] Indeed, there were seven cuttings of alfalfa, five of which the army purchased for 12,000 francs, 400 francs for each family.[76] Tallec's experiment provided strong testimony that modern irrigation development for natives was feasible.

Beyond the site where the nearly completed siphon under the Oum er Rbia would surface was a block of 30,000 hectares relatively unaffected by European land speculation. Tallec's experiment could be extended here on a massive scale. In short, the administration decided in 1936 to create a major irrigation perimeter for Moroccan peasants. This perimeter would counterbalance the irrigation perimeter in the Gharb, which was intended primarily for Europeans. It would therefore serve as a showcase of development, giving "to our protégés, already infected with nationalist propaganda, a tangible measure of our solicitude."[77] The irrigation perimeter would help halt the exodus ("fix the natives to the soil") because irrigation would multiply the necessary labor inputs by a factor of two to ten, depending on the crop. Further, not only would it greatly improve the lot of the 2,500 Beni Amir families within the perimeter, it could be used to settle other factions of the Beni Amir tribe living outside the perimeter, and possibly refugees from the famine-ridden south.[78]

To follow Tallec's logic in a confidential report: Using the estimate that 3 hectares of irrigated land were sufficient to support a Moroccan peasant family, it would be possible to settle the 2,500 families then

[75] Surugue, "La Renaissance," p. 166.
[76] "Une Tournée résidentielle," *BIM*, p. 152.
[77] Tallec, "L'Equipement hydraulique," p. 14.
[78] G. Carle and J. Gattefosse, "Le Problème général de l'Extrême Sud marocain," *RGM* 21 (1937): 191.

living in the perimeter on 7,500 hectares. Adding 5,000 more hectares for their future growth, and subtracting 6,000 hectares for land unsuitable for irrigation, this meant that some 12,000 hectares would still remain of the 30,000-hectare native irrigation perimeter. Another 4,000 Moroccan families could be settled.[79]

The first phase of the new Beni Amir irrigation perimeter, to irrigate 500 hectares belonging to the Chorfa and Oulad Abdalla clans, began in 1936. However, the project encountered resistance and had to be delayed for several months. According to one newspaper account,

> European Marxist agitators did not hesitate to join forces with Moroccan nationalists to cast suspicion on the protectorate's project, to argue that it was in conflict with traditional customs, and—all the while seeking to acquire land for themselves in the irrigable zone—to incite the Beni Amir to refuse the water that would only lead to the confiscation of their plain after they had given their labor to develop it.[80]

The Chorfa clan was able to be brought around by the appointment of a new shaykh.[81] The Oulad Abdalla, however, had to be excluded from the project, apparently to their later regret.[82] Thus, the first phase included only the 255-hectare plot of the Chorfas, not the entire 500 hectares. The Chorfa plot was divided up into eighty-five lots of 3 hectares each, and received its first water in the fall of 1937. The Chorfas were guided by a team of French monitors. Although after two years of famine they were reputedly listless participants,[83] the first season in the new Beni Amir perimeter was described as "brilliant."[84] Relatively high yields of wheat, cotton, and alfalfa were obtained.

This same season, cotton was also introduced to the 50-hectare Oulad Ziane irrigated plot.[85] In both cases, cotton and alfalfa were "contracted." Moroccan peasants were required to put fixed percentages of their irrigated land in crops the administration considered economically desirable. They were also required to follow a strict schedule of crop rotation. In exchange, they received government-supplied irrigation water, complete technical and material assistance (including

[79] "L'Equipement hydraulique," p. 16.

[80] Sermaye, "L'Irrigation," p. 3.

[81] Tallec, "L'Equipement hydraulique," p. 31.

[82] Sermaye, "L'Irrigation," p. 3; "Une Tournée résidentielle,' *BIM*, p. 152.

[83] Surugue, "La Renaissance," p. 167.

[84] "Une Tournée résidentielle," *BIM*, p. 152.

[85] Surugue, "La Renaissance," p. 166. The army bought all the alfalfa; the Association Cotonnière du Maroc, all the cotton.

fertilizer, select seed varieties, and insecticides), and a guaranteed purchaser and price at harvest. Contracts, total assistance, a highly interventionist structure—these were the essential characteristics of the "authoritarian" pattern of Moroccan irrigation development that Tallec
established in the Tadla. It was diametrically opposed to the laissez-
faire pattern established in the Gharb during the same period, in which
water was supplied by the government to the much larger settler holdings, on equally favorable terms, but with far fewer government inter-
ventions—particularly for private settlers.

As might be expected, the new Beni Amir perimeter became a major
cynosure of colonial press coverage. It was promoted as a demonstration of

> the firm and patient will of France progressively to bring well-
> being to the backward populations of Morocco while making
> them enter, almost despite themselves, a stage of civilization that
> turns them away from the misery of nomadism and fixes them to
> a soil rendered productive by the efforts of our technicians.[86]

On 29 May 1938, at Kasbah Tadla, Resident General Noguès inaugurated the new "perimeter of native colonization." Noguès had
given approval to Tallec's plan to develop the Beni Amir Plain soon
after his arrival in Morocco in September 1936. Now, at the inauguration, Noguès declared that this irrigation project had always been
intended solely for the benefit of the native Moroccan population:

> A rumor has been circulated for quite some time by ill-informed
> or perhaps ill-intentioned individuals, that these major works
> were undertaken with the goal of creating a perimeter of Euro-
> pean colonization in the Beni Amir Plain.
>
> I would like to affirm . . . that the government seeks here only
> the amelioration of the lot of our Moroccan protégés.[87]

To support the last claim, Noguès revealed that important new legislation was pending. This legislation would preserve for the Beni
Amir "their rightful patrimony and protect them against their own
improvidence and against speculation that would ultimately dispossess
them of their land."[88]

The legislation in question had been sought by Tallec for several
years. However, the experience in the Gharb, in which massive dis-

---

[86] J. Sermaye, "La Politique de l'eau au Maroc français," *L'Illustration*, 22 October
1938, p. 251.
[87] "Une Tournée résidentielle," *BIM*, p. 153.
[88] Ibid.

possession followed the construction of the Beth Dam, also had a strong influence.[89] Noguès's legislation was officially promulgated on 13 July 1938.[90] It prohibited any type of land transaction between tribal members whose lands were located in the new irrigation perimeter (the Beni Amir and Beni Moussa tribes) and nonmembers of these tribes. It did authorize transactions with other members of the same tribe. However, at the end of any such transaction, the original owner had to retain a minimum holding of at least 2 hectares, and the new owner or holder could not possess any more than 5 hectares.[91] Similar legislation was directed towards the Beni M'Tir, Guerrouane du Sud, and Oulad Yahia tribes—this last in the Gharb Plain within the zone potentially irrigable by the Beth Dam.[92] The legislation seems effectively to have prevented any further concentration of landholdings within the Beni Amir and other targeted areas.

At the inauguration, Noguès also hinted that the Beni Amir native irrigation perimeter was not to be a unique manifestation of the protectorate administration's solicitude. It was only one part of a vast economic and social program the government intended to implement for native Moroccan farmers.[93] Protectorate policy was rapidly changing.

The Million-Hectare Plan

In 1937, during the height of the famine, Théodore Steeg, Morocco's former resident general, undertook an official mission to North Africa "to determine measures to take against the native misery."[94] Steeg particularly recommended a series of small hydraulic works and made funds available for their construction. In February 1938, a special Commission de la Petite Hydraulique met in Rabat. Present were the heads of most of the regions affected by the drought, as well as the directors of Public Works, Finance, and Economic Affairs. The commission decided to implement the greatest possible number of small water projects in each region in order to develop local water resources and create work for natives. The goal was "to cure and at the same

[89] Surugue, "La Renaissance," p. 169. Priou, then president of the Rabat Chamber of Agriculture, would claim in 1939 that the Rabat colons had demanded such legislation since 1935, and that when it finally appeared in 1938 it was too late. See *BCAR*, 1939, p. 264.

[90] *BO*, 1342 (1938): 932–934.

[91] Ibid., p. 933.

[92] Ibid., pp. 933–934.

[93] "Une Tournée résidentielle," *BIM*, p. 153.

[94] "La Politique de l'eau au Maroc," *BIM*, p. 52.

time prevent the calamities caused by the drought . . . to maintain the peasant on his land."[95] These *petite hydraulique* projects included the following:

(1) Improvement of existing water-supply systems, for example by lining canals with cement
(2) Drilling wells and digging new canals
(3) Construction of qanats—locally called rhettaras
(4) Construction of check dams on slopes and in wadis, to help retard floods and recharge the water table
(5) Construction of stone weirs in streams to create pools for irrigation
(6) Construction of new underground cisterns and renovation of existing cisterns
(7) Diversion of watercourses into basins to create natural reservoirs.[96]

Elsewhere, the administration planned larger projects to improve native agriculture. A 180-hectare block of collective land at Hajjaoua, near Sidi Slimane, was developed for forty families in 1938, with one-third of it put into irrigated cotton production. Similar projects were studied for a nearby collective in the Gharb, and for a half-dozen other locations in southern and eastern Morocco.[97] All such projects visualized the introduction of high-value, labor-intensive crops, grown on irrigated land under the supervision of French monitors.

These numerous small and medium-scale projects represented an evolution of government policy towards the goal advocated by Lebault, president of the Casablanca Chamber of Agriculture. As noted earlier, Lebault had persuaded the Government Council in December 1935 to adopt a set of recommendations regarding water development. These included the following:

(1) That the government should establish a comprehensive plan for the complete harnessing of Morocco's water resources
(2) That water resources should be exploited wherever found, whether this involved large or small projects
(3) That the government should introduce labor-intensive crops such as cotton, sugar beets, and flax into the new irrigation perimeters in order to "fix the native to the soil."[98]

[95] *AG*, 1938, p. 535.
[96] Ibid., pp. 536–539; *BIM*, 1938, pp. 14–15, 52–53.
[97] *BIM*, 1939, p. 51.
[98] *BCAC* 69 (1936): 2; 71 (1936): 7–8.

These recommendations were included as part of an economic reform program submitted to Resident General Ponsot. He rejected the entire program in early 1936. However, 1936 was a tempestuous year. In March, Ponsot was replaced; in September, his successor, Peyrouton, was also recalled. The arrival of General Noguès finally gave leadership responsive to Lebault's proposals.

In June 1937, Lebault argued before the Government Council for a national irrigation plan. This was not the first time he had urged the creation of such a plan. However, the plight of rural Morocco gave his argument an urgency previously lacking.

Lebault pointed to the fact that between 1925 and 1931 Morocco's population had increased by 96,000 per year. Between 1931 and 1936, however, it had increased by 170,000 a year. A further acceleration in population growth could be expected as a result of the protectorate's health program. With 200,000 additional births a year, the Moroccan population would nearly double in twenty-five years. However, "If one examines the present situation in Morocco's nonirrigated lands . . . one perceives that cultivation will soon reach its absolute limits and will not be sufficient to support this population. There remains only one resource . . . water."[99] "We must not," Lebault insisted, "one day suddenly discover that our growing population has overrun us, and that we have not been provident enough to give it adequate means of existence."[100] He urged the Government Council immediately to establish a special commission to formulate a master irrigation plan and oversee its realization. Lebault was successful in his appeal.

The Government Council established a Commission de l'Hydraulique. Its first action was to demand from the administration a preliminary plan based on existing water development projects. To meet this demand, the administration created a special committee on 12 November 1937 that consisted of Normandin, director of Public Works, Picard, the Public Works chief hydraulic engineer (who had gone on the official mission to California eight years earlier), and Lefevre, director of Agriculture.[101] On 22 November 1938, the Commission de l'Hy-

[99] *BCAC* 97 (1938): 9.

[100] Ibid., p. 11.

[101] "Dahir du 12 novembre 1937 relatif aux attributions respectives de la direction générale des travaux publics et de la direction des affaires économiques en matière d'hydraulique," *BO* 1317 (1938): 86–87. This same decree effectively centralized control over all aspects of water development under the director of the Public Works Department.

draulique finally approved a plan developed by Normandin and Picard. Morocco's first comprehensive irrigation plan thus came into being.

The report introducing the plan clearly expressed the Malthusian motives behind it:

> The irrigation program . . . responds to a pressing need: that of feeding a rapidly growing population. The extension of irrigated agriculture is a powerful means of responding to this necessity. Without demanding the Moroccan soil to nourish, as do certain regions of Spain, up to 10 families per hectare, one can allow the figure of one family per hectare. Now, experience demonstrates that irrigation requires . . . 1/3 liter-second per hectare. Thus, a liter-second corresponds to 3 hectares, 3 families.
>
> At present, the average amount of water used in all of Morocco for irrigation can be estimated at 45 cubic meters per second. The amount immediately utilizable without new dams is 75 cubic meters per second. The estimated amount of water which can be retained behind future dams is 150 cubic meters per second. There are thus at our disposal: $75 + 150 = 225$ cubic meters per second, of which approximately one-fourth can be used again after infiltration into the ground. We can thus count on: $225 + 55 = 280$ cubic meters per second, which corresponds to $3 \times 280,000 = 840,000$ families, or approximately 4,000,000 inhabitants. At the present rate, it would take 26 years to generate this new population. However, the total harnessing of Morocco's waters need not be accomplished by the end of this period, because irrigation is not the only means of increasing production. . . . One should equally undertake efforts to improve the agricultural methods of the Moroccan peasant with the hope of producing for the Moroccan table twice what is produced today. Given these conditions, the Moroccan soil should be capable of feeding a population of: $2 \times 6 + 4 = 16$ million inhabitants. At the present population growth rate, it would take sixty years to attain this figure. This is the maximum delay given us to achieve the total harnessing of Morocco's waters.[102]

The report, it should be emphasized, *implicitly established the official goal of one million irrigated hectares.* Using Normandin and Picard's figures: 280 cubic meters per second of new irrigation water plus the

---

[102] "Rapport sur le programme d'hydraulique," *BCAC* 101 (1938): 3–4. See also A. Normandin, "Une Grande Oeuvre française: l'utilisation agricole des eaux au Maroc," *Annales des Ponts et Chaussées*, 1939, pp. 316–317.

existing 45 cubic meters per second already used for irrigation equalled a total of 325 cubic meters per second—enough to perennially irrigate 975,000 hectares.

The protectorate's plan to develop Morocco's water resources was divided into three phases, corresponding to the priority given to the respective projects:

Phase I   Estimated cost: 1,110,000,000 francs

(1) Completion of all canal networks for already existing dams (El Kansera, N'fis, Kasbah Tadla)
(2) Construction of all feasible small- and medium-scale projects
(3) Construction of a 40-meter-high storage dam at Imfout, with canal networks, to irrigate 120,000 hectares in the Abda–Doukkala Plain
(4) Construction of a diversion dam on the Moulouya, with canals, to irrigate 30,000 hectares in the lower Moulouya Plain near Berkane
(5) Construction of a diversion dam on the Sebou, with canals, to irrigate 15,000 hectares in the Fez region.

Phase II   Estimated cost: 1,600,000,000 francs

(1) Heightening of the Imfout Dam to 110 meters and construction of additional canals, to irrigate 80,000 more hectares in the Abda-Doukkala Plain
(2) Construction of storage dams at Melaina on the Sebou and M'jara on the Ouerrha, with canals, for flood control and irrigation of 200,000 hectares in the Gharb
(3) Construction of a storage dam on the Lakhdar, with canals, to irrigate an additional 10,000 hectares in the Haouz
(4) Construction of a second storage dam on the Sebou, with necessary canals, to complete the irrigation development of the Tadla region on the left bank of the Oum er Rbia.

Phase III   Estimated cost: 2,100,000,000 francs

(1) Construction of pumping stations along the Sebou to irrigate all land below 200 meters in elevation between the Bou Regreg and Oum er Rbia
(2) Cement-lining of all previously constructed canals.[103]

---

[103] Normandin, "Une Grande Oeuvre française," pp. 326–329; "Rapport sur le pro-

The total estimated cost of the comprehensive plan was 5 billion francs. Phase I was to begin on 1 January 1940, following a year of preparation, and was to be completed at the end of five years. Of the 1.11 billion francs necessary for the first phase, only 50 million already existed in the treasury.[104] However, the entire irrigation plan was to be financed by Morocco's own funds, with as little recourse to loans from France as possible. Funds were expected to increase rapidly from the geometric increase in tax revenues on agricultural production following irrigation development.[105] In sum, without creating a heavy financial burden for future generations, Morocco would completely develop its water resources and put a million hectares into perennial irrigation. It would thus solve the problem of feeding its own rapidly growing population.

The master plan was ambitious, idealistic, and farsighted. Speaking of the plan, which would not be finally completed until the year 2000, General Noguès noted to the Government Council on 7 December 1938, "None of us will live to see its achievement. But we will have served both Morocco and France well if, after the passage of the decades, not a drop of water from rivers born in the Rif or Atlas is uselessly lost to the sea or to the desert sands."[106]

Unfortunately, World War II broke out less than a year later. It disrupted all normal economic activity in Morocco. Following the war, both the context and character of French colonization in Morocco were profoundly different. Despite bombastic rhetoric, very little irrigation development was accomplished between 1939 and 1956, when the protectorate ended. Chapter 5 will analyze wartime and postwar agricultural development in the protectorate.

When Morocco achieved its independence in 1956, the new government immediately launched a campaign to compensate for the long-standing neglect of traditional dryland agriculture. By 1960, however, political and economic considerations had prompted Moroccan leaders to return to the 1938 colonial irrigation plan. The fulfillment of the colonial plan, and its implications for Morocco, will be examined in Chapter 6.

---

gramme d'hydraulique," *BCAC*, pp. 4–8; "Programme d'hydraulique au Maroc," *L'Entreprise au Maroc*, 23 March 1939, pp. 1–2; 30 March 1939, pp. 1–2; *BESM* 23 (1939): 27. This comprehensive plan was assembled from the congeries of projects then existing in Public Works files.

[104] *BESM* 23 (1939): 27.

[105] Normandin, "Une Grande Oeuvre française," p. 329.

[106] *BESM* 23 (1939): 27. The irrigation plan would commonly be known as the Plan Noguès.

1. Roman ruins at Volubilis near Meknes: key symbol of the colonial granary-of-Rome image.

2. Moroccan peasants. Cereal cultivation's predominance in Moroccan native agriculture helped inspire the protectorate's wheat policy.

3. Plowing by traditional means. Note wooden scratch plow.

4. Rendezvous in Casablanca, 1931. Left to right: William Hodgson, the American "spy"; Paul Guillemet, the great initiator of California methods in Morocco; prominent settlers.

Cette photographie d'orangeraie au pied des monts de Californie ne fait-elle pas songer à une vue future de la plaine de Marrakech au pied de l'Atlas marocain.

▼

5. The California Dream in Moroccan colonial agriculture. Propaganda photo taken in California by Paul Guillemet.

6. Colonial advertisement (1932) for Californian irrigation technology.

7. Water for colons: the El Kansera Dam on the Oued Beth. The dam was completed in 1935.

8. Protectorate triumph: the Bin el Ouidane Dam on the Oued el Abid. When completed in 1953, this was Africa's largest dam.

9. Tadla irrigation landscape. Fruit tree windbreaks reveal location of tertiary irrigation canals. (Compare with Fig. 7.)

10. Orange orchard of a former French settler on the upper Oued Beth, now owned by a member of the Moroccan elite. The orchard covers approximately 250 hectares, or 620 acres.

11. Gharb village dispossessed by colonization (left). Settler residence (center) is surrounded by orange orchard and settler fields. This former colonial farm is now the country estate of a wealthy urban Moroccan.

12. Field patterns in the Gharb revealing disparities between traditional and modern agricultural holdings.

13. A monument in the reign of Hassan II: the Moulay Youssef Dam near Marrakech, completed in 1970.

14. Contemporary Moroccan irrigation landscape: sugar cane in the Gharb.

15. Traditional agricultural village on marginal lands near the Middle Atlas. The haystacks are covered with sun-baked mud. Note erosion from overgrazing.

16. Hassan II, King of Morocco (1961–).

PART III

1940 – 1986

5

Pioneering Morocco's
Development Formula

The California image, which originally guided Morocco's orientation towards irrigation agriculture, had been subsumed by the million-hectare vision by the end of the 1930s. The protectorate administration had decided to undertake the complete harnessing of Morocco's surface waters. Irrigation would compensate for the vagaries of precipitation and make colonial agriculture more viable. It would extend the "useful" surface of Morocco, absorb the surplus rural labor force, and "fix the native to the soil." Above all, it would provide for the expansion of Morocco's indigenous population. Upon completion of the irrigation plan (it was often referred to as the "century plan" because its horizon was the year 2000), one million hectares would have been transformed by perennial irrigation. Henceforth "not a drop" of Morocco's surface waters would flow unused to the sea.

It was unclear, however, exactly how "native irrigation perimeters" would translate into a reliable food supply for Morocco's rapidly growing population. Indeed, the prevailing trend, as reflected in policy statements and Tallec's experiments in the Beni Amir Plain, was in the opposite direction: towards production of nonedible crops such as cotton and alfalfa. Coherent production plans for the new irrigation perimeters did not emerge until after World War II. During the war years, however, the administration developed the basic formula that has since characterized irrigation projects for Morocco's peasants.

For settlers, the long-sought adoption of a national irrigation plan was a highly encouraging sign. They demanded that large-scale official colonization be reinstated to settle Frenchmen in the future irrigation perimeters, arguing that settler farms could employ rural Moroccans, and that with Germany again flexing imperialist muscles, France urgently needed to demonstrate that its ties to Morocco were too tight to become unbound.[1]

Yielding to settler pressure in spring 1939, General Noguès decided to reactivate official colonization. Now, however, the ostensible goal was one of native policy: to lead to a distribution, as geometric as possible, of French farms amidst the native population in the future irrigation zones so that they might serve as centers of diffusion for the new crops and examples for the natives.[2]

The California dream was still alive: In spring 1939, the Rabat Chamber of Agriculture organized a "study voyage" to the United States. Its primary objective was to enable interested settlers to visit California's orchards, producer cooperatives, and packing plants—indeed, "all that might interest Morocco's fruit growers."[3] This study voyage was to take place in fall 1939.[4] Unfortunately, the outbreak of war in September canceled plans for the trip.

World War II seriously disrupted the initial phase of the comprehensive irrigation plan, which was to have been completed by the end of 1944. It also prevented a renaissance of French colonization in Morocco. By war's end, both the irrigation and colonization questions were very differently posed. This chapter will analyze the evolution of agricultural policy up to Morocco's independence in 1956. Its primary purpose is to explain how the basic patterns of present-day agricultural development in Morocco became established.

The Office de l'Irrigation
aux Beni Amir–Beni Moussa

The wave of resistance in the Beni Amir Plain in fall 1937, which troubled Tallec's efforts to implement the new "perimeter of native colonization," resulted in a partial relaxing of authoritarian measures. Planting directives were made less rigorous, and the procedure known as *remembrement* was for the time being given up.

Remembrement, or land consolidation, was designed to rearrange small, dispersed holdings of irregular size and shape into a new, geometric landscape conforming to the technical requirements of modern irrigation agriculture. It involved the expropriation and consolidation

---

[1] *BCAR*, 1939, p. 43.
[2] Ibid., p. 193.
[3] Ibid., p. 119.
[4] *BCAC* 109 (1939): 52.

of existing holdings, followed by the redistribution of "regularized" rectangular parcels forming the interstices of the new irrigation network. The procedure had been introduced by Tallec in 1935 in the Oulad Ziane experiment, then extended to the Beni Amir irrigation perimeter in 1937. The heavy-handed, *tabula rasa* nature of the procedure was an important factor behind the Oulad Abdallah's resistance. Remembrement would not reappear in Morocco for another decade.

In 1938 and 1939, although Tallec's native irrigation work proceeded without land consolidation, it still encountered opposition. According to one account, "the agitation was in large part provoked by the notables in the area, possessors of large flocks, who perceived in the extension of irrigation the disappearance of pasturelands and the loss of their influence."[5] Irrigation development progressed slowly. Nonetheless, the irrigated area amounted to 1,500 hectares in 1939 and to 2,000 hectares in 1940.

In 1940, with funds diminishing due to the outbreak of war, Tallec organized a ceremony to inaugurate a new section of the Beni Amir perimeter. This ceremony was intended as a political ploy: It was to put pressure on the administration to ensure commitment to the scheduled pace of development in the plain. The ceremony ended in disaster. A large crowd, supposedly manipulated by "nationalist extremists," stoned the sluice gates that were to be opened by Tallec's superior, the *chef de région*. Shaken by the incident, the *chef de région* yielded and announced that because the peasants did not desire irrigation, water would not be let into the canal.[6]

Tallec resigned from his post in protest and joined the central administration in Rabat. He engineered the appointment of a Moroccan friend, "who shared his ideas and possessed a powerful influence over . . . the Beni Amir," as caid of their region.[7] Within a year, Tallec himself was back in Beni Mellal, this time as *chef du territoire* as well as director of the newly created Office de l'Irrigation aux Beni Amir–Beni Moussa, an institution he had personally designed. The train of events clearly testifies to the force of his personality.

During the war, agricultural Morocco became subject to a regime of command production and requisitioned harvests that lasted through

[5] C. Mingasson, "Le Périmètre d'irrigation du Tadla," *Annales Algériennes de Géographie* 1 (1966): 55.

[6] J. LeGray, "Une Oeuvre franco-marocaine," *Revue Politique et Parlementaire* 631 (1953): 172–173.

[7] Ibid., p. 174.

1947.[8] All European settlers owning more than 5 hectares, for example, were required to put at least 10 percent of their land into either oilseed or textile crops, with strict penalties in the case of noncompliance. In this authoritarian atmosphere, the Office de l'Irrigation was created on 5 December 1941. The official "statement of motives" behind the creation of the Office is particularly revealing:

> The hour has come for Our subjects, the Beni Amir and Beni Moussa tribes, to gather the fruits of the State's efforts.
>
> It has appeared timely to initiate the concerned parties into modern irrigation practices and to teach them the methods requisite for the implementation . . . of crops up to now foreign . . . notably cotton, which are particularly appropriate to the vocation of a land revivified by water. These preoccupations . . . have led Us to create an organism that will assume responsibility for the agricultural education of Our subjects and . . . take all measures necessary to direct their efforts towards appropriate management of their land.[9]

The Office's official objective was the comprehensive development of the Beni Amir Plain. It was invested with a social as well as economic mission: to make the tribal member of the Tadla Plain participate in the radical transformation of his resource base, leading him out of "his laziness, his taste for mediocrity, his strange passivity,"[10] and hastening his evolution from a "medieval seminomad" to a modern cash-crop farmer.[11]

All means were placed at Tallec's disposal in this task. First, his Office was given complete autonomy in the development of the 200-square-kilometer region. Second, the technical staff of all the various administrative agencies in the region (Agriculture, Public Works, Rural Engineering, Horticulture, and Agricultural Research) were placed under Tallec's direct command. Finally, the Office was endowed with financial independence: It received low-interest loans from the government, which it repaid by charging for irrigation water and services performed. After 1947, when legislation permitted it to become a ma-

---

[8] Mingasson, "Le Périmètre d'irrigation," p. 56.

[9] "Dahir du 5 décembre 1941 portant création d'un Office de l'irrigation aux Beni Amir–Beni Moussa," *BO* 1525 (1942): 40.

[10] E. Laxan, "L'Irrigation et la rémunération du travail agricole chez les Beni Amir," unpublished *Mémoire* (1947), ENA, Paris, p. 46.

[11] F. Renard, "Les Problèmes humains posés par l'irrigation dans le périmètre des Doukkala," unpublished *Mémoire* (1949), ENA, Paris, p. 20.

jor landowner, the Office de l'Irrigation also generated profits from its own agricultural production.

Tallec now possessed full power to extend the work he had begun in 1935. Within less than a decade, the Tadla region would offer to admirers "the golden perspectives of a new California or of a new Tennessee Valley."[12] What makes the Office de l'Irrigation far more than an interesting colonial experiment, however, is the fact that it pioneered a basic formula of development that continues in Morocco to the present.

The Office energetically extended the canal network and increased the irrigated area from approximately 2,000 hectares in 1940 to 13,000 hectares in 1949. As the irrigated area expanded, it was divided into sectors that varied in size from 630 to 1,752 hectares. Each sector was placed under the command of a French monitor, who was responsible for seeing that the sector's production plan was followed. Predetermined percentages of each sector were devoted to particular crops, and a crop rotation schedule was introduced. Every peasant's parcel—most were less than 5 hectares—was subdivided into four approximately equal plots. A typical peasant, in a given year, might have wheat, wheat, cotton, and fallow on his respective plots. The French monitor was charged with seeing that the planting assignments and rotation schedule were obeyed. Among many other tasks, he also distributed seeds and fertilizer, guided the two to four hundred peasants in his sector through the agricultural calendar, and governed the distribution of irrigation water.[13]

Peasants theoretically were permitted to perform all the work on their own parcels. However, because many of the required tasks were beyond their means, they were forced to contract with the administration to have clearing, plowing, or other operations performed with Office machinery. Depending on the period, they might be given a choice of what they could grow on a portion of their land. However, in all other matters, they were required to follow the strict directives of the Office de l'Irrigation, under threat of stiff penalties for noncompliance.[14]

Before the creation of the Office in 1941, cereals accounted for most of the Beni Amir perimeter's production. Barley was the dominant winter cereal, cultivated in relationship to wheat on a nine to one ratio,

[12] R. Jambardan, *Les Débuts de la modernisation rurale*, CMR 6 (1948): 5.
[13] *ITOM*, 1954, pp. 353–362.
[14] A. Colombier, "La Gestion des grands périmètres d'irrigation au Maroc," unpublished *Mémoire* (1953), ENA, Paris, p. 5.

and maize was the principal summer crop. With the creation of the Office, measures were taken to:

(1) Prohibit maize production
(2) Substitute wheat for barley
(3) Decrease cereal cultivation in general
(4) Expand cultivation of such new crops as cotton, broad beans, and alfalfa.[15]

These measures were largely successful.[16]

In 1949, the Office de l'Irrigation's operations entered a decisive new phase following the recommendations of an official mission sent to California by Trintignac, now in charge of Morocco's irrigation development. (This mission will be discussed in detail later.) There was an intensified effort to "rationalize" the landscape. Remembrement was reintroduced, new irrigation canals were lined with cement, and drainage canals were systematically included in the network. In addition, the Office attempted to impose a fixed five-year crop rotation cycle composed of equal parts of hard wheat, soft wheat, cotton, broad beans, and alfalfa.[17] Fig. 7 compares the appearance of the new landscape with the traditional landscape. (See also Illus. 9).

The new irrigation landscape consisted of a series of long strips, each planted with a different crop, and each 80 meters wide and 1,000 to 1,500 meters in length. The strips ran perpendicular to the secondary irrigation canals and parallel to the tertiary canals. The production scheme was arranged so that the assigned plantings and crop rotation cycle were the same for all parcels in a given block. Each parcel—each peasant's landholding—included land in all five strips. Thus, each farmer grew equal amounts of five different crops. The long strips greatly facilitated mechanization and simplified control over the entire operation.[18]

By 1953, in the twilight of the protectorate, Moroccan small landholders owned 19,000 hectares of perennially irrigated land in the Office de l'Irrigation's perimeter. Table 3 demonstrates that the production scheme visualized in 1949 had been mostly implemented by this time. Table 4 shows the total distribution of landholdings in the

[15] Mingasson, "Le Périmètre d'irrigation," p. 56.
[16] Ibid., pp. 56–58.
[17] Ibid., p. 58.
[18] See, for example, F. Giscard d'Estaing, "L'Office de l'Irrigation au Beni Amir–Beni Moussa et la mise en valeur de la plaine du Tadla," unpublished *Mémoire* (1949), ENA, Paris.

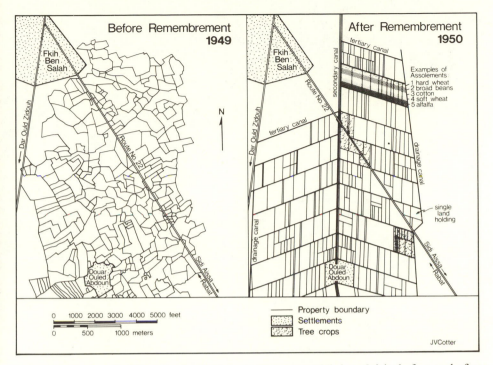

FIGURE 7   Landholdings in the Beni Amir Plain near Fkih ben Salah, before and after *remembrement*, 1949–1950
SOURCE: *Encyclopédie Mensuelle d'Outre-Mer*, June 1954, p. 7.

perimeter at the end of 1953, revealing that Moroccan small landholders owned nearly three-fourths of the irrigated land.

Table 4 requires several explanatory comments. First, the land held by Europeans was either former collective land that had been purchased before the protectorate administration's cadastral surveys, or former privately owned Moroccan land purchased before the 1938 decree prohibited land transactions with nonmembers of the Beni Amir–Beni Moussa tribes. None of the European-owned land was subject to the directives of the Office de l'Irrigation, and settlers purchased their water direct from the Public Works Department.[19] The "Office de l'Irrigation/Collectives" category was collectively owned tribal land developed by the Office under a twenty-year contract with the following terms: The collectives furnished the land and received one-fifth of the profit; the Office furnished the other factors of production and received four-fifths of the profit. Upon termination of the

[19] Ibid., p. 36.

TABLE 3 Crops on *Melk* Holdings in
the Beni Amir Perimeter, 1953

Crops	Total area (hectares)
Cotton	3,800
Hard wheat	3,700
Broad beans	3,100
Soft wheat	2,400
Alfalfa	1,100
Barley	950
Fruit crops	350
Market vegetables	300
(Fallow)	3,300
TOTAL	19,000

SOURCE: *ITOM*, 1954, p. 355.

TABLE 4 Ownership of Landholdings in the Beni Amir Irrigation
Perimeter, 1953

Category of landholding	Area (hectares)	
	Irrigated area	Total area
Melk (privately owned by Moroccans)	19,100	21,000
European colonization	3,235	3,235
Office de l'Irrigation/Collectives	2,310	2,750
Office de l'Irrigation	1,010	2,354
Public domain	245	245
TOTAL	25,900	29,584

SOURCE: Mingasson, "Le Périmètre d'irrigation," *Annales Algériennes de Géographie* 2
(1966): 86.

contract, the collectives could elect either to renew it or to have their
land returned. On these terms, for example, the Yacoubia (1945) and
Sidi Moussa (1946) collective lands were developed by the Office.[20]
Finally, the Office itself became a major landowner after a 15 October
1947 decree permitted it to purchase land. It argued successfully for
the 1947 legislation on the grounds that it needed to be able: (1) to

[20] *ITOM*, 1954, p. 359.

buy excess land from impoverished Moroccans so they would have the capital to invest in their irrigated parcels; (2) to buy holdings too small to be viable; and (3) to accumulate land on which to resettle Moroccans whose land was to be expropriated for the massive Bin el Ouidane Dam project. Most of the Office's land was arranged in blocks of 20 to 100 hectares that its own staff farmed mechanically.[21]

The Office justified its existence particularly well during the catastrophic drought of 1945—the worst Moroccan drought of this century (see Fig. 2). Wheat yields per hectare in the nonirrigated areas of the Beni Amir Plain were 0 in 1945 and 1.5 quintals in 1946. In the Office's irrigation perimeter, however, they were respectively 9 and 13.[22] One Casablanca journalist covering the drought reported:

> After an arduous voyage across a devastated land, one is suddenly in the heart of a fertile and inviting region. . . . The verdant fields of alfalfa, cotton, and maize contrast agreeably with the sepia-colored landscape we have just traversed. Here water is not lacking. . . . On these 15,000 hectares, nature is dominated by man. The consequences of a drought without precedent have had only negligible effects.
>
> The livestock have not been decimated . . . [and] it is cheering to behold hardy beasts that in no way resemble the ambulatory skeletons we have become accustomed to seeing.[23]

It is indisputable that the Office had a dramatic effect upon the development of the Beni Amir region. By 1953, its irrigated area supported a stable farming population of at least 20,000, triple the population of two decades earlier, on land where harvests formerly had failed "six times out of seven."[24] Moreover, a bustling town of over 8,000 inhabitants had sprung up where in 1940 there was only a dusty village of two or three hundred.[25]

Despite these facts, the Office de l'Irrigation had many detractors. It was sharply criticized by certain colonial administrators on technical and fiscal grounds—although in many cases these attacks seem to con-

---

[21] C. Mingasson, "Aspects techniques, économiques et sociaux de développement en zone irriguée d'Afrique du Nord: le périmètre du Tadla," unpublished doctoral thesis, 3d cycle, Geography, University of Strasbourg, 1964, p. 114.

[22] Laxan, "L'Irrigation et la rémunération," p. 18.

[23] "Intensifier les travaux d'irrigation au Maroc," Libération, 27 September 1945, p. 4.

[24] C. Tallec, "L'Equipement hydraulique de la plaine des Beni Amir et ses incidences politiques," unpublished confidential report, Mémoire no. 556, red series (1941), CHEAM, Paris, p. 1.

[25] ITOM, 1954, p. 360.

ceal daggers thrust for other reasons.[26] For the Moroccan Communist Party, it was "a marvelous idea, full of generosity and possibilities, from which only misery and oppression have resulted."[27] According to the party's official organ, *Espoir*, the Office's staff had "gnawed away at the peasants like a cancer," destroying their traditional lifestyle, overburdening them with water taxes and charges for services they never requested, and using them as slave labor for the Office's cotton production.[28] For other critics, the Office represented merely a unique French colonial experiment of "authoritarian native colonization . . . as atypical as its methods were questionable."[29]

For its admirers, the Office represented France's finest work in North Africa and constituted eloquent proof of this colonial power's tenacious and generous efforts to improve the lot of its Moroccan protégés. They proudly pointed to the fact that "numerous French and foreign missions of technicians and economists who . . . have come to visit the Beni Amir perimeter are practically unanimous . . . in recognizing its success."[30]

What makes the Office de l'Irrigation so important, regardless of how it is viewed, is that the basic formula of development that it pioneered has been employed by the government in Morocco ever since. Its specific method of remembrement, known as "Trame A," would be applied in the Doukkala Plain in 1952, then extended to all the other irrigation perimeters. This specific method would be largely replaced by the slightly different "Trame B" method after 1964. However, what is primarily significant is that the Office established remembrement as the absolute precondition of irrigation development for Moroccan peasants. The Office's highly authoritarian modus operandi, involving directed plantings in the context of a mandatory crop rotation cycle, is also an essential feature of irrigation development in Morocco today. On an institutional level, the Office would serve as a model for both the Office National des Irrigations (1960–64) and the

[26] R. Trintignac, "Note pour M. le Directeur de l'Agriculture . . . a/s: situation actuelle des périmètres irrigués des Beni Amir," confidential note, Service de la Mise en Valeur, 1 September 1946; R. Dumont, "Les Beni Amir, ou 'Les travaux forcés à perpétuité,' " unpublished report, September 1947. Both reports are in the archives of the Office des Beni Amir, and are on Centre National de Documentation microfiche 00511.

[27] "La Grande Misère des paysans de l'Office des Beni Amir," *Espoir*, 17 August 1947, p. 2.

[28] Ibid.

[29] A. Ayache, *Le Maroc: bilan d'une colonisation* (Paris, 1956), pp. 236–237.

[30] J. Pourtauborde, "Qu'est-ce que l'Office de l'Irrigation aux Beni Amir–Beni Moussa?," unpublished report, 1949, p. 14 (Centre National de Documentation microfiche 00511).

present-day Offices Régionaux de Mise en Valeur Agricole, each of which controls the development of a single region.

In all, the Office de l'Irrigation and its legacy represent the manifestation of a single individual's distinctive vision for the development of traditional agrarian Morocco. Tallec's vision was one of a highly ordered geometric landscape, dominated by man and revivified by irrigation water provided by *grands barrages*. It was a vision of a rationalized landscape composed of the lush, rearranged, privately owned parcels of peasant small farmers—seminomads rooted to the soil through water development—who would grow crops required by the state according to a rigid, predetermined production plan and adhering to strict rotation schedules. These settled people would be given total supervision and assistance by the government; however, they would be fully charged for water and aid to ensure the economic viability of the development scheme.

Tallec's vision has indeed proven influential in shaping the present rural Moroccan landscape. But it was not the only such vision during the protectorate period. Immediately after World War II, an alternative experiment was initiated. This experiment represents a path to development Morocco might have taken, but did not. More important, this initiative established the infrastructure of government intervention upon which all subsequent rural modernization efforts have been grafted. The point of departure for this second experiment was the now-legendary drought of 1945.

L'Année Terrible

The traditional Moroccan peasant, armed only with a wooden scratch plow, cannot begin planting until autumn rains have softened the earth. Because of Morocco's short winter growing season, planting normally must be completed by early January. In autumn 1944, the rains came late. Planting could not begin until the end of December; consequently, the total planted area was reduced. This situation threatened a shortfall that would only be averted if rainfall during the rest of the winter was above normal. Instead, disaster struck on an unprecedented scale: "After January, a period of drought without precedent since the beginning of the Protectorate set in; for eight months, not a drop of water fell on Morocco."[31]

The danger of catastrophic famine was increased by the fact that

---

[31] J. Nouvel, "La Crise agricole de 1945–1946 au Maroc et ses conséquences économiques et sociales," *Revue de Géographie Humaine et d'Ethnologie* 1 (1949): 87–88.

grain reserves were already depleted through wartime requisitioning and poorer-than-normal preceding harvests. The drought, furthermore, was not primarily localized in the south, as in 1935–38; it occurred over all of Morocco. Crop yields averaged only 1.5 quintals per hectare, as opposed to the normal 7.4 quintals for the period.[32] (See Fig. 2.) The total Moroccan harvest was only 5.1 million quintals for a population whose annual food needs amounted to 21 million quintals.[33]

While half of Morocco's livestock perished, grain shipments from the United States, Canada, and Argentina came to the aid of the human population. A massive relief operation succeeded in distributing grain to even the most remote parts of Morocco.[34] Nevertheless, relief stations were able to distribute only 6 to 9 kilograms per person per month.[35] Because cereals constitute the major part of the rural Moroccan diet, and 15 kilos per person per month is considered the threshold for normal nutrition,[36] widespread starvation resulted.

A full-scale effort was needed to prevent mass exodus to the cities. The immediate danger was looting and epidemics; the long-term threat was permanent social disruption stemming from the wholesale disappearance of small landholdings. This threat was due, in part, to the inability of small farmers to repay the loans made at planting time by rural notables and urban merchants. However, starvation itself caused peasants to sell land simply to save their families. According to one source, the going rate during this desperate period was one quintal of wheat for 2 hectares of land.[37]

In direct response, the protectorate administration passed legislation in 1945 and 1946 establishing a *bien de famille* for the rural Moroccan population—a minimum holding size below which all land transactions were prohibited.[38] In its own words, the legislation was designed "to protect the Moroccan peasant against the risks of dispossession, to assure him . . . a viable holding for his family's subsistence, and enable

[32] A. M. Jouve, "Démographie et céréaliculture: évolution comparée de la démographie et de la céréaliculture au Maroc depuis le début du siècle," *RGM* 4 (1980): 6, 11.

[33] Ibid., p. 6; Nouvel, "La Crise agricole," p. 88.

[34] Nouvel, "La Crise agricole," p. 88.

[35] Ibid.; "Intensifier," *Libération*, p. 4.

[36] A kilo of grain represents approximately 4000 calories.

[37] Istiqal Party, *Morocco under the Protectorate: Forty Years of French Administration* (New York, 1954), p. 32.

[38] Dahirs of 8 February 1945; Arrêtés Vizeriels of 19 May 1945, 4 July 1945, and 6 July 1946. This legislation was inspired by the Egyptian "5 feddan law" of 1913. See Nouvel, "La Crise agricole," p. 89.

him to participate in the economic development of the country."[39] The bien de famille was to be 7.5 hectares of dry land, 1.5 hectares of irrigated land, or 0.75 hectares of orchard land.[40] This holding size, it should be noted, was now considerably smaller than the most brazen colonialists had recommended two decades earlier.

Unfortunately, the legislation was only partially successful. An undeniable major consequence of the drought was a large reduction of small holdings.[41] The drought and its associated social consequences forcefully refocused the protectorate administration's attention on the plight of the traditional agricultural sector.

The extension of cereal cultivation had already reached a barrier which subsequent efforts have never significantly breached. (For example, 4.4 million hectares of cereals were cultivated annually during 1941–45, versus 4.5 million hectares during 1974–79.)[42] Further, yields in many areas seemed to be declining as a result of soil exhaustion. As Marchal, the plenipotentiary minister, concluded in 1946:

> Still today many are loath to admit it. However, we must accept the fact. Morocco is no longer, or can be only occasionally, an exporter of cereals. . . . Since 1940, the rural population has increased by at least a million, and yet the food to be shared has increased very little.[43]

For France's future in Morocco, if for no other reason, corrective measures were urgently demanded.

Unfortunately, an irrigation solution would not work. The Office de l'Irrigation development model, based on large-scale water projects, was applicable to only a select portion of agrarian Morocco: Both Morocco's water resources and the administration's finances were far too limited. Called for, instead, was a vigorous "native agriculture policy" that would raise agricultural yields in the dryland areas.

Before 1945, there was no real policy for the traditional agricultural sector other than the oft-repeated faith that the native would learn from the European's superior example. What was called a Direction

[39] "Dahir du 8 février 1945 créant un bien de famille marocain," *BO* 1687 (1945): 97.

[40] A. Barbarin, "La Protection de la petite propriété agricole dans la zone française du Maroc: étude de bien de famille," unpublished report, *Mémoire* no. 1569 (1950), CHEAM, Paris, p. 32.

[41] Nouvel, "La Crise agricole," p. 89.

[42] Jouve, "Démographie et céréaliculture," pp. 6, 8.

[43] L. Marchal, "Les Principes, les méthodes et les buts de la modernisation rurale au Maroc," *BIM*, 1946, p. 308.

de l'Agriculture was essentially a department of colonization. Native agricultural matters were divided up among four departments: Economic Affairs, Finance, Public Works, and, most important, Interior. The only significant action taken to assist the native farmer was the creation of Sociétés Indigènes de Prévoyance in 1917. These provident societies were inspired by the traditional collective granaries.[44] In one Frenchman's words, they were designed to lend assistance "to the poor or unfortunate fellah, aid rendered necessary by the difficulties these naturally improvident folk have balancing their resources and needs."[45] The SIPs lent out seeds and made minor short-term loans for fertilizer and equipment. All Moroccan peasants were automatically members of the local SIP and had to contribute when they paid the annual agricultural tax, or tartīb. These funds, in turn, were augmented by state funds. Unfortunately, the entire pool amounted to only a few dollars per member. Loans of any significant size did not reach beyond a narrow circle of notables and "modern Moroccan farmers."[46] While the SIPs had a secondary function of extending modern agricultural methods, their efforts were so diffuse that they had virtually no effect on the Moroccan peasantry as a whole.

The new postwar development experiment would derive from two important observations: (1) average settler yields were significantly higher than Moroccan peasant yields (typically nearly double for both hard and soft wheat); and (2) settler production was much less susceptible to fluctuations in annual weather conditions. On the latter point, for example, during the period 1940–44 the worst settler grain harvest was only 26 percent poorer than the best, whereas for Moroccan peasants the variation was 55 percent.[47] For the drought year 1945—l'Année terrible—the settler harvest was still approximately half of normal; the Moroccan harvest, however, was only one-sixth.[48]

The principal factor accounting for these differences was believed to be the settlers' use of the tractor. Tractors enabled plowing to begin before the autumn rains, so that the entire cultivable area could be put into production and seeds immediately benefited when rain arrived. Tractors permitted deep plowing, so that the soil could store moisture

---

[44] J. Despois, L'Afrique blanche (Paris, 1964), pp. 408–409.

[45] M. Bonnefous, Perspectives de l'agriculture marocaine (Bordeaux, 1949), p. 29.

[46] C. F. Stewart, The Economy of Morocco, 1912–1962 Cambridge, Mass., 1964), p. 108.

[47] Marchal, "Les Principes," pp. 307–308.

[48] Nouvel, "La Crise agricole," p. 88; Jouve, "Démographie et céréaliculture"; Marchal, "Les Principes," p. 307.

for more effective growth during the dry season, and so that the deeply rooted dwarf palm and jujube tree could be eradicated; the wooden plow had to scratch its way around these hardy weeds and the productive area was thereby reduced. Finally, tractors enabled the harvest to be gathered much more rapidly, reducing the ever present threat from locusts, hot dry winds from the Sahara, and summer drought conditions.[49] In short, it was believed that the introduction of the tractor into the traditional agricultural sector would result in greatly increased harvests. "Famine in Morocco will be finally vanquished only when the tractor has come into general use," Resident General Puaux declared in 1946.[50]

The Secteurs de Modernisation du Paysannat Experiment

The architects of the Secteurs de Modernisation du Paysannat (SMP) scheme, in which the introduction of the tractor was to play a key role, were Jacques Berque and Julien Couleau. Berque, a civil controller like Tallec, had already distinguished himself through research on rural Moroccan society; Couleau was an agronomist and intellectual committed to improving the lot of the Moroccan peasant. They had the support of some of the most liberal leaders during the entire protectorate period: Marchal as plenipotentiary minister and Gabriel Puaux and Eirik Labonne as residents general.[51]

"Modernizing the peasantry" was already one of the pillars of a reform package that Resident General Puaux had submitted to the sultan at the beginning of 1944. With these reforms, Puaux claimed, "Morocco will achieve its rightful place in the evolution of the world."[52] Following the advent of famine in 1945, full support was given to the experiment proposed by Berque and Couleau.

Berque and Couleau held it essential to view rural life as "a coherent whole."[53] In their view, rural society in each corner of Morocco had achieved a certain level of equilibrium with its environment. Each rural

---

[49] Stewart, *The Economy of Morocco*, p. 103.

[50] *BIM*, 1946, p. 15.

[51] P. Marthelot, "Histoire et réalité de la modernisation du monde rural au Maroc," *Tiers-Monde* 2 (1961): 144–145. Puaux was resident general from June 1943 to March 1946; Labonne from March 1946 to May 1947.

[52] *BIM*, 1946, p. 14.

[53] J. Berque and J. Couleau, "Vers la modernisation du fellah marocain," *BESM* 26 (1945): 18.

group's annual cycles, agricultural techniques, technology, and social customs were parts of "an ensemble." Given this fact, efforts to change a single part of the whole, as by replacement of the wooden plow with the European steel plow, would not succeed. Berque and Couleau's rallying cry became, "Le progrès sera total, ou ne sera pas!"[54] Their formula was designed to change the whole.

What they visualized was an *action de synthèse*: a concentrated, comprehensive development effort in certain well-defined sectors. The experiment drew inspiration from Berque and Couleau's own understanding of rural Morocco, as well as from the Tennessee Valley project in the United States and Soviet farm collectivization.[55] (Indeed, depending on the point of view, the experiment would be proudly labeled "le New Deal marocain"[56] or described as a dangerous kolkhoz operation.)[57] The rural modernization sectors (SMPs) were to be concerned with both social and economic development; thus, schools, infirmaries, and other social institutions would be attached to their headquarters. The headquarters would serve as the nuclei of model farms that would introduce the peasant to the use of the tractor and to modern farming techniques. On these model farms, the peasant would serve, so to speak, "his apprenticeship as modern man and informed cultivator."[58] In sum, the SMPs were to function as the growth poles of rural modernization.[59]

Berque and Couleau's second key concept was *action de choc* (shock therapy). The *action de choc* would operate in tandem with the *action de synthèse*. Rural transformation, Berque and Couleau believed, could only take place when a psychological jolt had burst the bonds holding the old "ensemble" together. This jolt would come from the introduction of the tractor. The tractor would compensate for the disruption of the peasant's ancestral modes by giving him an almost immediate increase in powers of production and by emancipating him from the tedium of his traditional existence.[60] To hold the social body together on its rapid journey of modernization, Berque and Couleau proposed the substitution of the *jmaʿa* (the traditional Berber governing council) for the prevailing patronage network controlled by caids and rural

[54] Marchal, "Les Principes," p. 314.
[55] Ibid., p. 303; Berque and Couleau, "Vers la modernisation," p. 21.
[56] J. Célérier, "La Modernisation du paysannat marocain," *RGM* 1 (1947), p. 13.
[57] Marthelot, "Histoire et réalité," p. 146; L. Papy, "Une Réalisation française au Maroc: les secteurs de modernisation rurale," *COM* 36 (1956): 328.
[58] *BCAR*, 1956, p. 306.
[59] F. Joly, "La Modernisation rurale au Maroc," *AG* 55 (1946): 212.
[60] Berque and Couleau, "Vers la modernisation," p. 19.

notables. The "jmaʿa on the tractor," in short, was the basic formula of the SMP program.[61]

Legislation creating the SMP program was passed on 5 July 1945, in the middle of *l'Année terrible*. Rural modernization sectors quickly began to be established, nearly always on collective land. Theoretically they were established in areas where "the conditions of the milieu, the degree of evolution of the rural population, and the possibilities offered by the intervention of modern machinery or by the accomplishment of certain mechanized tasks permit and justify a concentration of effort."[62] A select portion of the land chosen as an SMP site was reserved for the model farm. This was theoretically to be 2,000 hectares in size. Members of the local tribe were compelled to participate in the program. Under the watchful eyes of a French staff, they helped clear the land, construct roads and buildings, plant and harvest, and perform numerous other tasks.

The SMPs generally operated on four functional levels, each of which was reflected spatially. First, there was "direct exploitation" on the central model farm, the profits of which accrued to the state and were considered necessary to finance the development venture.[63] Second, surrounding the model farm was a "zone of development" comprising uncultivated land that the SMP's heavy machinery would clear for the Moroccan owners—usually a collective—after which the land would be returned for cultivation. The SMP's work was paid at cost. Third, there was a "zone of work-to-order." (This might overlap with the second zone geographically but not temporally.) In this zone, the SMP's machinery would plow and harvest on contract. Again, work was paid at cost. These first three zones were intended to constitute a beachhead "of a modernized Morocco within medieval Morocco."[64] Finally, surrounding this central core of direct intervention was a much broader, unbounded "zone of diffusion" through which, in theory, modernization would automatically diffuse until it covered the whole of rural Morocco.[65]

Each SMP was to respond to local conditions of man and milieu. Most were located in the Atlantic plains and specialized in dry farming of cereal crops. However, some were intended to serve as the vanguards of irrigation development (for example, SMP no. 44 in the

[61] Marthelot, "Histoire et réalité," p. 145.
[62] Claude Ecorcheville, cited in Papy, "Une Réalisation française," p. 329.
[63] *Encyclopédie Mensuelle d'Outre Mer* (1954), p. 111.
[64] Bonnefous, *Perspectives*, p. 34.
[65] See Papy, "Une Réalisation française," pp. 337–340, for a fuller description of these zones.

TABLE 5   Proposed Development Schedule of the Secteurs de Modernisation du Paysannat Program (hectares)

	1945 (5)ᵃ	1946 (20)	1947 (50)	1948 (110)	1949 (220)	1950 (220)	1951 (220)	1952 (220)
	2,500	5,000	7,500	10,000	10,000	10,000	10,000	10,000
	—	7,500	15,000	22,500	30,000	30,000	30,000	30,000
	—	—	15,000	30,000	45,000	60,000	60,000	60,000
	—	—	—	30,000	60,000	90,000	120,000	120,000
	—	—	—	—	55,000	110,000	165,000	220,000
TOTAL	2,500	12,500	37,500	92,500	200,000	300,000	385,000	440,000

SOURCE: See note 67.

NOTE: This scheme needs some explanation. In 1945, 5 model farms of 500 hectares each were to have been put into production. These 5 farms were supposed to have been expanded to 1,000 hectares each in 1946; to 1,500 hectares each in 1947; and to a final size of 2,000 hectares each in 1948, for a total of 10,000 hectares. Simultaneously, in 1946, 15 new model farms of 500 hectares each were supposed to have been established, and they were to have been progressively enlarged to 2,000 hectares each by 1949. In 1947, 30 new model farms of 500 hectares each were to have been established; in 1948, 60 new model farms; and in 1949, 110 new model farms. By 1949, a total of 220 model farms were to have been established, for a total of 440,000 hectares when all had achieved their final 2,000 hectares by 1952.

ᵃ Figures in brackets indicate proposed total number of SMPs.

Doukkala Plain). And a few specialized in horticulture, oasis agriculture, and stock raising.[66]

The program was ambitious. Each SMP was annually to put 500 hectares into direct cultivation for the model farm, until it reached the optimum 2,000-hectare size after four years. Five SMPs were to be established the first year, 15 the second, 30 the third, 60 the fourth, and 110 the fifth. On this basis, at the end of the eighth year (1952), 440,000 hectares—10 percent of cultivated Morocco—were to have been brought under direct cultivation (see Table 5).[67] When each SMP's 2,000-hectare model farm had been put into full production, rural modernization would rapidly spread outward.

The vision, unfortunately, remained unfulfilled. By the end of the protectorate, only fifty-seven SMPs were in operation and their activities extended to only 75,000 hectares: 22,000 on the model farms and another 53,000 in the "work-to-order" zones.[68] The SMP experiment

[66] Ibid., pp. 330–335.
[67] Berque and Couleau, "Vers la modernisation," p. 24.
[68] Papy, "Une Réalisation française," p. 348. The protectorate authorities claimed an

thus became the second of a string of failed efforts to modernize Morocco. As Marthelot lamented, "the road to modernization in Morocco . . . is paved with aborted endeavors."[69]

There were certain conceptual weaknesses in the scheme itself. First, the "zone of diffusion" proved to be a nonfunctional concept. This was clearly the crucial zone in the scheme, for it was here that modernization was automatically to diffuse outward on the basis of the example set in the core. However, as Stewart points out, there is nothing automatic about the diffusion of a major new technology.[70] Among other things, it takes capital—far more than was available to either the Moroccan fellahin or the protectorate administration during the lean postwar years. The SMPs had very little influence outside their core areas.

Second, the scheme viewed the "feudal mentality" of the peasant and his "archaic" *genres de vie* as the root of the problem. In fact, the root of the problem was colonization itself. Colonization's usurpation of the heartland of agrarian Morocco (and its planned future extension) was inherently contradictory to the goals of the program. This seems to have been missed even by the plan's architects. For example, Berque stated, "If we commit the will, the men, and the means, it will be possible . . . to reconcile the rise of the native with the expansion of France."[71]

The main reason for the SMP program's failure, however, was its threat to the status quo. The program generated opposition on all sides. Settlers decried it as a subversive kolkhoz movement, but feared most that it would raise the native standard of living and absorb unemployment, thereby making their work force more expensive.[72] In addition, they were concerned that investment in rural modernization would reduce funds spent on colonial agriculture.[73] Settler opposition to the program was influential enough to ensure that its budget remained small. As the French geographer Papy noted, the contrast between the magnitude of the SMP program's task and the modesty of its resources was striking.[74]

---

additional 136,000 hectares for the SMP's extension work in the "zones of diffusion." See ibid.

[69] Marthelot, "Histoire et réalité," p. 143.

[70] Stewart, *The Economy of Morocco*, p. 110.

[71] Cited in M. Naciri, "Les Expériences de modernisation de l'agriculture au Maroc," *RGM* 11 (1967): 105.

[72] Marthelot, "Histoire et réalité," p. 146.

[73] Stewart, *The Economy of Morocco*, p. 110.

[74] "Une Réalisation française," p. 348.

The Moroccan rural elite, whom the French used to control the countryside, were also against the SMP program: They rightly feared a loss of their traditional authority. Ironically, this group profited most from the program. In many regions, only large landowners modernized their techniques.

Finally, peasants, the intended beneficiaries of the SMP program, stubbornly resisted. In part, this was due to the program's heavy-handed, paternalistic approach. Participation was compulsory. And the jma'as, which were supposed to run the model farms with the French directors, were rarely consulted.[75] Much more important, however, peasants feared expropriation of their land. This fear was well placed. By the end of the protectorate, none of the land "borrowed" to establish the model farms had been returned to its rightful owners as it theoretically should have been after development had taken place.

Resistance often took overt forms. One famous and symbolic incident occurred in autumn 1946 at SMP no. 2 in Dkhissa, near Meknes. This SMP had been singled out to commemorate the first harvest of the SMP program. Assembled were Resident General Labonne and other high protectorate functionaries. A battery of tractors was lined up, scheduled to commence clearing the next section of the model farm. Just as the ceremony began, the collective members, upset at the way the harvest had been distributed, lay down before the tractors or opposed them with force. Five hundred soldiers had to be summoned to restore public order.[76]

When the liberal Resident General Labonne was replaced by the conservative General Juin in May 1947, settlers regained control over agricultural development decisions and the steam quickly went out of the SMP movement. The great scheme became simply another minor government bureau, of little consequence.

The significance of the SMP program lies in its legacy. The fifty-seven SMPs operating at the end of the protectorate constituted a basic network of "intervention centers" upon which all subsequent national development efforts have focused.[77] Second, its formula of massive rural transformation through introduction of the tractor was adopted by the ill-fated Operation Plow program (1957–62) shortly after in-

---

[75] R. Dumont, *Etude des modalités d'action du Paysannat, CMR* 3 (1948): 24–26.

[76] Papy, "Une Réalisation française," pp. 328–329; Marthelot, "Histoire et réalité," pp. 146–147; R. Bidwell, *Morocco under Colonial Rule: French Administration of Tribal Areas, 1912–1956* (London, 1973), p. 229. After this incident, the military authorities would claim that the SMPs constituted a threat to public order. See Marthelot, "Histoire et réalité," p. 147.

[77] Naciri, "Les Expériences de modernisation," p. 105.

dependence, and is again being resurrected in Morocco (see Epilogue). Its vision of social transformation, through substituting the jma'a for the prevailing power structure of rural notables, would strongly influence both the Office National des Irrigations (1960–64) and the Sebou Project (1963–68) in their respective searches for a new "cell of development." Finally, the SMP program firmly established a pattern of state farms in Morocco that has continued to the present. Despite this important legacy, the rapid collapse of the program in 1947 cleared the way for a return to irrigation development.

The Grands Périmètres d'Irrigation

As earlier noted, World War II seriously disrupted Phase I of the comprehensive irrigation plan, which was to have been completed by the end of 1944. The war retarded the development of the plains dominated by the N'fis, El Kansera, and Kasbah Tadla dams, construction of the Imfout Dam, and most *petite* and *moyenne hydraulique* projects. The Imfout Dam, begun in 1939, was not completed until 1945, three years later than originally planned.[78] Both the Moulouya and Sebou projects were completely tabled by the war, the former until May 1947; the latter indefinitely.

A report drafted in July 1946 by Bauzil, adjunct director of Public Works, inventoried the war's effect on the irrigation plan. Instead of 265,000 hectares, which successful completion of Phase I would have accomplished, only some 30,000 hectares had been put into modern irrigation: 15,000 hectares in the Tadla Plain (Kasbah Tadla Dam), 10,000 hectares in the Gharb Plain (El Kansera Dam), and 5,000 hectares in the Haouz Plain (N'fis Dam).[79]

Nonetheless, despite the setback, the national irrigation plan was still in force. Indeed, the massive new Bin el Ouidane Dam project was initiated in 1945. This dam, to be Africa's largest and the world's fifteenth largest when completed, theoretically would permit the irrigation of 120,000 hectares in the Tadla.[80] (See Illus. 8.) Bauzil's 1946 report estimated Morocco's irrigable area at 1.3 million hectares.[81] The latent riches this water represented—which each year flowed idly to the sea—were now estimated at 9 billion francs.[82]

Immediately after the war, when liberal administration in France

[78] *RGM*, 1945, p. 27.
[79] V. Bauzil, "L'Hydraulique agricole au Maroc," *BESM* 8 (1946): 376–377.
[80] *ITOM*, 1954, p. 618.
[81] Bauzil, "L'Hydraulique agricole," p. 371.
[82] Ibid.

was reflected in the colonies, the SMP program represented the central thrust of Morocco's agricultural development policy. However, by summer 1947, conservative forces in France had begun to reconquer "ground lost in the aftermath of the Liberation."[83] When General Juin was sent to Morocco in 1947 to replace the liberal Resident General Labonne, *grande hydraulique* again assumed center stage. The government now placed major emphasis on "profitability," an emphasis that replaced the SMP's previous emphasis on social action. The SMP program was sharply criticized for "nineteenth-century socialistic utopianism" that had led it to sink funds in unproductive regions.[84] René Dumont, a prominent agricultural expert who made an official visit to Morocco in 1947, for example, claimed that the majority of SMPs had been established in environments too marginal to justify such investments. "We must not," he emphasized, "confuse social action with the squandering of public funds."[85]

Dumont concluded in an influential report presented to the protectorate administration in September 1947 that Morocco should develop its *best lands*, those that would pay for funds invested in them.[86] Instead of government intervention on a vast country-wide scale, he recommended limited but much more intensive actions. Specifically, he recommended that the administration concentrate investments in irrigation. Dumont's recommendations carried great weight. He was officially charged with developing a program for increasing North Africa's agricultural production as part of the postwar Monnet Plan. His recommendations became a central feature of Morocco's 1949–52 plan.[87]

Dumont's recommendations lent support to a policy already strongly favored by the settler community. "Investment in the best lands" closely corresponded to "investment in settler lands," because Europeans already owned the most productive part of agricultural Morocco. Table 6 reveals the strong proportion of European landholdings in the six major irrigation perimeters in 1951.[88] Of the land already

[83] Marthelot, "Histoire et réalité," p. 147.

[84] Dumont, *Etude des modalités*, p. 6.

[85] Ibid., p. 20.

[86] Ibid., p. 19.

[87] *BCAR*, 1949, p. 1691.

[88] Sources for Table 6 are the following: R. Trintignac, "La mise en valeur agricole du Maroc," unpublished report presented at the Centre d'Etudes Méditerranéen d'Ankara, 12 December 1951; L. Garnier, "Rapport sur les problèmes majeurs de la mise en valeur des grands périmètres marocains," unpublished report, Service de la Mise en Valeur. Both reports are in the archives of the Direction de l'Agriculture in the Centre

TABLE 6   European Landholdings within the Irrigation Perimeters, 1951

| | | Percentage of land ownership | | Perennially |
Perimeter	Irrigable area (hectares)	European	Moroccan	irrigated area (hectares)
Sidi Slimane (Gharb)	40,000	60	40	12,000
Triffa (Moulouya)	40,000	60	40	—
N'fis (Haouz)	35,000	20	80	5,000
Beni Moussa (Tadla)	120,000	20	80	—
Beni Amir (Tadla)	45,000	10	90	18,000
Doukkala	120,000	10	90	—
TOTAL	400,000			35,000

SOURCES: See note 88.

irrigated at this date, virtually all of that in the N'fis perimeter, 80 percent of that in the Sidi Slimane perimeter, and 12 percent of that in the Beni Amir perimeter—in other words, half of Morocco's perennially irrigated land—belonged to settlers, who represented a mere .5 percent of Morocco's landowners.

Another major force behind irrigation development in this period was the hydroelectric lobby, dominated by the powerful Banque de Paris et des Pays-Bas. "Paribas" owned a controlling interest in EEM, which had been granted exclusive rights to develop Morocco's hydroelectric potential. EEM contributed three-quarters of the financing for hydroelectric projects, the Moroccan government one-quarter. In many cases, as earlier noted, conflict between hydroelectric and agricultural interests helped retard irrigation development. However, the converse was ultimately far more significant: Had it not been for powerful lobbying and heavy financial contributions by private hydroelectric interests, many of Morocco's predominantly multipurpose dams might never have been built. This interpretation is confirmed by a confidential letter from the protectorate's secretary general to the plenipotentiary minister on 16 July 1952:

> The motive behind the primacy given to large-scale irrigation appears to reside in the dynamism with which large-scale hydroelectric works have been established in this country. Irrigation has thus appeared as a by-product of electric energy. . . . Since dams were necessary for the production of electric energy, the oppor-

National de Documentation, Rabat. The microfiche number for Trintignac's report is 02560; for Garnier's report, 02955.

tunity existed to use the water accumulated by these dams for irrigation purposes.[89]

The same confidential letter also drew attention to a study that estimated the respective "profitability coefficients" of different modes of agricultural investment:

1.2   for investment in dryland agriculture for small Moroccan farmers
0.2   for investment in European agriculture in *grands périmètres d'irrigation*
0.17   for investment in modern Moroccan agriculture in *grands périmètres d'irrigation*.[90]

This study thus demonstrated that the return on investments in traditional dryland agriculture was six times that expected from large-scale irrigation development for Europeans and more than seven times that from irrigation development for Moroccans. Thus, although the protectorate administration now undertook irrigation development in the name of profitability, top administrators were aware that the path chosen was by far the least profitable.

A final major force behind irrigation development in the postwar period was the "showcase factor." From 1948, France was conscious of the hypothetical nature of its future in Morocco.[91] This caused it to gradually apply the brakes to expensive development projects. Phrases such as "a million hectares of irrigation," "assuring the food needs of the Moroccan population," and "the key to Morocco's future prosperity" became primarily rhetoric for propaganda purposes. Irrigation development would still proceed, but cautiously. Meanwhile, France needed to make a spectacular demonstration of its efforts to develop Morocco.

One foreign analyst, J. M. Houston, aptly described the postwar situation in an address to the Royal Geographical Society:

> Morocco is being watched by the Moslem world and by all the nationalist elements now awake on the African continent. . . . With the spot lights of world publicity focused on Morocco and the thrice repeated motion of the Moroccan question tabled at the United Nations, the protectorate powers of France and Spain

[89] Confidential letter of 16 July 1952, p. 8. This letter is on microfiche 03447 at the Centre National de Documentation, Rabat.
[90] Ibid., p. 7.
[91] Interview with Paul Pascon, 1 December 1982.

cannot afford to fail in their policies for the future of the country.[92]

Here the Office de l'Irrigation aux Beni Amir–Beni Moussa provided the key. It had already demonstrated that, with an authoritarian formula, irrigation could be developed for Moroccan small farmers. The Office, indeed, had already pioneered the formula. Nearly half of the perennially irrigated land in Morocco was owned by fellahin governed by the Office. With France's future in Morocco in question, the Office constituted one of the strongest cases in the protectorate's dossier.

In short, according to the policy that emerged in 1948 and remained in force until the end of the protectorate, large-scale irrigation development was both to benefit settlers and constitute a showcase of France's "impartial" efforts to develop Morocco. *Grande hydraulique* would constitute the protectorate's principal agricultural policy. For settlers, irrigation would take place under the relatively liberal conditions evolved in the Gharb. For Moroccans, it would take place according to the authoritarian formula pioneered by the Office de l'Irrigation in the Tadla, with remembrement and an imposed crop rotation cycle as the key features. Settlers would grow high-value export-oriented crops such as citrus and market vegetables. Moroccans would grow crops for Morocco's processing industries (cotton, oilseeds, and sugar beets), forage crops for improved stock raising and a dairy industry, and food for the domestic economy (wheat, market vegetables, rice, and legumes). The now-neutralized SMP program was to constitute the administrative gesture towards traditional dryland Morocco.

The new policy was fully reflected in both postwar protectorate development plans in Morocco, 1949–52 and 1953–56. For example, total funding for *grande hydraulique* in the 1953–56 budget represented the second largest item, after "basic infrastructure" (roads, ports, railroads, and communications).[93] Of agriculture's 1953–56 share of 38.5 billion francs, *grande hydraulique*, or large irrigation projects, accounted for 20 billion francs, as opposed to 3.8 billion for traditional dryland agriculture. This distribution supposedly demonstrated, in comparison to the 1949–52 budget, an "accent . . . on the need for stronger action to modernize traditional agriculture."[94]

[92] "The Significance of Irrigation in Morocco's Economic Development," *Geographical Journal* 120 (1954): 314.
[93] *ITOM*, 1953, pp. 14–15.
[94] *ITOM*, 1954, p. 198.

Irrigation development in the postwar period became concentrated in six major irrigation perimeters (*grands périmètres d'irrigation*): the Sidi Slimane perimeter in the Gharb, the Beni Amir and Beni Moussa perimeters in the Tadla, the N'fis perimeter in the Haouz, and the Abda-Doukkala and Triffa (Moulouya) perimeters in the plains of the same names (see Fig. 8). All except the Beni Moussa perimeter, to be irrigated with water from the massive Bin el Ouidane Dam, had been part of Phase I of the 1938 irrigation plan. Indeed, the 1938 plan as a whole was still considered to be in effect.

From 1949, as the first postwar development plan began to make funding available for irrigation, there was a strong emphasis on "rational development" (a fact earlier noted with regard to the Beni Amir perimeter). In part, this reflected the recommendations of Dumont following his official mission to Morocco. More directly, it reflected the recommendations of a mission sent to California by the protectorate administration in 1948.

The 1948 mission represented the decision of Roger Trintignac, a key member of the protectorate's official mission to California twenty years earlier. Trintignac was now head of Morocco's Service de la Mise en Valeur et du Génie Rural. In short, he was charged with establishing development policy for Morocco's irrigation perimeters. He sent one of his assistants, Louis Garnier, to the United States in 1948 in order to update the protectorate administration's information on California's irrigation agriculture, including methods of conditioning, packing, and processing fruits and vegetables, and to examine American methods of soil conservation. Garnier's report on his mission was made widely available to settlers and administrators in Morocco upon his return.[95]

Certain of Garnier's observations or recommendations became directly translated into policy. For example, Garnier drew attention to the fact that drainage canals had become "an absolute rule" in California.[96] Following his mission, drainage canals likewise became de rigueur in Morocco. (As earlier noted, drainage canals were systemati-

[95] Garnier also visited a "giant" (26,500-hectare) wheat ranch in eastern Montana owned by General Campbell. He took detailed notes on the dry-farming procedures that had enabled the ranch to obtain impressive yields, and he recommended that these procedures be immediately tested by the SMPs and "the most advanced colons" in each region. See *LTM*, 1949, p. 317. On a side trip, he also inspected the California date industry in the Coachella Valley (*LTM*, 1950, p. 16). Garnier's report was published in *LTM*, 1949, pp. 189–193, 237–239, 313–317; 1950, pp. 16–17, and in more complete form in *BCAR*, 1948, pp. 1374–1379; 1949, pp. 1746–1750, 1773–1784, and 1870–1875.

[96] *LTM*, 1949, p. 238.

cally included in the Beni Amir perimeter beginning in 1949.) Garnier also emphasized that it had become standard practice in California to plan for the development of entire watersheds. He recommended that the protectorate administration draw up development plans for the Moulouya, Sebou, and Oum er Rbia watersheds, or, failing this, one for each irrigation perimeter. Watershed planning was not implemented until the 1960s. However, immediately following the Garnier mission, the administration drafted comprehensive plans for the *mise en valeur* of the major irrigation perimeters. It initiated reforestation and soil conservation measures to help prolong the life of Morocco's dams. And it hired an American expert, W. C. Lowdermilk, to advise it how to combat erosion.[97] On the basis of Lowdermilk's recommendations, a new government agency was created in 1949: Défense et Restauration des Sols, or DRS.

In other areas, Garnier's report also had a direct effect. His observations on California's fruit juice industry served as the point of departure for fruit processing in Morocco.[98] His recommendation that Morocco extend its citrus growing season, as California had, by emphasizing production of early and late varieties, helped encourage a similar production pattern in Morocco. In addition, both his report and Dumont's report focused attention on the need to rationalize development procedures in the irrigation perimeters. What resulted was: (1) the reintroduction of remembrement in the Beni Amir perimeter in 1949 and its subsequent diffusion to the other perimeters; (2) the simultaneous effort to impose a five-year crop rotation cycle on Moroccan peasants in the irrigation perimeters; and (3) the systematic lining of new irrigation canals with cement.

The Garnier mission also paved the way for at least three further missions from Morocco to the United States and particularly California before the end of the protectorate.[99] These study missions and numerous references in the French agricultural literature indicate that California was the primary model for Morocco's irrigation development in the postwar era, just as it had been two decades earlier.

Settlers enthusiastically embraced the protectorate administration's postwar *grande hydraulique* strategy. They envisaged irrigation as the key to a renaissance of colonization. Irrigation would solve Morocco's

---

[97] Lowdermilk, "L'Eau et la conservation du sol au Maroc," *Bulletin de la Société des Agriculteurs du Maroc* 17–18 (1948): 25–51. See also L. Garnier, "Les Leçons d'une mission aux Etats-Unis," in *La Mise en valeur du Maroc*, ed. F. Malet et al. (Paris, 1949), pp. 13–17.

[98] *BCAR*, 1949, pp. 1746, 1784.

[99] See Chapter 3, note 55.

land shortage problem because it would greatly increase the productive capacity of native land; consequently, through land consolidation, large new areas could be opened for colonization. Numerous arguments were made to justify official colonization. "Events of recent years," according to some, revealed a pressing need to reinforce the French rural population in Morocco, which amounted to only 30,000 total in 1946.[100] Chambers of Agriculture also claimed to be besieged with demands from prospective settlers in France.[101]

The protectorate government viewed a new program of colonization favorably; there were, however, serious obstacles. Shortage of land was the overriding problem, just as it had been since the early 1920s. But the government was confronted with a more specific problem. Its bien de famille legislation of 1945–46, which reserved a minimum holding size for Moroccan peasants, made it nearly impossible to expropriate any new land for colonization. Population pressure was already too intense.

A loophole was found to alleviate the problem. On 19 March 1951, the administration issued a decree "on the development of collective lands." Known as the "dahir Juin," after Resident General Juin, this decree enabled a private land development company to acquire a sizable portion of the not-yet-irrigated Beni Moussa perimeter. According to the terms of the decree, the Société d'Etudes et de Gestion (SEG) received 3,265 hectares of land expropriated from several tribal collectives, for which it was obligated to pay a minimal price and clear the remainder of the collectives' land. The SEG immediately sold this land to forty-seven colons in lots of approximately 60 hectares.[102]

More effective means, however, were sought. By 1952, a strong lobby of settlers and land companies was pressing for abrogation of the legislation protecting Moroccan peasants. Their demands were due to the fact that the first water from the Bin el Ouidane Dam (Illus. 8) was scheduled to arrive in the Beni Moussa Plain in 1954.

The protectorate government yielded to the pressure. On 7 February 1953, the bien de famille decree was replaced by much less restrictive legislation.[103] Intense land speculation followed. Companies and individual settlers acquired holdings wherever available in the irriga-

---

[100] *BCAR*, 1946, p. 189.

[101] They argued that if nothing was done by the protectorate to respond to these demands, young Frenchmen instead would take their "youthful energy and eagerness" to South America or Canada (ibid., p. 190).

[102] Mingasson, "Le Périmètre d'irrigation," p. 86; *Echo d'Oran*, 6 August 1953, p. 6.

[103] "Dahir du 7 février 1953 abrogéant et remplaçant le dahir du 8 février 1945 créant un bien de famille," *BO* 2109 (1953): 442–444.

tion perimeters in the belief that they would be automatically consolidated by the administration when the network of irrigation canals was installed.[104]

In 1953, the administration decided to implement a limited program of official colonization in the irrigation perimeters. One project involved the allotment of domainal land in the Triffa (Bassa Moulouya) perimeter, which was scheduled to receive water from the Mechra Homadi Dam in 1955. The project was to reserve 42 percent of the irrigable 2,924 hectares for Europeans and 58 percent for Moroccans. The European lots would be 43 to 49 hectares in size, the Moroccan lots 6 to 8 hectares.[105]

However, the Triffa project, other similar projects, and the hopes that settlers and speculators invested in the irrigation perimeters remained unfulfilled. On 2 March 1956, Morocco became an independent state.

The Balance at Independence

There is perhaps no better symbol of irrigation development under the protectorate than the Rocade Canal. At independence in 1956, this canal was a monument to the political currents that had continuously undermined colonial efforts to harness Morocco's waters, as well as to the great unfulfilled potential in the protectorate's legacy.

The canal had an aura of mystery. It was a major earth canal, with a capacity greater than the summer flow of the Sebou. It abruptly began in an arid plain northeast of Marrakech, over 40 kilometers from any source of water. Its parched mouth lay more than 80 kilometers "downstream" to the southwest. The Rocade Canal was to have opened the central and western Haouz to colonization and irrigated some 40,000 to 60,000 hectares.[106] Instead, the canal became a casualty in the conflict between agricultural and hydroelectric interests.

The Rocade Canal was to have tapped the Tessaout and Lakhdar rivers further to the east, both major tributaries of the Oum er Rbia. Damming these tributaries and diverting water to the Haouz Plain for irrigation, however, would have reduced the flow in the Oum er Rbia at hydroelectric facilities downstream at Imfout, Daourat, and Sidi Maachou. The hydroelectric potential upstream at the Tessaout and

---

[104] Mingasson, "Le Périmètre d'irrigation," p. 86.

[105] *Réalités Marocaines*, 1954, p. 265.

[106] J. Pilleboue, "Aspects de l'irrigation dans se Haouz de Marrakech," *Mémoire*, 3d cycle, Geography, University of Paris, 1962, p. 181; ORMVAH, "Les Ressources naturelles et la mise en valeur actuelle de la plaine du Haouz," *RGM* 17 (1970): 34.

Lakhdar dam sites could have replaced the loss, but only at considerably greater cost.[107] Settlers tugged one way, hydroelectric interests the other.

In 1950, in an attempt to force the issue, the Haouz settlers secured funding to enable vigorous digging of the canal to begin—from the downstream end first. This was an all-or-nothing gamble. The canal would remain totally useless until it tapped the rivers 126 kilometers to the east. Settlers reasoned that the administration would not cancel the project after it had reached an advanced state: Funds already expended would be completely wasted. They underestimated their foes. The powerful Banque de Paris et des Pays-Bas and other financial groups behind Morocco's hydroelectric development prevailed. In 1953, the government canceled work on the canal.[108]

The Rocade Canal is singular in one way. The protectorate government's legacy in irrigation infrastructure was generally "upstream." That is, the unfulfilled potential almost exclusively involved water controlled or impounded by dams that was not able to be used for irrigation because the principal canals had not yet been constructed, the secondary and tertiary canal network did not yet exist, or the land had not yet been cleared, leveled, consolidated, and otherwise prepared for irrigation. Table 7 portrays the protectorate's legacy and reveals these progressive disparities.[109] The table demonstrates that existing dams had the potential to irrigate 246,000 hectares. However, existing main

[107] J. Rossano, "La Colonisation européenne dans le Haouz de Marrakech," *COM* 7 (1954): 352–353.

[108] Ibid.; interview with Paul Pascon, 1 December 1982.

[109] Sources for Table 7 are the following: *La Documentation Française* 2388 (1958): 37; *ITOM*, 1954: 87–89; A. M. Jouve, "L'Evolution des superficies equipées et irriguées dans les grands périmètres irrigués de 1957 à 1977," *HTE* 4 (1972): 60; Morocco, Direction des Travaux Publics, *L'Equipment hydraulique du Maroc* (Rabat, 1954), p. 10. Figures given for Morocco's perennially irrigated area at independence vary widely. This is principally due to the interpretation given to irrigation in the N'fis perimeter. In this perimeter, only 5,000 hectares (belonging almost exclusively to colons) could be perennially irrigated by the Cavagnac Dam. However, up to another 25,000 hectares (belonging principally to Moroccans) could be irrigated via earthen canals by flood waters of the N'fis in wetter-than-normal years. In 1956, it was possible to irrigate not quite 5,000 hectares in the N'fis perimeter. See *La Documentation Française* 2388 (1958): 37 or *ITOM*, 1954, pp. 84, 89. Disparities between the "irrigable" and "irrigated" figures led to settler accusations that dams were mainly being constructed for hydroelectric purposes. This charge caused Bauzil, adjunct director of Public Works, to write an article entitled "Dans la conception de ses programmes hydroélectriques, le Maroc a toujours donné la priorité à l'hydraulique agricole." See *ITOM*, 1954, pp. 611–614. In this article, Bauzil explained the disparities as due to lack of funds, to delays in remembrement operations, and to the difficulty of teaching the fellah the new discipline of irrigation.

TABLE 7   The Protectorate Government's Legacy in Irrigation Development, 1956 (hectares)

Perimeter	Irrigable with existing dams	Irrigable with existing main canals	Outfitted with secondary and tertiary canals	Perennially irrigated areas
Sidi Slimane (Gharb)	32,000	30,500	22,000	10,500
Triffa (Moulouya)	46,000	3,000	1,500	0
N'fis (Haouz)	5,000	5,000	7,500	5,000
Beni Moussa (Tadla)	85,000	0	4,000	0
Beni Amir (Tadla)	38,000	36,000	28,000	20,000
Doukkala	40,000	9,700	4,000	300
TOTAL	246,000	84,200	67,000	35,800

SOURCES: See note 109.

NOTE: Figures for irrigated area do not include private irrigation areas established by settlers and wealthy Moroccans. Much of this private irrigation (some 20,000–30,000 hectares) involved pumping from streams regularized by protectorate dams; it therefore constituted an indirect legacy of irrigation development efforts by the protectorate.

canals, to convey water from dams to the irrigation areas, had the capacity to irrigate only 84,200 hectares. Secondary and tertiary canal networks, necessary for actual irrigation, had only a 67,000-hectare capacity. Finally, only roughly 10 percent of the land within the irrigation perimeters was actually irrigated.

In conclusion, after forty-four years of the French protectorate, the government's legacy of irrigated acreage was tiny: only 36,000 hectares out of Morocco's potential of over a million hectares. Because the protectorate had rapidly evolved into a de facto colony after Lyautey, it is perhaps not surprising that approximately 47 percent of this irrigated land belonged to settlers. Moreover, though they represented under .5 percent of Morocco's landowners, settlers owned roughly 25 percent, or 100,000 hectares, of all land within the government-established irrigation perimeters. On the other hand, some 20,000 to 30,000 additional hectares had been put into irrigation by settlers and wealthy Moroccans who had established private pumping stations on streams regularized by protectorate dams. This was an indirect legacy of protectorate development efforts. Furthermore, Morocco's water resources had been well inventoried and nearly all promising dam sites had been identified by French engineers. Most potential irrigation projects had already been studied, and a comprehensive irrigation plan had been formulated. Finally, the protectorate government already had constructed dams that would enable a quarter-million hectares to be irrigated. Visible results were embarrassingly small. However, the protectorate government's legacy was vast in potential. Fulfilling this potential would soon become a major goal of the independent Moroccan government.

6

Fulfilling the Colonial Vision

This chapter focuses on agricultural development in Morocco since independence. Its purpose is, first, to examine the striking continuities between colonial and postcolonial policies; second, to explain how the colonial objective of irrigating a million hectares evolved into a central national development goal; and third, to analyze the present irrigation policy's impact on Morocco.

The Dilemma at Independence

At independence in 1956, perhaps the most complex problem confronting Morocco was the disparity between its modern and traditional agricultural sectors. As Joly, a French geographer, noted, "The net effect of colonization has been to juxtapose a modern mechanized economy against a preserved antique economy."[1] The problem had several important political and economic dimensions. First, there were glaring inequalities in land ownership (see Illus. 10–12). These had resulted primarily from colonization's disruptive forces and rapid population growth. Roughly 1.3 million hectares in the modern agricultural sector, generally Morocco's best land, were concentrated in the hands of 5,900 Europeans and 1,700 Moroccans.[2] On the other hand,

[1] F. Joly, "Données sur l'agriculture marocaine," *COM* 1 (1948): 97.

[2] C. Bénier, "Essai statistique sur l'économie agricole marocaine," *BESM* 74 (1957): 181–182; A. Belal and A. Agourram "Les Problèmes posés par la politique agricole dans une économie 'dualiste,'" *BESM* 122 (1973):3. Europeans owned a total of 1,017,000 hectares at independence, of which private colonization accounted for 728,000 hectares and official colonization for 289,000 hectares. Private colonization had taken place primarily on privately owned Moroccan land that settlers purchased.

TABLE 8   European-Owned Agricultural Land in Morocco, 1956

Holding size (hectares)	No. of holdings	Total area	% of total area
0–10	1,800	11,000	1.0
10–50	1,500	51,000	4.9
50–300	1,700	352,000	34.7
300–500	500	202,000	19.8
Over 500	400	401,000	39.6
TOTAL	5,900	1,017,000	100.0

SOURCE: Morocco, Ministry of Agriculture, unpublished statistics.

approximately 6.5 million hectares in the traditional sector were shared by 1.4 million Moroccan families.[3] The average modern holding was about 170 hectares. The average traditional holding was less than 5 hectares.

Land concentration, however, was even greater than these aggregate figures indicate. In the modern sector, averages of holding size were distorted by *petite colonisation*—mostly market gardening on the outskirts of the urban areas. In reality, fewer than half of the settlers owned 94 percent of the European agricultural land (refer to Table 8). For these 2,600 European large landowners, the average holding size was approximately 365 hectares.[4]

In the traditional sector, statistical distortion also appears. Some 5,800 rural Moroccan notables had developed latifundia during the course of the protectorate period—large, traditionally cultivated, sharecropped operations with an average size of 225 hectares.[5] With latifundia factored out, the average peasant holding falls to less than 4 hectares, a holding far too small to be viable unless irrigated. This is particularly true because fallowing was typically the only means employed to maintain soil fertility. As much as 40 percent of the tradi-

---

Official, or government-sponsored, colonization had taken place on lands drawn from the public domain (52 percent, including *jāysh* lands), expropriated "surplus" tribal or collective lands (26 percent), expropriated private lands (20 percent), and *ḥabūs* or religious-foundation lands (2 percent). See *LQA*, p. 404, and I. W. Zartman, "Farming and Land Ownership in Morocco," *Land Economics* 39 (1963): 190.

[3] Bénier, "Essai statistique," pp. 181–182.

[4] A number of large holdings were registered as land corporations. However, many of these were essentially family operations.

[5] Bénier, "Essai statistique," p. 182; also figures in Zartman, "Farming and Land Ownership," pp. 188, 193.

tional sector lay fallow in a given year.[6] Again, however, averages are misleading: Some 500,000 rural Moroccan families were virtually landless.[7]

Government surveys following independence established that, for the country as a whole, 5 to 10 percent of the agricultural heads of household owned more than 60 percent of Morocco's land, 50 to 55 percent owned less than 40 percent of the land, and roughly 40 percent owned essentially no land.[8] Of the three North African countries colonized by the French, Morocco had been left with the highest percentage of rural population (estimated at 70 percent in 1956) as well as of landless peasants and holdings too tiny to support a family.[9]

The modern sector had been the principal beneficiary of governmental assistance during the protectorate period. This sector employed up-to-date techniques, planted improved crop varieties, was generally mechanized, and had significantly higher yields than the traditional sector—often double for cereal crops. It moreover accounted for most of Morocco's agricultural exports. The principal problem after independence was that this sector was still three-fourths owned by foreigners. In stark contrast to the prosperity of the modern sector stood the traditional agricultural sector, steadily deteriorating after forty-four years of the protectorate.

The Moroccan government did not immediately nationalize foreign holdings for two main economic reasons. First, it did not wish to jeopardize the privileged trade agreements with France that had been established during the protectorate period. Second, it feared economic disruption if European agricultural expertise suddenly departed. This was particularly the case for the citrus and other high-value irrigated operations. Exports of citrus and market vegetables provided approximately 20 percent of Morocco's foreign revenue in 1955.[10]

Strictly political factors also came into play. While nearly all factions in Morocco agreed that "land reform" should take place, the nature of this reform generated considerable debate. Additionally, during the period 1956–62, Morocco was politically shaky. The united independ-

[6] Leaving land fallow was not entirely a matter of choice; to a significant degree, fallow land resulted from the fellah's inability to put land into production when the autumn rains, which softened the earth so that it could be worked with a scratch plow, arrived late or were reduced.

[7] *LQA*, p. 390. "Virtually landless" indicates a holding of less than 0.5 hectares or being totally landless.

[8] Morocco, *Plan Quinquennal, 1960–1964* (1960), p. 75. See comment, note 7.

[9] D. E. Ashford, "The Politics of Rural Mobilization in North Africa," *Journal of Modern African Studies* 7 (1969): 195.

[10] *Annuaire Statistique du Maroc*, 1958, p. 98.

ence movement became fragmented, and rural rebellions in the Rif and Middle Atlas had to be settled. The net result of these economic and political factors was a *politique d'attente*—a policy of procrastination. Indeed, the final and largest block of settler lands would not be expropriated until 1973, seventeen years after independence.

Only minor land reform took place from 1956 to 1960. In the first flush of independence, a few wealthy shaykhs, "who had enriched themselves more rapaciously than the *colons*," had part of their large domains and power stripped away.[11] (In one case, this involved an estate of 56,000 hectares.)[12] Additionally, leases held by settlers on collective lands were annulled by legislation passed on 9 May 1959. Following this legislation, approximately 23,000 hectares were recovered from foreign owners.[13] Similar legislation on 30 June 1960 expropriated the 3,265 hectares acquired by the SEG in the Beni Moussa irrigation perimeter.[14]

Using a portion of the recovered land, the government distributed nearly 16,000 hectares from 1956 to 1960.[15] Most of this land was in the irrigation perimeters. The average plot distributed was relatively large—about 9 hectares.[16] However, these distributions, as well as the expropriations of foreign holdings, amounted to feeble political gestures. The average number of land reform beneficiaries per year, three hundred, amounted to less than 1 percent of the annual rural exodus. Glaring disparities in land ownership persisted.

In short, colonization in rural Morocco lasted well beyond 1956. Most settlers continued farming. The profitability of many operations made selling out an unattractive option. For an orange orchard, for example, net annual profit was roughly one-third of the market value of the land.[17] What often did change, however, was the degree of reinvestment in the land. Many settler farms became essentially "mining operations," where short-term profits were made to the long-term detriment of the land. Gradually, however, settlers began to sell their holdings. The French embassy in Rabat has estimated that over

[11] Zartman, "Farming and Land Ownership," p. 193.

[12] The Amharoq family of Khenifra owned this vast estate. Other "land baron" families included the Layadi of the Rehamna (30,000 hectares), the Glawi and al-Biaz of Marrakech (18,000 hectares each), and the Boujemas of Beni Mellal (12,000 hectares). See ibid. Some of this confiscated land, however, was later restored. See *LQA*, p. 406.

[13] *LQA*, pp. 16–17, 406.

[14] Ibid.

[15] Ibid., p. 409.

[16] K. Griffin, *Land Concentration and Rural Poverty* (New York, 1976), p. 91.

[17] C. Mingasson, "Le Périmètre d'irrigation du Tadla," *Annales Algériennes de Géographie* 2 (1966): 87.

200,000 hectares of French holdings were transferred to Moroccans from 1956 to 1959, nearly all from private colonization.[18]

These land transfers were a clear threat to the success of the expected land reform. Consequently, the government passed legislation on 17 November 1959 making sales of colonization land conditional upon authorization by a minister of Agriculture, Interior, or Finance.[19] To prevent the deterioration of the modern sector. King Mohammed V also tried to reassure settlers.[20] However, whether still owned by Europeans or newly purchased by the Moroccan elite, Morocco's modern agricultural holdings remained relatively intact and the sector in general remained a pillar of the economy. Indeed, the modern sector began to expand as latifundia owners modernized their operations with government assistance. Unfortunately, the problems of Morocco's peasants also remained intact.

The Plight of the Traditional Sector

Cultivated acreage in Morocco greatly expanded during the protectorate period. Cereals, the mainstay of the Moroccan diet, increased from a preprotectorate average of 2 million hectares to around 4.3 million hectares by 1955.[21] Most of this expansion took place in the traditional agricultural sector. In 1951, for example, settler farms accounted for only 7 percent of the total acreage of the four main cereals (barley, hard wheat, soft wheat, and maize) and only 9 percent of their total production.[22] Only in soft wheat, the principal commercial cereal, did settlers make a major contribution to cereal production.[23]

Despite the doubling of sown area, however, Morocco's total cereal production increased by less than 60 percent during the protectorate period.[24] Furthermore, some of this increase was due to improved yields in the modern sector. The distressing truth is that yields were declining in much of Morocco. Despite a considerable extension of cultivation, production hardly increased in many areas.

Traditional agriculture's plight resulted from a set of processes ini-

[18] Griffin, *Land Concentration*, p. 101.

[19] O. Marais, "Le Maroc," in *Terre, paysans et politique*, ed. H. Mendras and Y. Tavernier (Paris, 1969), p. 284; *LQA*, p. 17.

[20] Marais, "Le Maroc," p. 284.

[21] A. M. Jouve, "Démographie et céréaliculture: évolution comparée de la démographie et de la céréaliculture au Maroc depuis le début du siècle," *RGM* 4 (1980): 6–7.

[22] C. F. Stewart, *The Economy of Morocco, 1912–1962* (Cambridge, Mass., 1964), p. 87.

[23] Ibid. Settler production of soft wheat amounted to 45 percent of the total in 1951.

[24] Jouve, "Démographie," p. 10.

tiated by French colonization. To generalize, agriculture in the coastal plains and plateaus before the start of the protectorate was an extensive system of cereal cultivation and animal husbandry. Most land was collectively owned by tribes. The land often had an underutilized appearance due to fallowing and low population pressure.

Colonization dislodged Moroccans from much of the best land (see Illus. 11). In addition, the establishment of the protectorate enabled Moroccans allied with the French to amass large private holdings.[25] The Moroccan peasantry was crowded onto poorer lands, often land used only for pasture in former years. The wheat policy's higher prices for cereal crops also encouraged expansion onto marginal lands. Poorer lands gave lower yields.

Simultaneously, health measures introduced by the French caused population to mushroom. Indeed, during the protectorate period, the Moroccan population tripled. Rapid population growth (estimated at 3.25 percent by the 1960 census) and capture of over 30 percent of the agricultural base by settlers and Moroccan large landowners resulted in a "convergence process."[26] Peasants progressively decreased their percentage of fallow land and extended cultivation onto poorer soils and unfavorable slopes. Holdings became smaller and smaller. In brief, less and less land per peasant, and progressively poorer land, was fallowed less and less often.

Compounding the problem, landholdings were traditionally dispersed in Morocco to provide for equity, where communal traditions were observed, and as a strategy to counter the vagaries of rainfall and reduce the risk of crop failure.[27] With population pressure, this system became largely dysfunctional: Dispersed plots tended to become too small through division at inheritance to remain viable. Fragmentation of holdings, the gradual disappearance of fallow, soil exhaustion, and declining yields were all elements of a resulting vicious circle in the traditional agrarian sector.

One of the surest signs of distress was the rural exodus. It usually indicated either that a peasant's holding had fallen beneath a critical

[25] Private ownership of land greatly increased in Morocco after the arrival of the French. Greater security and the Torrens registration system adopted by the French were major factors. (This system had been pioneered by the British in Australia.)

[26] H. van der Kloet, *Inégalités dans les milieux ruraux: possibilités et problèmes de la modernisation agricole au Maroc* (Geneva, 1975), esp. pp. 24–60.

[27] These plots were normally 1 to 2 hectares in size. They had the shape of long strips and were called *flij* after the strips sewn together to make a tent. See Zartman, "Farming and Land Ownership," p. 192. Pascon estimates that the average dryland holding today is composed of seven different plots. See P. Pascon, "Agriculture, faillité et perspectives," *Lamalif* 145 (1983): 19.

size for viability or that he had become completely landless. Morocco's rural exodus began around 1920. It was estimated by authorities in the latter part of the protectorate period to amount to some 30,000–50,000 annually. Drought years transformed the exodus into a human flood. The percentage of rural population decreased from approximately 90 percent in 1921 to 70 percent in 1960, largely as a result of outward migration from the countryside.[28]

Morocco's rural exodus was initially viewed by protectorate authorities as simply a threat to the public order. Only gradually did it come to be seen as symptomatic of an alarming deterioration of traditional dryland agriculture. As Miège noted in 1950 regarding Morocco's wheat production, "Yesterday's problem of finding markets has become, today, a problem of subsistence."[29] Since 1938, Morocco's per capita cereal production had been steadily dropping (Fig. 10). By 1960, annual per capita cereal production for the first time fell below 300 kilograms—a figure regarded as the critical minimum for normal nutrition.[30] Ironically, not long after the protectorate ended, the former "granary of Rome" had become a net importer of cereals.

A rescue effort was soon under way, however. In 1957, the newly independent Moroccan government enthusiastically launched Operation Plow.

Operation Plow

Operation Plow (Opération Labour) stands out today as the single committed effort by the independent Moroccan government to raise dryland agricultural productivity. In several ways, it was strongly influenced by the SMP program. This is perhaps not surprising: Julien Couleau, one of the architects of the SMP program, helped the Moroccan Minister of Agriculture to design Operation Plow.[31]

Like the earlier SMP program, Operation Plow was supposed to administer shock therapy to traditional agrarian Morocco through massive introduction of the tractor. Its goals were virtually identical to the SMP program's:

1. To lead to a rapid increase in cereal production by overcoming the peasant's need to wait for autumn rains before planting

[28] D. Noin, *La Population rurale du Maroc*, vol. 1 (Paris, 1970).
[29] J. Miège, *Le Maroc* (Paris, 1950), p. 87.
[30] Jouve, "Démographie," p. 13.
[31] Marais, "Le Maroc," p. 292.

2. To simultaneously introduce more advanced agricultural methods, including use of fertilizers and improved seed varieties
3. To introduce a new nucleus of organization, the cooperative (as opposed to the SMP program's jmaʿa)[32]

Operation Plow was grafted onto the network of already existing SMPs. These SMPs, rebaptized Work Centers, served as the focal points of intervention for the new program.[33]

Operation Plow was imbued with revolutionary fervor. Government tractors were to start from the Work Centers and progressively expand the area of deep mechanized plowing through all of the traditional agricultural sector. During the first five-year phase, the plowed area was to grow from an initial 150,000 hectares to 1 million hectares.[34] The Ministry of Agriculture provided nearly a thousand tractors for this herculean task.

The basic plan was as follows: Large blocks of land composed of myriad small holdings were to be plowed and disk-harrowed as if a single holding.[35] This was intended to reduce costs, facilitate introduction of improved techniques, and maximize the psychological impact. After government machinery had plowed and harrowed the land, the fellah was to perform the remaining tasks of sowing, scratch-plowing under the seed, fertilizing, and harvesting on his own holding. However, these operations were to be performed under the guidance of Work Center personnel. Each block was to be divided in half, with each half subject to compulsory crop rotation. In a given year, one half was to be planted in winter wheat or barley, the other half in a summer crop (maize, beans, or peas) or else fallowed if soils were poor. In the first year, the government's tractor labor was to be provided at minimal cost, and fertilizer was to be distributed free of charge. However, beginning the second year, more realistic charges were to be levied. Operation Plow was to become entirely self-financing by the end of the third year; peasants would pay for the program's true costs through the annual *tartīb* or agricultural tax.[36]

[32] Kloet, *Inégalités*, p. 117.

[33] Morocco's Centres de Travaux (SMPs) increased in number from 57 at independence to 110 by 1961. Fifty-four, located primarily in the Gharb, Chaouia, and Doukkala wheat-producing areas, participated in Operation Plow. See H. J. van Wersch, "Rural Development in Morocco: *Opération Labour*," *Economic Development and Cultural Change* 17 (1968): 37, 40–41.

[34] *LQA*, p. 16.

[35] In practice, these blocks would vary greatly in size, from 150 to 200 hectares in hilly areas or where there was extreme fragmentation of land, up to 12,000 hectares on collective land in the plains. See van Wersch, "Rural Development," p. 40.

[36] Ibid., pp. 38–40.

In autumn 1957, Operation Plow was inaugurated amidst widespread national optimism. King Mohammed V drove a tractor over field boundaries in an opening ceremony to symbolize the revolutionary, communal nature of the undertaking. The area covered by the operation rapidly expanded from an initial 100,000–150,000 hectares in the first season to 300,000 in the second, mostly in the Gharb, Chaouia, and Doukkala plains. Then, disappointingly, the program declined to 100,000 hectares by 1961–62. After 1963, no further government data on the program were released. Operation Plow quietly died.[37]

What killed Operation Plow? Analysts advance numerous reasons for the program's demise.[38] All these reasons, however, merge into a primary cause: The program became highly unpopular with Morocco's peasants.

Coercion was applied by local authorities to overcome peasant reluctance to enter the program; this caused deep resentment. The program's disregard for traditional field boundaries was also mistrusted and resented. In addition, Operation Plow's design was seriously flawed: Peasants required to leave their land in fallow received no income from their land that year. If a summer crop was assigned, livestock were deprived of traditional summer pasturage.

For many reasons the program did not achieve the desired improvements in agricultural yields. For example, because peasants were not sufficiently educated about the program, the government's fertilizer often was not used. It remained stacked at the edge of the fields, got sold to neighboring settlers, or was even scattered to the wind. Furthermore, the fertilizer provided was high in phosphate; soil conditions called for applications of nitrogen. The plowing depth was also inappropriate in many areas. Finally, select seeds were diverted by certain local authorities to the black market.[39]

Compounding these problems, the weather seemed to conspire to sabotage Operation Plow. Flood damage in the Gharb and frost damage in the Chaouia helped to lower yields significantly during the second season. The net result was that total yields were scarcely higher than they had been prior to the program.[40] This confirmed peasant misgivings and began to cause a mass exodus from Operation Plow.

[37] Kloet, *Inégalités*, p. 119; A. Gayoso, "Agricultural Development Strategies in Morocco, 1957–1970," unpublished USAID report (1970), Rabat, pp. 10–11.

[38] For example, van Wersch, "Rural Development," pp. 39, 43–45; Kloet, *Inégalités*, pp. 118–121.

[39] Ibid.

[40] Van Wersch, "Rural Development," pp. 42–43.

Finally, peasants, many chronically indebted to wealthy landowners or urban merchants, had great difficulty paying for the new services and materials. With all the other problems, therefore, the government's attempt to impose "true charges" for Operation Plow at the end of the second year functioned as the coup de grâce to the program. This authoritarian attempt to rescue traditional dryland agriculture rapidly collapsed. When the collapse occurred, Morocco's government quickly reoriented agricultural policy towards irrigation.

The Office National des Irrigations

While Operation Plow occupied the center stage of agricultural development, pressure for a national irrigation program was quietly building. A 1959 editorial in *Al Istiqlal*, the newspaper of the main political party, was representative. Entitled "The Irrigation Perimeters: An Insufficiently Exploited Heritage," the editorial claimed that the lands within the irrigation perimeters could greatly improve Morocco's agricultural production.[41] Not only were these lands capable of becoming much more productive than the nonirrigable lands, but their production could be diversified. Sugar, which annually required expensive imports, could be produced, as could textile fibers to supply industry, or export crops to garner foreign currency. The problem, the editorial claimed, was that irrigation development was stalled because it was the responsibility of several competing agencies. Billions already invested in dams were being wasted:

> In a country such as ours, where the low standard of living and demographic pressure demand that agricultural yields be elevated, production diversified, and employment provided for peasants, it is tragic to see such a state of affairs persist; it is unpardonable that such important investments lie unproductive; it is criminal to let such a rich legacy remain untapped.[42]

The solution, the editorial concluded, was the creation of a national irrigation office.

Both in the movement for a national irrigation office, then for the new office itself, the old colonial Office de l'Irrigation aux Beni Amir served as the primary model—though this role generally was not acknowledged. In fact, the new Office National des Irrigations repre-

[41] "Un Patrimoine insuffisamment exploité: les périmètres irrigués," *Al Istiqlal*, 28 March 1959, p. 11.
[42] Ibid.

sented little more than the old Office de l'Irrigation transposed to the national level.[43]

What had been particularly controversial about the old Office during the protectorate period became part of its attraction after independence, particularly after Operation Plow's failure. As Marais noted in 1969, "Still today . . . certain young Moroccan bureaucrats regard Tallec, at least privately, with a certain fascination."[44] Tallec's rural development approach of total control over man and milieu within a tightly confined sector was seen as much better adjusted to Moroccan realities than idealistic schemes like the SMP program or Operation Plow, which attempted to modernize all of rural Morocco. "These same leaders," Marais added, "have little faith in the possibility of modernizing peasant mentality."[45]

Called ONI, the new Office National des Irrigations was established within the framework of the 1960–64 five-year plan. It was specifically charged with completing the protectorate administration's unfinished task in the five major irrigation perimeters: the Gharb, Tadla (Beni Amir and Beni Moussa), Haouz, Abda-Doukkala, and Basse Moulouya (Triffa). At the end of fifteen years, all 246,000 hectares irrigable by existing dams were to have been brought into intensive production. ONI brought under a single roof all the various bureaus involved with Morocco's irrigation development. In addition, it took command of the thirty-one Work Centers (the former SMP headquarters) existing in the irrigation areas. These regional centers were to serve as operational nodes for the new program of irrigation development.[46] The new Office was animated by the following philosophy:

> To attain the desired objectives. . . . it is not sufficient to simply construct irrigation canals as rapidly as possible. The State must [also] create the conditions enabling development to take place, and *make this development obligatory* [italics added].[47]

The Moroccan government's decision to reemphasize irrigation was due, in part, to pressure from large landowners. To a minor degree, it was also stimulated by recommendations from an FAO advisory study

---

[43] P. Marthelot, "Histoire et réalité de la modernisation du monde rural au Maroc," *Tiers-Monde* 2 (1961): 149. Marthelot notes that, instead, reference was made to initiatives in Italy, Spain, and France.

[44] Marais, "Le Maroc," p. 282.

[45] Ibid.

[46] *BONI* 1 (1961): 6–13; Morocco, *Plan Quinquennal, 1960–1964*, pp. 126–131.

[47] *BONI* 1 (1961): 7–8.

in 1959.[48] However, in order fully to understand the ONI period, as well as all subsequent irrigation development, it is necessary to examine the evolution of the land reform question.

Operation Plow's failure was a sobering lesson for the Moroccan government. It forcefully demonstrated the stubborn and deeply rooted nature of traditional agriculture's problems. These problems could not simply be cleared away with an enthusiastic government plowing scheme; indeed, they could not be uprooted without major changes in agrarian Morocco's underlying social, political, and economic matrix. The program's failure appeared to confirm what the political left and many independent observers had maintained since independence: that agricultural development in Morocco could not take place without a comprehensive agrarian reform. Operation Plow's collapse occurred while the leftist Ibrahim-Bouabid cabinet was in power (24 December 1958–27 May 1960). The program's failure enabled this cabinet to interject a new vision for agrarian Morocco's reconstruction into the 1960–64 plan, then in preparation.

The 1960–64 plan called for heavy investment in irrigation. However, to ensure that this investment was fully productive, the plan called for a basic agrarian reform to establish "rational farming operations." The measures proposed to achieve reform were particularly revolutionary in the Moroccan context. They included the following:

1. Establishment of a maximum holding size to prevent further land accumulation by large landowners
2. Expropriation without indemnity of a portion of the larger holdings benefiting from state-supplied irrigation water
3. Expropriation (with indemnity) of insufficiently exploited land, particularly in the irrigation perimeters
4. Expropriation of all official and private colonization lands.[49]

ONI was to work out the details, then implement the proposed reform. Land would be expropriated by legislation drafted by ONI. This land would be distributed to peasants without land and to those with holdings too small to be viable. The goal was to create a new rural landscape structured by cooperatives of small peasants with modern irrigated holdings. ONI was to take all requisite steps to ensure that land became developed in a way that contributed to the national economy.

This audacious agararian reform program was far too revolutionary

[48] A. El Kabir, "Les Tentatives de modernisation de l'agriculture marocaine," unpublished *Mémoire*, Law and Economic Sciences (1971), University of Paris, p. 79.
[49] Morocco, *Plan Quinquennal, 1960–1964*, pp. 15, 87–91.

for Morocco, then or now. It drew opposition from King Mohammed V, the increasingly conservative Istiqlal Party, and the rapidly expanding class of Moroccan large landowners (many of whom were Istiqlal members), who by 1960 had already gained possession of approximately 207,000 hectares of colonization land. In other ways, the 1960–64 plan was also offensive to the prevailing powers. Consequently, the Ibrahim-Bouabid cabinet was dissolved by the king in May 1960. Mohammed V personally took control of the government, with Crown Prince Hassan as his assistant.

The fall of the Ibrahim cabinet cast a long shadow over land reform. Nonetheless, ONI supervised the distribution of 4,746 hectares in the Haouz, Tadla, and Gharb irrigation perimeters to some 536 beneficiaries in autumn 1960, shortly after its formation.[50] Then the death of Mohammed V on 26 February 1961 further destabilized Morocco and put the entire reform program in question.

Mohammed V's death was a major turning point. In general, the 1959–61 period was characterized by an incessant power struggle between the monarchy and the various political parties. The critical choice for the monarchy during this period was between (1) a comprehensive agrarian reform which would improve agricultural production and the lot of the Moroccan peasant, but which would also deeply alienate large landowners—the monarachy's principal base of support; and (2) measures to postpone or evade the necessary reforms in order to ensure the support of the elites with, in consequence, increasing disparities in landownership, growing exodus from the countryside, and resulting economic and political problems.[51] Mohammed V's heir, Hassan II, chose the second option:

> In 1961, the die was cast, and an orientation was chosen which has continued to this day. In short the monarchy opted for the maintenance of the status quo . . . the support of the urban and rural elites being attained on condition of the nonapplication of the plan in question.[52]

Following Hassan's succession to the throne on 26 February 1961, the 1960–64 plan was completely rewritten. The section on agrarian reform was ominously absent from the new version.[53]

[50] *BONI* 2 (1962): 74–75; *LQA*, p. 409. Beware of errors in tables in *BONI* 2 (1962), p. 76.

[51] R. Leveau, *Le Fellah marocain: défenseur du trône* (Paris, 1985), p. 61; Marais, "Le Maroc," pp. 296–297; P. de Mas, *Marges marocaines* (The Hague, 1978), pp. 149–152.

[52] Mas, *Marges marocaines*, p. 152.

[53] The original version of the 1960–64 plan has a blue cover and a publication date of November 1960. In Leveau's estimation, the passages on agrarian reform had already

"Agrarian reform," however, would remain a useful political device for Hassan II (Illus. 16). It would constitute an ever-ready threat to ensure the allegiance of the land-owning elite. It would serve as a handy bargaining chip in discussions with France over the colonization lands. And it would function as a promise to the political left and the rural poor. Thus, in November 1961, in the same month that the rewritten 1960–64 plan appeared, a government commission was established to prepare a "legislative dossier" for land reform. The commission consisted of ONI leaders as well as representatives from most government ministries. The dossier in question would not be completed until 1963. Until then, land reform was completely tabled.

Meanwhile, other events sapped ONI of its effectiveness. The 1960–64 plan was abandoned altogether at the end of 1962 as a result of economic difficulties and political distractions.[54] This sharply curtailed ONI's financial resources, impeding irrigation development.

This same year, ONI became embroiled in political conflict. The context was its effort to introduce sugar beets into the Gharb. Because sugar beets were totally new, a massive campaign was launched to persuade Moroccan peasants to grow this crop. A team of ONI agents, directed by rural sociologists, wandered the countryside, organizing village meetings and giving demonstrations. This activity greatly disquieted both landowning elites and the Ministry of the Interior. ONI agents were accused of promising land reform, fomenting peasant unrest, and stirring up opposition to King Hassan's new constitution, to be the subject of a referendum on 7 December 1962. In consequence, ONI's activist director, Mohamed Tahiri, was fired in January 1963.[55] From this point on, ONI became simply another failed development program.

The legislative dossier for Morocco's land reform officially appeared on 19 February 1963. It amounted to a slightly diluted and redirected version of the 1960–64 plan's land reform package. Specific proposals

---

been "sweetened" by the government—now directly controlled by the king—before the plan's appearance. See Leveau, *Le Fellah*, p. 61. The revised version of the plan has (appropriately) a black cover and a publication date of November 1961. Mas incorrectly gives the revised "black" version a publication date of November 1960 (P. de Mas, "The Place of Peripheral Regions in Moroccan Planning," *Tijdschrift voor Economische en Sociale Geografie* 69 [1978]: 89).

[54] M. Louafa, "La Politique hydraulique et le développement économique au Maroc," unpublished *Mémoire*, Law and Economic and Social Sciences (1974), University of Paris, pp. 25–26; C. F. Gallagher, "The Moroccan Economy in Perspective," *American Universities Field Staff Reports, North African Series* 12 (1966): 6; Mas, 'Peripheral Regions," p. 89.

[55] Leveau, *Le Fellah*, p. 63; Marais, "Le Maroc," pp. 289–290.

included the following: expropriation without indemnity of a certain portion of large landholdings benefiting from government-supplied irrigation water; establishment of a ceiling on holding sizes (50 hectares of irrigated land and 100–300 hectares of dry land, depending on soil quality); the permanent distribution of all collective lands; and strict controls on sales of colonization land.[56] The first three proposals were too extreme to be acceptable. However, the last proposal was adopted seven months later, in September 1963.

On 26 September 1963, the government issued a decree that subjected all sales of private colonization land to prior approval of the royal cabinet. This decree was part of the first major action to recover foreign-owned land. The same day, the government issued a more important decree that provided for the nationalization of all official colonization lands, a total now of roughly 256,000 hectares.[57]

The new legislation was embraced with enthusiasm by ONI's staff; approximately 81,500 hectares of official colonization land were located in ONI's irrigation perimeters.[58] Imani, ONI's new director, noted that ONI could distribute this land to some 20,000 landless peasants—distributions that would serve as "the leaven" for an overall land reform.[59] In 1964, his office distributed 2,560 hectares in the Tadla.[60] However, this was the last land distributed by ONI. On 7 May 1965, ONI was absorbed into a new Office de Mise en Valeur Agricole (OMVA) which was charged with development of all of agricultural Morocco, not just the irrigated areas. Then, on 22 October 1966, the new office was dissolved, for reasons that will soon be examined.[61]

ONI had been created to put a quarter-million irrigable hectares into production and, simultaneously, to supervise a sweeping agrarian reform program. In both areas it failed. It put only some 43,000 hectares into perennial irrigation and distributed only 7,306 hectares to only 891 of Morocco's half-million landless peasants.[62]

---

[56] BONI 5 (1963): 6–7. The 50-hectare limit in irrigated areas was apparently inspired by similar measures in Spain and Italy.

[57] Official colonization land was recovered as follows: 48,783 hectares in 1963, 66,511 hectares in 1964, 109,340 hectares in 1965, and 31,628 hectares in 1966 (LQA, p. 408. Beware of addition errors for 1965 recuperations and total recuperations in table on p. 408).

[58] Colonization land in the ONI irrigation perimeters was located as follows: Gharb, 40,000 hectares; Haouz, 25,000 hectares; Abda-Doukkala, 12,500 hectares; Tadla, 4,000 hectares. See BONI 7 (1964): 280.

[59] Ibid., p. 282.

[60] LQA, p. 409. This land went to 355 beneficiaries.

[61] Ibid., pp. 23–28.

[62] See M. Ben-Elkadi, "L'Evolution de l'exploitation des ressources hydrauliques au

Nonetheless, ONI's contribution to Moroccan irrigation development was significant. First, there was the legacy of its extensive research: "Its technical and socioeconomic dossiers constitute the inexhaustible fount . . . from which the government continues to draw its inspiration."[63] Second, ONI was responsible for the introduction of sugar beets, a crop that today plays a vital role in the national economy. Probably ONI's most important legacy, however, was its formula for irrigation development. The principal components of this formula were not original; they had been pioneered earlier by the Office de l'Irrigation in the Tadla. Nonetheless, ONI's formula represented a refinement of earlier techniques. It has been used by the Moroccan government ever since.

The key features of ONI's formula were: (1) a new method for organizing the irrigated landscape, and (2) a policy of contracts. ONI organized peasants into service cooperatives and restructured their holdings according to a system of remembrement termed Trame B. This new system represented a response to technical problems encountered with the earlier Trame A system.[64] In Trame B, the long strips of crops run parallel to the secondary canals (or main canals, where irrigation water is pumped directly from rivers) instead of perpendicular to them (Fig. 9). Because of this arrangement, irrigation is able to be more easily supervised by the government, and the water dosage can be better adjusted to the requirements of each crop.[65] The Trame B system became widely used after 1964. Other features of the Beni Amir office's authoritarian formula for irrigation development (assigned plantings and a mandatory crop rotation cycle) remained intact under ONI.

ONI additionally initiated a policy of contracts which, like the Trame B system, has since become general. This, too, was not original. Contracts had been imposed by Tallec in his experiments with "native irrigation" in the Tadla, and had also been used to encourage oilseed production during World War II. However, agricultural contracts be-

Maroc," unpublished *Mémoire*, 3d cycle (1976), Institut Agronomique Hassan II, p. 36, for perennial irrigation figure. Land distribution and beneficiary figures represent the cumulative total of figures given earlier in the text.

[63] A. Benhadi, "La Politique marocaine des barrages," *Annuaire de l'Afrique du Nord, 1975* 14 (1976): 279. "A. Benhadi" is the pseudonym of a prominent Moroccan social scientist.

[64] See the lengthy technical comparison of the two systems by F. Sauze in *BONI* 3 (1962): 15–34.

[65] Ibid.; also SAHM, pp. 38, 66.

came widespread in Morocco only when ONI launched its campaign to introduce sugar beets into the Gharb.

In sum, ONI had been called upon to execute a vast environmental vision. It was supposed to complete development of the colonial irrigation perimeters along the lines traced by the old Office de l'Irrigation. The new irrigated areas were to reflect social justice and economic development. The end result was to be a rational, geometric landscape, structured by modern irrigation networks, with cooperatives of small peasants operating as partners with the state, producing valuable crops for the national economy upon viable new holdings. ONI was dismantled before it could effectively undertake its given task. It was dissolved in 1965. However, its development formula, comprising cooperatives, Trame B, and contracts, has continued to the present. This formula has been usefully employed as a political tool, as will be seen.

La Politique des Barrages: Towards a Million Hectares

By 1963, Morocco's government was so alarmed at the country's drift into economic disarray that it invited the World Bank to help it find a path to "sustained development."[66] A World Bank economic survey mission spent three months in Morocco during spring 1964. The mission had an immediate impact: Morocco's new three-year plan for 1965–67 closely reflected its recommendations. The mission's long-term impact on Moroccan agricultural policy, however, has been even more significant. The mission's recommendations justified a course that the Moroccan government was already in the process of taking.

In a number of ways, the mission's suggestions became directly translated into actions. It initially criticized the lack of coordination resulting from two autonomous agencies for agricultural development: ONI for the irrigated areas and ONMR for the dry lands. This criticism led to a merging of the two agencies on 7 May 1965. The previously mentioned Office de Mise en Valeur Agricole (OMVA) resulted. However, in its 1966 official report, the mission subsequently criticized the new tendency towards "undue" centralization: "Agricultural development takes place on the land and not in Rabat."[67] It recommended regional administration at the level of irrigation perimeter or province.

66 Gallagher, "Moroccan Economy," p. 6.
67 World Bank, *The Economic Development of Morocco* (Baltimore, 1966), p. 111.

From this recommendation came the dissolution of OMVA and creation of seven regional development offices on 22 October 1966.

Each of the five existing modern irrigation regions—the Gharb, Haouz, Tadla, Moulouya, and Doukkala—became endowed with a new Office Régional de Mise en Valeur Agricole (ORMVA). In addition, on the same date, regional development offices were created in the Ziz and Draa river valleys—termed the Tafilalet and Ouarzazate offices, respectively. (Two additional ORMVAs were later established: the Souss-Massa in 1970 and the Loukkos in 1975.) Each ORMVA was basically identical to the old colonial Office de l'Irrigation in the Tadla, suggesting that it was a conscious model. Nominally, the ORMVAs were under the control of the Direction de Mise en Valeur of the Ministry of Agriculture, but financially and administratively they were virtually autonomous.

The mission also emphasized that Morocco's primary task was to increase agricultural production quickly, efficiently, and with Morocco's limited financial resources. It believed that this increase should primarily come from the modern sector because raising the productivity of over a million traditional farmers could be accomplished only with great difficulty and over a long time span. Morocco, in short, should attempt to maximize growth in the areas of greatest opportunity. It recommended that government investment be concentrated in favored geographic zones and on "the more advanced segments of the agricultural community."[68] The mission also strongly recommended completion of existing irrigation projects. Faithful to these recommendations, the Moroccan government has subsequently heavily concentrated its investments in the modern agricultural sector and on the development of irrigation.

With regard to a comprehensive land reform, the World Bank mission pointed to the impossibility of conducting the necessary surveys and studies within a reasonable period of time. It recommended that the government—for the time being—limit land reform to those "areas where it is of importance either for raising production or for soil conservation."[69] For the irrigation perimeters, specifically, it presented a detailed blueprint for limited land reform. Where collective, ḥabūs (religious foundation), or state land existed in the irrigation perimeters, the mission recommended that this land be redistributed on a rent/purchase basis. Distributed holdings should be of a relatively small size, but "sufficient to produce a gross income large enough to cover

[68] Ibid., p. 103.
[69] Ibid., p. 107.

the repayment over time of the capital and current costs . . . together with a surplus to provide a net personal income somewhat above the levels presently pertaining among small farmers."[70] Where holdings were fragmented, they should be consolidated. Where they were of a less-than-viable size, they should be augmented. All these recommendations were adopted. They would inspire both the agrarian reform law of 4 July 1966 and the 1969 Code des Investissements Agricoles. Indeed, the World Bank mission's mid-1960s recommendations have essentially defined Morocco's land reform policy to the present.

The World Bank mission strongly advised Morocco to ensure that the full benefits of government investment in irrigation became realized. The government was to create legislation requiring that, both on the redistributed land and on private land benefiting from state investments in irrigation, development took place within a reasonable period of time. Specifications of required farming methods were to be established for each perimeter, and they were to be firmly backed by sanctions.[71] All these recommendations, too, were adopted. They became an integral part of the 1969 Code des Investissements Agricoles.

However, not all the World Bank mission's recommendations were slavishly adopted. The Moroccan government, it is clear, was selective. For example, the mission suggested in its official report that measures be taken to recoup excessive windfall gains from the enhanced capital value of large landholdings resulting from government investment in irrigation.[72] (Virtually identical recommendations had already been made by the 1960–64 plan and the ONI legislative commission, as documented earlier.) The World Bank mission's recommendation in this regard fell on deaf ears. The mission also criticized the Moroccan government for initiating new irrigation projects before "the full exploitation" of irrigation infrastructure already in place.[73] Its advice in this regard would soon be flagrantly disregarded.

Nonetheless, the Moroccan government obviously accepted enough of the mission's recommendations. In 1964, the World Bank began to provide substantial loans to Morocco. By 1985, cumulative World Bank loans for Moroccan development exceeded $2.7 billion, the bulk associated with irrigation projects.[74]

---

[70] Ibid., p. 109.
[71] Ibid.
[72] Ibid.
[73] Ibid., p. 119.
[74] *The World Bank Annual Report, 1985* (Washington, D.C., 1985), p. 167. USAID, the Soviet Union, Saudi Arabia, Kuwait, the UAE, Iran, the United Nations Development Program, and West Germany have also been major financers of Morocco's irriga-

Morocco's all-out new emphasis on irrigation development would become clear only near the end of the 1965–67 period; a mere 8,350 hectares were put into irrigation during these three years. Development of tourism temporarily preoccupied the government. However, the 1965–67 plan signaled the government's new resolve to ignore the traditional agrarian sector (an "ensemble which resists the slightest innovation")[75] and determination to concentrate its investments "in the most profitable sectors."[76] This determination fully materialized when the *politique des barrages* emerged near the end of the 1965–67 period. Since then, large-scale irrigation development has constituted the central thrust of Moroccan development efforts.

The 1968–72 plan revealed the official motives behind the government's decision to embark upon its *politique des barrages*, a major dam-building campaign. The plan's wording closely followed the thinking of the World Bank mission. The plan acknowledged that, in the past, increased agricultural output in Morocco had primarily been achieved through extension of cultivation. However, the limits of the sown area had been reached. Since independence, agricultural production had grown at the feeble rate of 1.5 percent per year—half the annual rate of population growth. The consequences for Morocco's trade balance were disastrous. Accelerating Morocco's agricultural development was the "number one imperative."[77]

In this vital endeavor, the traditional sector could unfortunately contribute very little: The cultivated area could not be extended further; existing structures of land tenure constituted a major impediment; and changing the mentality of peasants was an inevitably slow procedure.

On the other hand, only a minor fraction of Morocco's annual endowment of 110 billion cubic meters of water had been harnessed for irrigation. Morocco had at its disposal one million hectares of irrigable land. To irrigate a million hectares was fully equivalent to clearing 5 million new hectares for dry farming, because yields were higher and of greater value. For all these reasons, the Moroccan government had decided to launch a vast irrigation program.[78]

Irrigating a million hectares was to be accomplished via an accelerated program of dam construction. The completed harnessing of Mo-

---

tion development. As of 31 December 1983, Morocco's total outstanding external public debt amounted to slightly over $13 billion, a figure roughly equal to its GDP. See ibid., p. 180.

[75] Morocco, *Three-Year Plan, 1965–1967* (1965), p. 82.

[76] Ibid., p. 87.

[77] Morocco, *Plan Quinquennal, 1968–1972* (1968), p. 102.

[78] Ibid., numerous pages.

rocco's surface waters through dams would permit over 850,000 hectares in the major irrigation perimeters to be put into perennial irrigation. With small modern irrigation systems and traditional irrigated areas added to the *grande hydraulique* figure, the million-hectare objective would be more than exceeded.

In short, the Moroccan government had resurrected the colonial vision of a million irrigated hectares by the year 2000 and elevated it into a national imperative. The new development policy was referred to either as "la politique des barrages" or "la politique du million d'hectares," depending on whether the focus was on spectacular means or ambitious end.

Steps towards this new policy, it should be noted, had been initiated several years before. By 1961, the Moroccan government was already hoping to undertake the comprehensive development of the Sebou basin.[79] Massive flooding in the Gharb in 1963 prompted the government to request immediate assistance from the United Nations. An exhaustive study of the basin resulted. An international team of fifty-five engineers, economists, and sociologists, augmented by a myriad of consultants, examined every aspect relevant to the basin's development. Their multivolume report, completed in 1968, constituted a long-term master plan. It called for seven to twelve major dams for flood control and the irrigation of 250,000–300,000 hectares in the Gharb.[80] The Sebou Project subsequently became an integral part of the *politique des barrages*.

In addition, when flash flooding in the Ziz valley devastated the lower riverine oases in November 1965, the king decided upon construction of a dam for flood control and the social development of the valley. He made an emotional radio broadcast appeal on 11 November 1965. Moroccans could choose to have the government-set price of sugar lowered by 0.35 dirhams per kilogram. Or they could elect to maintain the current price and thereby finance a dam on the Ziz to aid their southern brothers. The response was overwhelmingly in favor of the latter.[81] This popular response undoubtedly encouraged adoption of Morocco's dam-building strategy.

La politique des barrages was launched in 1968. By the early 1970s, the policy had attained almost mythic proportions. The king personally officiated over ground-breaking or inauguration ceremonies. Media coverage emphasized:

[79] P. de Mas, "Opinion à propos du Projet Sebou au Maroc," *LMA* 122 (1980): 21.
[80] S. Grigory, "A propos du Projet Sebou au Maroc," *Maghreb-Machrek* 85 (1979): 61.
[81] *LQA*, p. 25.

the vastness of the works erected, volumes of water retained, spaces dominated, and resources mobilized; the profound transformation of the landscape: the rigorous geometry of the hydraulic network, of the parcels consolidated, of the crop assignments imposed ... the magic of certain golden figures ... : a quintupling of production, 100 billion cubic meters, one million hectares by the year 2000.[82]

In all, the *politique des barrages* was extolled as the path to Morocco's "green revolution." Its physical achievements alone were impressive, as Table 9 demonstrates. (See also Fig. 8.)

Only fourteen dams had been constructed during the 1912–56 protectorate period. In the interim period, 1957–67, only three dams were completed. However, after the emergence of the *politique des barrages*, a continuous succession of new dams began to appear on the Moroccan landscape. Since then, nearly twenty new dams have been constructed. At least six other dam projects are in progress. However, dams already constructed are more than sufficient, with the addition of existing small and medium-scale irrigation systems, to fulfill the old vision of a million irrigated hectares.

On 8 January 1969, King Hassan II officially declared "one million irrigated hectares" to be a national objective.[83] The occasion was his commencement address for a government conference convened from 8 to 27 January to prepare a new "agricultural development code." This Code des Investissements Agricoles was completed on 25 July 1969. It was both an explicit statement of Morocco's new strategy and a voluminous body of legislation giving this strategy the force of law. It has defined Morocco's agricultural development policy ever since.

The official objectives of the Code are the following:

1. The concentration of government agricultural investment in a few well-defined and favored geographical areas: the irrigation perimeters.
2. Within these limited perimeters, land reform on the following basis:
   (a) The division of collective lands among their rightful owners
   (b) The distribution of state land to landless peasants or owners of less-than-viable holdings
   (c) Remembrement, to facilitate irrigation development and create rational units of production

---

[82] Benhadi, "La Politique marocaine," p. 275.
[83] *LQA*, p. 31.

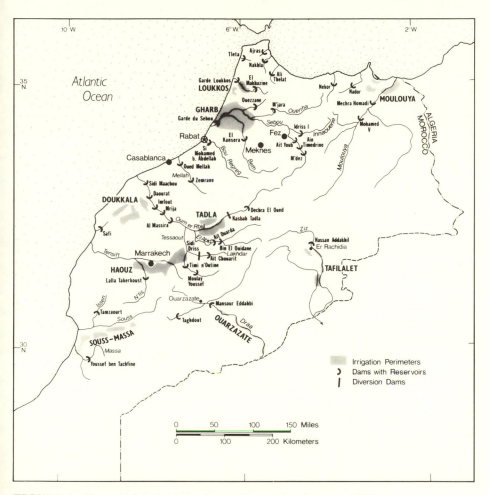

FIGURE 8 Dams and major irrigation perimeters in Morocco, 1986
SOURCE: Morocco, Travaux Publics, unpublished documents.

     (d) The establishment of 5 hectares as a minimum holding size.
Land in the irrigation perimeters should be divided in such a
way as to create no holding smaller than 5 hectares. The owner
of a holding less than 10 hectares in size is required to select a
single heir so as not to create, through division, a holding
smaller than 5 hectares.

  3. Total government intervention. Government intervention not only
includes "external operations" necessary to deliver water to the
farmer's land, but "internal operations" as well. The ORMVAS, or

TABLE 9 Register of Morocco's Dams and Dam Projects, 1986

No.	Name	Year completed	Watercourse	Height (meters)	Reservoir capacity (1,000 m³)	Purpose	Irrigable area (hectares)
1	Sidi Maachou	1929	Oum er Rbia	23	1,520	E, D	—
2	Kashah Tadla	1930	Oum er Rbia	5	—	I, E	23,000
3	Oued Mellah	1931	Mellah	33	18,000	I, D	800
4	Ali Thelat	1934	Laou	36	25,000	I, E	1,400
5	El Kansera	1935	Beth	68	290,000	I, D, E	28,000
6	Lalla Takerkoust	1935	N'fis	62	31,000	I, D, E	4,000
7	Ouezzane	1937	Bou Droua	16	400	D	—
8	Imfout	1944	Oum er Rbia	50	25,000	I, E	40,000
9	Zemrane	1950	Mellah	20	600	N, D	—
10	Daourat	1950	Oum er Rbia	40	24,000	E	—
11	Bin el Ouidane	1953	El Abid	133	1,484,000	I, E	63,000
12	Air Ouarda	1954	El Abid	43	4,040	E	—
13	Mechra Homadi	1956	Moulouya	57	14,000	I, N, D, E	61,000
14	Taghdout	1956	Taghdout	28	3,000	I	250
15	Nakhla	1961	Nakhla	46	7,800	D	—
16	Safi	1965	Sahim	18	2,120	D, N	—
17	Mohammed V	1967	Moulouya	64	730,000	I, F, E	61,000
18	Ajras	1969	Ajras	25	18,000	I	700
19	Moulay Youssef	1970	Tessaout	100	199,400	I, E	30,000
20	Hassan Addakhil	1971	Ziz	85	355,400	I, F	21,300
21	Mansour Eddahbi	1972	Draa	70	560,000	I, F, E	19,000
22	Youssef ben Tachfine	1973	Massa	85	310,000	I, F	20,300
23	Idriss I	1973	Innaouene	68	1,250,000	F, I, E	75,000
24	Si Mohamed b. Abdellah	1974	Bou Regreg	100	493,000	D	—

25	El Makhaźine	1978	Loukkos	66	710,000	I, F, D, E, N	25,000
26	Timi N'Outine	1978	Tessaout	34	5,000	F, I	—
27	Tleta	1978	Mharhar	31	42,200	D, I, E	2,000
28	Garde Loukkos	1978	Loukkos	8	3,500	E, I	—
29	Nekor	1978	Nekor	40	43,000	I, D	5,000
30	Nador	1978	Mrader	20	2,200	I, D, N	—
31	Al Massira	1979	Oum er Rbia	82	2,800,000	I, D, N, E	102,000
32	Tamzaourt	1979	Issen	97	218,000	I, D	9,000
33	Sidi Driss	1980	Lakhdar	45	7,000	I, D	—
34	M'Dez	—	M'Dez	90	550,000	I, E, N, F	120,000
35	Garde du Sebou	—	Sebou	15	5,000	I, N	—
36	Ait Youb	—	Innaouene	—	—	—	—
37	Ain Timedrine	—	Sebou	40	4,000	E	—
38	Dechra el Oued	—	Oum er Rbia	103	740,000	I, N, E, D	35,000
39	Ait Chouarit	—	Lakhdar	—	200,000	E, I	35,000
40	Mrija	—	Oum er Rbia	40	130,000	E	—
41	M'Jara	—	Ouerrha	80	3,100,000	I, F, E	100,000
							881,750

SOURCE: Morocco, Travaux Publics, unpublished documents.

KEY: I = irrigation, E = electricity, D = drinking water, F = flood control, N = industrial.

NOTE: Dam functions in the "Purpose" column are listed in order of importance. Irrigation accounts for approximately 88% of water use in Morocco, compared with 8% for domestic purposes and 4% for industry.

regional development offices, are charged with clearing, leveling, canal construction, and other essential operations on each private holding in their respective perimeters.

4. The establishment of measures making development mandatory and ensuring the state an adequate return on its investment. Each irrigation perimeter is divided into "development zones," and each zone is subdivided into "hydraulic sectors" of 20–40 hectares having similar agronomic characteristics and constituting units of production. For each sector, the regional development office establishes the crops to be grown, the rotation cycle to be followed, the required agricultural techniques, and the specifics of water use. Landowners are charged with repaying the state in the following manner:

   (a) All landowners with more than 5 hectares owe a flat fee of 1,500 dirhams per hectare to be paid over seventeen years with a 4 percent rate of interest. (Owners of less than 20 hectares can deduct the first 5 hectares from this obligation)

   (b) An annual water tax is progressively introduced so that 100 percent of the tax is due only after five years for ground crops and ten years for tree crops. The minimum water tax is equal to that for 3,000 cubic meters per hectare—to encourage sufficient use of water.

   In theory, the state is to be reimbursed 40 percent of its investment.[84]

5. Measures providing for expropriation of existing water rights in the irrigation perimeters. Expropriated water rights are indemnified.[85]

The Moroccan government regards the Code des Investissements Agricoles as a contract between the state and the farmer to build the national economy through irrigation development. It pays for the dams, the irrigation network, and necessary on-farm development. It provides credit, select seeds, fertilizer, farm equipment, and certain mechanized operations, usually at subsidized prices. Finally, it guarantees the prices of crops such as sugar beets, sugar cane, rice, and cotton through contracts. In turn, the farmer is obligated to farm his

[84] The other 60 percent of the government's development expenses are considered a subsidy. In practice, the contributions from those benefiting from development do not even come close to 40 percent. Furthermore, farmers in the Tafilalet, Ouarzazate, and Souss-Massa perimeters are exempted from the land improvement tax and water charges.

[85] For a more detailed account of the Code, see H. Delannoy, "Le 'Code des Investissements Agricoles,'" *RGM* 16 (1969): 151–157.

TABLE 10   Planned Agricultural Production in
the Perennially Irrigated Areas, A.D. 2000

Production category	Hectares
Citrus	75,000
Market vegetables	200,000
Forage crops	200,000
Sugar cane	135,000
Sugar beets	70,000
Cotton	50,000
Cereals	180,000
Olives	275,000
Rice	35,000
Miscellaneous	40,000
TOTAL	1,260,000

SOURCE: SAHM, p. 21.

NOTE: In 1985, cereals accounted for 38% of Morocco's
modern irrigated area, industrial crops (sugar beets,
sugar cane, and cotton) for 18%, fruit trees for 16%,
forage crops for 14%, market vegetables for 9%, and
other crops for 5% (U.S. Agency for International
Development, "Morocco, Country Development
Strategy Statement" [Washington, D.C., 1986], p.
26). Figures for area in Table 10 take into account
both simultaneous and summer cropping.

irrigated land in the national interest, to follow the norms imposed for
his hydraulic sector, and to repay the state through a land improvement tax and water charges.

Official socioeconomic goals of Morocco's irrigation development
policy have consistently been defined as the following: to assure the
nutritional needs of the country through domestic production; to
maintain and develop agricultural exports to earn foreign currency;
and to raise the rural standard of living, thereby staunching Morocco's
rural exodus and contributing to regional development.[86]

The year 2000 is the horizon date of the million-hectare policy. In
that year, Morocco's population is expected to reach 36–40 million.
To provide for this population, the government has developed a comprehensive agricultural production plan for the perennially irrigated
areas (see Table 10). Additionally, it has developed a specific plan for
most of the major food commodities resulting from irrigation devel-

[86] SAHM, p. 19; *Annuaire de l'Afrique du Nord, 1975* (Paris, 1976), p. 291.

TABLE 11   Planned Perennial Irrigation by
Region, A.D. 2000

Region	Total hectares
Gharb	245,000
Haouz-Tessaout	155,000
Tadla	115,000
Doukkala	100,000
Souss-Massa	95,000
Moulouya	70,000
Tafilalet (Ziz)	40,000
Loukkos	40,000
Ouarzazate (Draa)	30,000
Remainder of Morocco	260,000
TOTAL	1,150,000

SOURCE: SAHM, p. 21.
NOTE: Of the total 1,150,000 hectares, 880,000 hectares are scheduled to be irrigated by large-scale irrigation systems (see Table 9) and 270,000 hectares by small and medium-scale modern irrigation systems. The total does not include an additional 140,000–200,000 hectares that will continue to be irrigated seasonally by traditional systems.

opment (i.e, a Plan Sucrier, Plan Laitier, Programme Oléagineux, Programme Viande, and Plan Primeurs).

Detailed water development plans have been established for Morocco's two major watersheds: the Sebou and the Oum er Rbia. The master plan for the Sebou is essentially the technical section of the Sebou report developed by the United Nations' international team during the 1963–68 period. The master plan for the Oum er Rbia was established in 1975. These two plans together embrace Morocco's four most important irrigation regions: the Gharb, Haouz, Tadla, and Doukkala. By region, Morocco's perennial irrigation in the year 2000 is to be distributed in the manner shown in Table 11.

In short, since 1967, a major irrigation program has monopolized Morocco's agricultural development. Indeed, it has constituted the dominant thrust of national development policy. For nearly twenty years, water impounded by rapidly constructed new dams has been oriented primarily towards the goal of irrigating a million hectares. Most of the dams envisioned have already been constructed, and *mise en valeur* of Morocco's irrigable cropland has rapidly proceeded. What has been the impact of this monolithic irrigation strategy?

"To Enrich the Poor without Impoverishing the Rich": From Credo to Crisis

The physical transformation of the Moroccan countryside has been impressive. A series of new landscapes has emerged: monumental dams and reservoirs, vast verdant expanses, far-flung latticeworks of irrigation canals, giant agricultural checkerboards (Illus. 13, 14). Extensive new clearing and leveling operations, moreover, testify to the determination behind the million-hectare policy and the national resources being consecrated to its fulfillment (approximately 70 percent of government investment in agriculture during the period 1965 to 1986).

Table 12 indicates the accelerated rate of irrigation development following the launching of *la politique du million d'hectares*, as well as Morocco's overall achievement since independence.[87]

The perennially irrigated area resulting from large-scale government irrigation development grew from approximately 36,000 hectares in 1956 to over 470,000 hectares by 1986. Drought and Morocco's economic difficulties slowed the pace of irrigation development between 1981 and 1986. However, the goal of 880,000 hectares in large-scale irrigation systems by the year 2000 could certainly be achieved. At least 600,000 hectares could be irrigated with existing dams, and other dams are under construction. Also, sprinkler irrigation has been emphasized in recent years; it will expedite mise en valeur of the irrigation perimeters.[88] Some 850,000 hectares were already under perennial irrigation in Morocco in 1986, if one includes areas irrigated by modern and traditional small-scale irrigation systems.[89] In short, the colonial

[87] Sources for Table 12 include A. M. Jouve, "L'Evolution des superficies équipées et irriguées dans les grands périmètres irrigués de 1957 à 1977," *HTE* 4 (1972): 60–61; *Annuaire Statistique du Maroc, 1980* (Rabat, 1981), p. 72; U.S. Agency for International Development, "Morocco, Country Development Strategy Statement (FYs 1987–1991), Annex C, The Agricultural Sector in Morocco: A Description," unpublished report, 1986 (Washington, D.C.: USAID), p. 24; plus my projection.

[88] Sprinkler irrigation was introduced in 1975. Plans call for 300,000–350,000 hectares ultimately to be irrigated by sprinklers. Though more expensive (48,000 Dh vs. 38,500 Dh per hectare for gravity irrigation in 1978), sprinkler irrigation has the advantages of a reduced need for leveling operations, more effective and efficient use of water, ease of introduction to farmers without previous experience with irrigation, higher yields, reduced erosion, reduced risk of water-borne diseases such as bilharzia, and reduced salinization. See *Afrique Agriculture* 34 (1978): 39–40.

[89] SAHM, p. 22; U.S. Agency for International Development, "Morocco, Country Development Strategy," p. 24; plus my projection.

TABLE 12   Estimated Expansion of Large-Scale Irrigation within Morocco's Major Perimeters, 1956–1986 (hectares)

Perimeter	1956	1965	1975	1986
Gharb	10,500	28,000	54,200	87,300
Haouz-Tessaout	5,000	4,000	30,300	38,000
Tadla	20,000	62,300	97,500	109,400
Doukkala	300	11,000	28,200	63,000
Souss-Massa	—	7,000	11,700	25,700
Moulouya	—	11,500	45,500	69,000
Tafilalet	—	—	20,700	36,200
Loukkos	—	—	900	17,200
Ouarzazate	—	—	7,300	26,000
TOTAL	35,800	123,800	296,300	471,800

SOURCES: See note 87.

NOTE: In 1986, approximately 155,000 hectares within the major irrigation perimeters were also being irrigated by small-scale irrigation systems, most of which were privately owned. Outside these major perimeters, another 220,000 hectares were being irrigated by small and medium-scale irrigation systems. In all, nearly 850,000 hectares were under perennial irrigation in Morocco in 1986.

vision of a million irrigated hectares will almost certainly become a reality by century's end.

What has the million-hectare policy meant for agrarian Morocco, and what has it meant for Morocco as a whole? One fact is undeniable: Major new forms of rural organization have been created. The infrastructural base of new organization is the irrigation framework. Almost exclusively, this base is the Trame B framework developed during the 1960s by ONI technicians.[90]

Within the Trame B framework, each irrigation or "hydraulic" sector (usually 20–40 hectares in size) varies according to the crops and rotation cycle imposed by the ORMVAs. The number of years in the rotation cycle corresponds to the number of *soles*, or strips of crops, and the specific types of crops. There are several basic patterns. For example where a four-year cycle or *assolement* is imposed, there are four soles—typically of sugar beets, wheat, cotton or sugar cane, and market vegetables or a forage crop (alfalfa, berseem clover, or maize). In the five-year assolement, there are five soles—typically sugar beets,

[90] The older Trame A framework is still employed in rare circumstances, however. For rice, a special framework has been developed that is characterized by rectangular submersion basins each .25 hectares in size.

wheat, cotton or sugar cane, market vegetables, and a forage crop. Where the development plan expressly calls for sugar cane, a six-year crop, there are six soles—four or five for sugar cane and one or two for the "farmer's choice," where wheat and sugar beets are commonly grown. Various other combinations also exist.[91] Fig. 9 depicts a hypothetical but typical irrigation sector in the Gharb in which both five-year and sugar-cane assolements have been imposed. The sector depicted could belong to a land reform cooperative, a tribal collective, or private landowners.

The irrigation framework with its assolements, then, represents a device for national agricultural planning and a technical and administrative mode of organization. In significant part, however, it also manifests the government's desire to create a small client class of peasants. This policy has its origin both in agrarian reform legislation passed on 4 July 1966 and in the Code des Investissements Agricoles.

Legislation passed on 4 July 1966 provided for redistribution of the recovered official colonization lands planted in annual crops or comprising pastureland. (Citrus, other orchard crops, and vineyards were to remain for the time being as state-run farms.) Land reform appli-

---

[91] Assolements have been imposed with varying degrees of success. The Code des Investissements Agricoles allows the government to expropriate holdings distributed in the land reform program if recipients do not follow the assolement for their sector. Such expropriations were not uncommon during the early years of land reform. Since this early period, assolements have been fairly well respected by land reform recipients. Private landowners, collectives, and managers of *ḥabūs* or religious foundation holdings, on the other hand, have been much less respectful of assolements. To a significant degree, however, respect and nonrespect depend on the type of assolement and crop. For example, the sugar-cane assolement is usually closely followed because sugar cane is not only the most profitable crop in any of the assolement plans because of heavy government price supports (up to three times more profitable), but also requires much less time and effort. (Sugar cane has only half the labor requirements of sugar beets and one-third those of cotton.) Where an assolement is not followed, it is often because sugar cane is grown instead of another assigned crop. The government, for its part, has generally been most vigilant and strict with regard to its sugar-cane, cotton, rice, and sugar-beet assignments. It accords greater tolerance with regard to the other assignments. In some regions, for example in the Souss-Massa and Basse Moulouya, assolements exist more on paper than in reality. It is important to note that many large landowners within the irrigation perimeters are exempt from assolements. This is because (1) they developed irrigation by private pumping before the entry into force of the 1969 Code des Investissements Agricoles or (2) they acquired already irrigated colonization land. In many cases, large landowners are also "exempt" by their political connections: They commonly flout government development directives with impunity, preferring to grow the most profitable crops. For greater detail on assolement theory versus Moroccan reality, see H. Popp, *Effets socio-géographiques de la politique des barrages au Maroc* (Rabat, 1984), pp. 103–126.

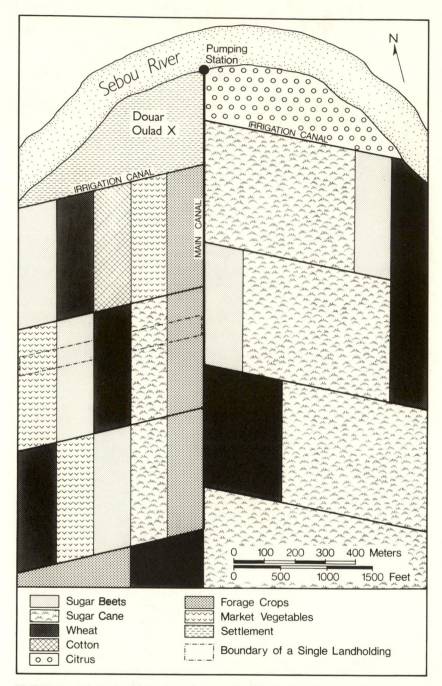

FIGURE 9   A typical irrigation sector in the Gharb with five-year and sugar-cane *assolements*

cants were supposed to be citizens of Morocco; earners of under 4,000 Dh a year—the upper end of the expected income of land reform beneficiaries; natives of the area where the land distributions were to take place or prior residents for at least five years; physically able; morally upright; younger than forty-five years of age; experienced in agriculture; and one of these: (1) totally landless or possessors of only very small plots, which were to be ceded to the state in exchange for viable new holdings, (2) members of the predominant tribe in the area, or (3) prior cultivators of the land to be distributed.[92]

Because the policy designated 3,500–4,000 Dh per year as the desired target income of land reform beneficiaries, the size of each allotment varied, depending on soil conditions and availability of irrigation water.[93] The typical size of the distributed lots, however, was 5–6 hectares in irrigated areas and 16–22 hectares in the dry lands. Prices charged for land in the program were often lower than prevailing prices, particularly in the early years. However, after 1973, when private colonization lands were recovered, prices were often significantly higher than the indemnities paid by the government for the land.[94]

Beneficiaries have been given eighteen to twenty years to pay for the land and are charged a minimal interest rate of 4 percent.[95] They are obliged to farm the land themselves according to specified norms and to participate in the local cooperative. The government has established three types of cooperatives: service cooperatives (approximately 60 percent of the total), in which members merely contract for services and supplies with the government; production cooperatives (6 percent), in which members work the land as a common unit; and "mixed" cooperatives (34 percent) that combine features of the pre-

[92] Morocco, Ministère de l'Agriculture et de la Réforme Agraire, *Réforme agraire* (Rabat, 1973), p. 2. There were cases of allotments of land to individuals who were clearly ineligible (for example, sons of wealthy local landowners). As can be expected, there was also much maneuvering within the traditional rural patron-client networks for allotments. Generally, however, the spirit of the requirements was maintained. A rough sketch of the average beneficiary is provided by the following 1979 statistics: 96 percent were younger than fifty-five years old; 78 percent were illiterate; 97 percent were married, and this group had six children on average, of whom only 23 percent had ever attended school (Ministry of Agriculture, unpublished documents, 1982).

[93] Lots varied in size from 2.75 hectares to 75 hectares (*Afrique Agriculture* 11 [1976]: 40).

[94] H. Akbour, "La Réforme agraire: un mythe et quelques réalités," *Lamalif* 120 (1980): 34.

[95] Many land reform beneficiaries, however, have never made any payments. See Popp, *Effets socio-géographiques*, p. 122. That this is tolerated by the government demonstrates that the motives for land reform are almost exclusively political. Theoretically, peasants will only have usufruct rights until their land is completely paid for.

TABLE 13 Land Distributions in Morocco,
1956–1986 (hectares)

Year	Total	Cumulative total
1956	3,410	3,410
1957	2,600	6,010
1958	1,090	7,100
1959	3,391	10,491
1960	4,746	15,237
1961	0	15,237
1962	0	15,237
1963	0	15,237
1964	2,560	17,797
1965	0	17,797
1966	5,666	23,463
1967	2,964	26,427
1968	0	26,427
1969	16,949	43,376
1970	19,016	62,392
1971	31,355	93,747
1972	90,857	184,604
1973	4,569	189,173
1974	70,527	259,700
1975	60,249	319,949
1976–82	52,447	372,396
TOTAL to 1986:		372,396

SOURCES: See note 96.

vious two types. The average cooperative has about thirty-four members, and there are approximately 740 cooperatives in all. In general, they function as the organizational link between the state and the peasant. The local agency of state intervention is the Centre de Mise en Valeur Agricole or CMV (the former Work Center or SMP headquarters), each of which has from 2,000 to 5,000 hectares under its control.

Table 13 reveals the pace at which land has been redistributed in Morocco. It suggests that the timing of distributions has been heavily influenced by political events. For example:

—The relatively minor distributions from 1956 to 1960 came immediately after independence when there was strong mass pressure for land reform. Following this, there were no further distributions until after the visit of the World Bank economic study mission in 1964.

—On 23 March 1965, Casablanca was rocked by riots. A month later, on 20 April 1965, the king announced the creation of a Common Fund for Agrarian Reform and the forthcoming redistribution of state lands. Minor distributions followed.

—Land distributions from 1969 to 1970 followed the promulgation of the Code des Investissements Agricoles. Besides legitimizing this charter, these distributions were probably intended to gain the good will of the World Bank.

—On 10 July 1971, rebel military officers initiated a bloody coup attempt at the king's summer palace at Skhirat. The following month, on 30 August 1971, the government announced that 140,000 hectares would be redistributed over the following two years. From 6 to 11 September 1971, 31,355 hectares were distributed.

—On 16 August 1972, as the king returned from Paris, his royal jet was attacked in a second nearly successful coup attempt. During the next two months, from 7 September to 31 October 1972, the government distributed 90,857 hectares. The king announced the debut of an "agrarian revolution" on 19 September 1972, and issued a decree on 2 March 1973 that provided for the nationalization of all remaining foreign holdings. Distributions totaling 187,792 hectares followed.[96]

Until 1972, land reform was largely concentrated within the irrigation perimeters. As its pace accelerated after the second coup attempt, however, it was primarily outside these perimeters and included pastureland.[97] In total, approximately 70,000 hectares were distributed within the irrigation perimeters.[98]

[96] My sources for land distribution figures are *LQA* 2, p. 221, and the U.S. Agency for International Development unpublished report of 1986, "Morocco, Country Development Strategy," p. 32. *LQA* 2 gives a total of 379,570 hectares, not counting preindependence figures. This total includes a distribution figure of 59,621 for 1976, when *LQA* 2 went to press. The 1976 figure represented the government's declared intentions. However, most of this land was not allotted in 1976, but instead was slowly distributed over the period lasting until 1982, when the land reform program was discontinued. Slightly over 7,000 hectares of the 1976 figure was never distributed. The probably quite reliable 1986 USAID report gives a total of 354,599 hectares for the period from 1966 to 1982. If one adds the *LQA* 2 figures for 1956 to 1965 to the USAID total, one gets a total of 372,396 hectares.

[97] The distribution in irrigated zones accounted for roughly 19 percent of the total. Approximately 190,000 hectares (51 percent) of the 372,396-hectare total were in the dryland agricultural sector, 89,000 hectares (24 percent) were in pastureland, and

The nearly 25,000 land reform beneficiaries are fortunate individuals, provided with land, heavy equipment, credit, agricultural supplies, and technical expertise. Those with irrigated allotments, however, are particularly fortunate. Incomes on typical 5-hectare land reform plots are commonly four to six times the government's ostensible target income of 4,000 Dh.[99] To put this into perspective, the target income by itself places a beneficiary in the uppermost 20 percent of the rural income spectrum.

To a limited degree, other Moroccan peasants have benefited from government irrigation development. Since the promulgation of the 1969 Code des Investissements Agricoles, tribal lands within the irrigation perimeters have been considered as belonging in "indivision" to a specified number of rightful owners. The Code requires each collective to establish a permanent list of such owners. The number of owners is theoretically not permitted to increase. Thus, as with redistributed land, for every owner there can be only one official heir. The collective's block is restructured through remembrement to fit the irrigation framework, and assolements are imposed. Collective members are grouped into cooperatives that interact with the local CMV. In the end, the collective block is nearly identical in appearance to blocks owned by land reform beneficiaries.[100]

What is strikingly different between collective and land reform blocks, however, is both the amount of land per collective member and the way this land is worked. Statistics on land holdings in Morocco are dated and in critically short supply. Nonetheless, two relatively recent studies suggest that the average number of hectares per collective farmer is closer to 1 than to 5.[101] This means that the aver-

23,000 hectares (6 percent) were nonproductive, being occupied by settlements, government compounds, roads, etc.

[98] SAHM, p. 24, plus my projection.

[99] Griffin, *Land Concentration*, pp. 107–108; Popp, *Effets socio-géographiques*. The 1986 U.S. Agency for International Development report ("Morocco, Country Development Strategy," p. 32) claims that the average land reform cooperative member had an annual income of 12,360 Dh in 1982. This average includes recipients of dryland plots.

[100] A major goal of the Code des Investissements Agricoles is to bring about private ownership of collective lands within the irrigation perimeters. This would theoretically constitute a significant socioeconomic change from the traditional system in which collective lands were periodically redistributed among the tribal members. In fact, however, since the late 1950s there have been relatively few redistributions of collective lands in Morocco. See P. Pascon, "Sur les terres collectives, l'état n'a plus d'idées," *Lamalif* 112 (1980): 22.

[101] Popp, *Effets socio-géographiques*; D. Soudho, "L'Evolution des structures foncières

age collective member is automatically much less prosperous than the land reform beneficiary. Disparity is further increased by the fact that land reform has taken place primarily on Morocco's better land—land originally expropriated by colonization.

In addition, the Code does not control how the members of the collective divide their land for purposes of working it. Consequently, under the seemingly rational, uniform appearance of the Trame B framework exist highly complex, idiosyncratic systems of land tenure. On the one hand, powerful members of collectives are able to amass relatively large holdings through various arrangements. On the other hand, old egalitarian traditions have persisted: Collective members maintain dispersed plots in different parts of the collective domain. Because most holdings are quite small to begin with, this means that the typical collective farmer cultivates pockets of land scattered here and there. It is consequently much more difficult for government technicians to ensure that specified farming and irrigation practices are obeyed. Fragmentation of collective land is increased by the fact that a great many collectives have never established official lists of rightful owners; consequently, the number of individuals owning land has continued to increase through inheritance.[102]

On privately owned (*melk*) small holdings that have benefited from irrigation development, many of the same problems are occurring.[103] Because the Code stipulates that divisions creating holdings smaller than 5 hectares are prohibited, in theory all peasants possessing under 10 hectares (over 90 percent of Morocco's peasants) must select a single heir. This heir should indemnify the others upon the peasant's death. Reality, however, is usually very different. Although a single individual may be officially listed as the new owner, the other heirs typically continue to participate just as though they had become owners following Islamic law. The net result is dispersed microholdings that run counter to planners' hopes for high efficiency. Given Morocco's high rate of demographic growth, fragmentation of holdings will increasingly become a problem in the irrigation perimeters.

However, small holdings, whether belonging to private farmers, collectives, or land reform beneficiaries, represent only about one-fifth of the land that has benefited from irrigation development in Morocco. Of the present 625,000 hectares of modern irrigated land located in the major irrigation perimeters, small landowners own only about

dans le Rharb entre 1965 et 1981: cas du secteur hydraulique S9 de la Première Tranche d'Irrigation," unpublished *Mémoire*, 3d cycle (1981), INAV, Rabat.

[102] Soudho, "L'Evolution," esp. p. 56.

[103] Ibid., esp. p. 128.

125,000 hectares. Large landowners own or are acquiring some 500,000 hectares.

Well over half of the 1,017,000 hectares formerly owned by Europeans, including both irrigated and dryland holdings, has fallen into the hands of the Moroccan elite. European settlers sold approximately 410,000 hectares to wealthy Moroccan nationals between 1956 and 1973, when remaining foreign holdings were expropriated.[104] This total alone is significantly larger than the total distributed under land reform (372,396 hectares). Until recently, the state retained some 245,000 hectares of former European land. Roughly 163,000 hectares of this total was composed of former colonial orchards and farms run by SODEA and SOGETA, two semiprivate corporations owned half by the state and half by a small group of Moroccans including members of the royal family.[105] These two corporations controlled some 40 percent of Morocco's citrus orchards, 80 percent of its vineyards, significant percentages of its other fruit and nut orchards, and much productive cereal land.[106] In a recent move, the Moroccan government has decided to divest itself of all former colonial land. This land is now being "privatized," i.e., sold outright to the Moroccan elite.[107] In short, the clandestine land transfers from European settlers to Moroccan elites and the present privatization of the state-controlled former

[104] This figure is based on the fact that of the 1,017,000 hectares of colonization land at independence, only 606,744 hectares were ultimately recovered: 26,265 hectares in 1959–60; 256,262 hectares in the wave of expropriations of official colonization land from 1963 to 1966; and 324,217 hectares of private colonization land in 1973. The French embassy in Rabat estimates that 386,000 hectares belonging to French settlers alone were sold to Moroccans from 1959 to 1973 (Griffin, *Land Concentration*, p. 101). It appears that at least some property titles were transferred from European settlers to Moroccans after the 2 March 1973 decree nationalizing all remaining colonization land; these titles were illegally predated. See Popp, *Effets socio-géographiques*, p. 62. Of the 410,256 hectares of colonization land acquired by wealthy Moroccans, approximately 404,000 hectares were from private colonization holdings, the remainder from official colonization. Most of the Moroccans who acquired European holdings are absentee urban landlords. Popp gives some insight into the nature of these new Moroccan colons: a businessman from Fez, an army colonel, a Rabat merchant, a former minister of tourism, a member of parliament from Nador, an attorney from Safi, etc.

[105] The remainder of the 245,000 total was mostly forest land.

[106] See, for example, M. Couvreur, "Une Nouvelle Forme de gestion des terres récupérées au Maroc: la Société de Développement Agricole (SODEA)," *Méditerranée* 29 (1977): 97–102; *Afrique Agriculture* 11 (1976): 60–63.

[107] The official motives behind privatization of the state's agricultural land are "to return to private enterprise everything which naturally belongs to it" and to help reduce rural depopulation and improve the food deficit. See *Middle East Economic Digest*, 26 April 1985: 28–29.

colonial holdings represent the real land reform in Morocco. Most of this land is irrigated or irrigable.

Measures recommended by the 1960–64 plan, ONI, the Sebou Project, and the World Bank to place limitations on holding sizes and recover the windfall gains from large holdings benefiting from irrigation development have never been implemented by the Moroccan government. In the absence of preventive legislation, land concentration has continued, widening the chasm between rich and poor. This has been particularly true within the irrigation perimeters. One analyst termed the *politique des barrages* the "spearhead" of land concentration, noting that it was sufficient merely to pronounce the word "dam" in a region to initiate a scramble for land.[108] Indeed, advance information concerning the location of areas to be irrigated seems to have been leaked in certain cases. Thus, it is claimed that in the Souss region three individuals were able to accumulate 40 percent of the irrigable land before construction of the Massa Dam.[109]

The requirement that private landowners in the irrigation perimeters pay a capital improvement tax of 1,500 dirhams per hectare to help defray government development costs is little more than a symbolic gesture for owners of large landholdings. The required sum, payable over seventeen years at 4 percent interest, amounts to a mere 169 dirhams per hectare annually. By contrast, in 1969, when the Code was issued, the profit on modern irrigated operations reached as high as 10,000 dirhams per hectare.[110] To add insult to injustice, the predominantly absentee landowners who acquired colonial holdings often neglect these holdings and ignore the directives of the regional development offices.[111] Much highly productive land is left fallow, and many formerly well-tended orchards are falling into disrepair. The pri-

---

[108] M. Benhlal, "Politique des barrages et problèmes de la modernisation rurale dans le Gharb," *Annuaire de l'Afrique du Nord, 1975* 14 (1976): 268.

[109] L. Oussalah, "Le Développement inégal au niveau national: Maroc utile/Maroc inutile," unpublished *Mémoire*, Law and Economic Sciences (1976), University of Aix–Marseille II, p. 129.

[110] "A qui profitera le Code des Investissements Agricoles?" *Al Kifah al Watani*, 17–24 January 1969, p. 11. Irrigation water charges, moreover, have been so low that they have not even covered the cost of maintenance. Additionally, the collection rate with respect to water charges was only about 43 percent in 1984. See U.S. Agency for International Development," Morocco, Country Development Strategy," p. 27.

[111] Field observations and anonymous sources in the Ministry of Agriculture, Rabat. Popp gives many examples of the way the former colonial holdings are farmed today. He also documents the fact that at least some of the former colonial holdings have been subdivided into small holdings by Moroccan colons and sold for enormous profits (Popp, *Effets socio-géographiques*).

TABLE 14   Morocco's Trade Balance in Agriculture, 1969–1982 (Millions of Dirhams)

Year	Agricultural imports	Agricultural exports	Balance
1969	751	1,495	744
1970	953	1,464	511
1971	1,123	1,450	327
1972	1,023	1,655	632
1973	1,623	2,242	619
1974	2,923	2,168	−755
1975	3,665	1,800	−1,865
1976	2,953	2,134	−819
1977	3,249	2,055	−1,194
1978	3,193	2,384	−809
1979	3,702	2,610	−1,092
1980	4,376	3,106	−1,270
1981	6,341	3,633	−2,708
1982	5,842	3,753	−2,089

SOURCE: U.S. Agency for International Development, "Morocco, Country Development Strategy," p. 110.

mary incomes of these "Moroccan colons" are from urban pursuits; their colonial estates function more as status symbols and country retreats than active investments (Illus. 11). Furthermore, because the colonial holdings were typically acquired at very low prices from settlers fearful of expropriation, they are often highly profitable even if farmed only extensively.

Hassan II's development policy was designed, in his words, "to enrich the poor without impoverishing the rich."[112] As recently as 27 December 1983, the same slogan was used by the Minister of the Interior to define the king's policy.[113] Irrigation development has indeed enriched a tiny percentage of the poor—some 1 or 2 percent. However, its primary effect has been to further enrich the wealthy and neglect, if not further impoverish, most of Morocco's peasants.

Has the policy produced the desired agricultural growth? Table 14 addresses this question. The table demonstrates that in 1969, soon after the launching of the *politique des barrages*, there was a trade surplus in agricultural commodities of about 750 million dirhams. In

[112] J.-P. Peroncel-Hugoz, "Le Roi Hassan désire se concilier le monde rural," *Le Monde Diplomatique*, 7 October 1972, p. 5.
[113] *Le Monde*, 24 January 1984, p. 3.

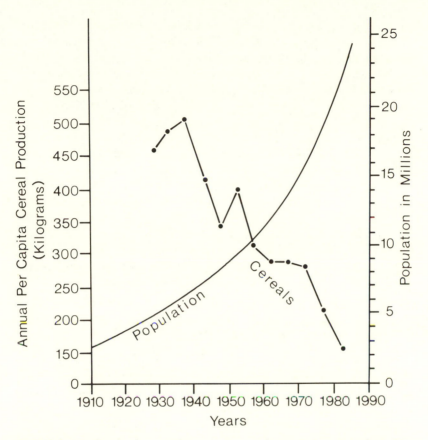
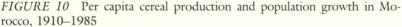

FIGURE 10   Per capita cereal production and population growth in Morocco, 1910–1985

SOURCE: Jouve, "Démographie et céréaliculture," p. 8; *FAO Monthly Bulletin of Statistics*, 1980–85.

NOTE: Points along the cereal production line represent five-year averages; however, the final point represents the 1981–84 average.

1974, however, this healthy surplus disappeared. It was replaced by a trade deficit of 755 million dirhams. A large and growing trade deficit in agriculture has persisted ever since. In short, in terms of all three of its objectives—to raise rural standards of living, earn foreign currency, and provide for the nation's food needs—the irrigation policy has clearly failed. Indeed, it has seemingly been counterproductive.

Fig. 10 places the present plight of Morocco in historical perspective. This graph compares Morocco's population growth during the period 1910–85 with per capita production of cereals. Per capita cereal production is a significant indicator because cereals constitute the major part of the average Moroccan's diet. Most of Morocco's cereals are grown in the traditional dryland sector.

Total Moroccan production of cereals has remained essentially unchanged since the 1950s. Morocco's average annual cereal production for the period 1951–55 was 39.2 million quintals; for 1974–84 it was 40.3 million quintals, an increase of less than 3 percent.[114] Agricultural production resulting from irrigation development has involved either export crops (particularly citrus, early vegetables, and cotton) or "strategic" import-substitution crops (such as sugar beets, sugar cane, and forage for the dairy industry). None of the resulting food commodities have, to any significant degree, replaced cereals in the Moroccan diet.

Fig. 10 reveals in the most striking, elemental terms that since the mid-1930s Morocco has steadily been losing its ability to feed itself. Until 1960, Morocco was a net exporter of cereals. The year 1960, however, marked the end of the "granary of Rome's" cereal exports. Since then, cereal imports have grown at an alarming rate: from an annual average of 3 million quintals in the early 1960s to over 20 million quintals in the 1980s.[115] Morocco must now import up to half of its cereal grains. In addition, it must import up to one-third of its sugar and 90 percent of the raw materials to produce comestible oils.

The present agricultural policy, focused on developing irrigation for a minor portion of arable Morocco, a tiny privileged segment of the agricultural community, and on export and "strategic" crops instead of basic foodstuffs, has not addressed the principal problem. For increasingly sizable numbers of Moroccans, both rural and urban, survival is the issue.[116] This is poignantly demonstrated by food riots. First in June 1981, then in January 1984, scores of Moroccans were killed protesting against government hikes in subsidized food prices.[117] These short-lived riots were easily put down by an army

[114] *FAO Monthly Bulletin of Statistics*, various issues.

[115] The growth of cereal imports has been steady: average annual imports of 2.9 million quintals for the period 1960 to 1964; 4.9 million quintals for the period 1965 to 1969; 6.5 million quintals for 1970 to 1974; 14.3 million quintals for 1975 to 1978; and 20.7 million quintals for 1980 to 1983 (ibid.).

[116] Authorities have estimated that between 30 and 40 percent of the urban population and 30 and 60 percent of the rural population suffer from malnutrition. See *Lamalif* 159 (1984): 26.

[117] On 20 June 1981, anywhere from 69 to 600 people were killed in Casablanca while rioting. See *Le Figaro*, 1 July 1981, p. 2. Between 19 and 22 January 1984, 20 to 200 people were killed during rioting in the Rifian towns of Tetouan, Nador, and Al Hoceima. See *Le Monde*, 26 January 1984, p. 4. The low figures represent the official account in each case.

equipped with modern tanks, helicopters, and machine guns. However, probably only an immediate and successful campaign to raise dryland cereal yields will be able to avert crisis.

In sum, the most striking fact about Morocco's contemporary agricultural development is its continuity with protectorate agricultural development. Agricultural policy has remained oriented towards the modern sector. Moroccan elites have replaced settlers. A million hectares are being put under perennial irrigation and a colonial development plan is being fulfilled. Agricultural policy, unfortunately, has stood still. Morocco's agricultural problems, unfortunately, have not.

Summary and Conclusion

Government policies have transformed Morocco on a massive scale during the past three-quarters of a century. In favored areas of the coastal lowlands, relatively prosperous enclaves of modern agriculture have been created. In most of the remainder of the country, traditional agriculture has progressively deteriorated as a result of forces introduced by French colonization, population pressure, and longstanding government neglect. The country's landscapes are artifacts of past policy decisions. Agrarian Morocco can only be comprehended through analysis of past government policies.

A wheat policy, designed to convert Morocco into a breadbasket for France, monopolized development efforts during the first two decades of the protectorate period. This policy was based on an idealistic image of Morocco as the former fertile granary of Rome; there was little objective resource appraisal. In reality, most of Morocco is a marginal environment for rainfed wheat production, particularly for export. Thus, the protectorate's wheat policy ultimately precipitated a crisis for colonization. The policy was replaced in the early 1930s by a new emphasis on irrigation agriculture. The wheat policy's legacy, however, stubbornly persists in the large holdings that the policy created in the coastal lowlands, holdings that largely remain to the present.

In order to create colonial wheat farms, European settlers expropriated the choicest part of lowland Morocco and crowded Moroccan peasants onto less productive lands. In all, 1 million hectares were taken over by fewer than 6,000 Europeans. This land should rightly have been returned to Morocco's peasants after independence. Instead, nearly two-thirds of the colonization land has passed or is passing into the hands of the Moroccan elite. Little more than a third has been redistributed to peasants.

French administration of Morocco also enabled individual Moroccans to amass large holdings by the same methods used by private European settlers. During the course of the protectorate period, some 7,500 Moroccans developed large landholdings on a total of 1.6 million hectares. Most of this land is now integrated into the modern agricultural sector. The army officers, government officials, urban merchants, and other wealthy Moroccans who have acquired colonization land since independence have joined this older landed elite, creating a powerful class of 8,500–9,000 large landowners. Today, they own some 2.2 million hectares—nearly 30 percent of Morocco's agricultural land, including most of its modern sector and perennially irrigated land.[1] Land concentration during and since the protectorate period has been perhaps the major cause of the gulf between rich and poor in Morocco.

The agricultural crisis that began in 1929 convincingly demonstrated the "economic heresy" of the wheat policy and prompted a new orientation. In this crisis period, inspiration was drawn not from Morocco's classical past, but rather from the fabled success that California had achieved through irrigation agriculture. Californian agricultural methods, crop varieties, and marketing techniques were transferred en masse to Morocco. By 1934, a major new form of colonial agriculture had emerged, based on irrigation and the export of citrus fruit and market vegetables *à la Californie*. This California-inspired policy has continued to the present. Fruit and vegetable production by irrigated means accounted for over four-fifths of Morocco's agricultural exports in 1986, and Morocco today is the world's second largest exporter of oranges.

The "California policy" was subsumed into a larger development strategy by the end of the 1930s, however. In response to a devastating four-year drought, the rise of the nationalist movement, and the alarming implications of Morocco's first real census, protectorate policymakers decided in 1938 to undertake the complete development of Morocco's water resources. They developed a highly ambitious and idealistic irrigation plan. One million hectares were to be put under perennial irrigation by the year 2000. Upon fulfillment of the plan, "not a drop" of Morocco's water was to flow unused to the sea. The 1938 plan has served as the basis of all subsequent irrigation development.

Agricultural development in Morocco today is essentially the implementation of French colonial policies; the colonial million-hectare plan

---

[1] This extreme concentration of landownership is only hinted at in statistics on landholdings in Morocco. It is disguised by the fact that wealthy landowners often own several "holdings," while statistics gathered at local levels and never cross-referenced do not reveal this; also by the fact that large landowners commonly have registered some of their land under the names of others (mainly relatives) as insurance against eventual government measures to expropriate excessive holdings.

is now being fulfilled. This plan envisioned the complete harnessing
of Morocco's streams by the end of the century. The present irrigation
program embraces identically the same goal. The main difference lies
in the increased pace of development, not in its overall methods or
rationale. Since independence, nearly twenty new dams have been constructed, and the modern irrigation area has grown from roughly
65,000 hectares in 1956 to some 625,000 hectares in 1986.[2] However, nearly all of the present dam and irrigation projects were originally drafted by protectorate technicians. In addition, nearly all of the
elements of the present agricultural development formula were pioneered during the protectorate period. Embedded within colonial development policies and plans is a strong political and economic bias.
This has been perpetuated along with the policies and plans.

As the 1938 plan began to be implemented after World War II,
protectorate policy called for (1) nearly exclusive concentration of investment in irrigation development in Morocco's coastal lowlands; (2)
production of irrigated export crops, such as citrus, on the large holdings of European settlers; (3) provision of irrigation water and special
assistance to a small number of dispossessed Moroccan peasants; and
(4) production of strategic crops for the national economy on the
small irrigated holdings of the state-supported peasants. In Morocco
today, virtually the same formula is being followed, with only one
major difference: The Moroccan elite have taken control of a majority
of the large European farms.

In both the colonial and postcolonial periods, irrigation development has served distinctly similar political ends. During the colonial
period, it was intended to benefit settlers and create a demonstration
of France's efforts to assist Moroccan peasants. In contemporary Morocco, its goal has been to ensure the king's base of support among
the landowning elite and create a showcase for agrarian reform.

The present agricultural policy took shape during the early 1960s.
According to King Hassan, the policy was designed to "enrich the
poor without impoverishing the rich."[3] The policy's specific characteristics have been the following:

(1) The Moroccan elite were allowed to acquire foreign-owned ag-

---

[2] The 65,000-hectare figure includes both the protectorate government's legacy of
36,000 hectares in large-scale irrigation systems and the land privately put into irrigation
by European settlers and wealthy Moroccans. The 625,000-hectare figure likewise includes land in large-scale irrigation systems and land under private irrigation.

[3] Privately, King Hassan is reported to have said, "If I had a million irrigated hectares
. . . *eh bien*, then you would see my monarchy defend itself" (*Le Monde*, 7 October 1972,
p. 5).

ricultural land and replace departing European settlers. This reflected a conscious political decision by Morocco's leaders. At independence, it was clear that all of the colonization land would be needed for redistribution if there was to be an effective land reform. Instead, King Hassan adopted a laissez-faire land policy. Not until nearly two decades after independence, with prompting from two coup attempts, did the Moroccan monarch stop private purchases of colonization land and nationalize remaining foreign holdings. No effective measures have ever been implemented to curtail excessive land concentration—for example, by establishing a maximum landholding size.

(2) Government-financed irrigation development has essentially followed the vision of the 1938 colonial plan. Irrigation water has benefited the landowning elite; it has expanded the modern export sector comprised of large private holdings and the state-controlled former colonial farms that are now being privatized; and it has served as the key element of a limited, preemptive land reform. Through this land reform, a small client class of relatively prosperous peasants has been created to grow strategic crops for the national economy, mollify international lenders, and serve as a shield between the impoverished rural masses and wealthy landowners.

(3) Traditional agriculture, which still occupies some 70 percent of Morocco's cultivated land and involves well over 90 percent of its farmers, has remained essentially untouched by government development efforts. This sector has been progressively deteriorating (Illus. 15). Statistics are scarce, but all indicate the present seriousness of rural Morocco's plight. For example, Morocco's cultivated area now amounts to less than one-half hectare per rural inhabitant. An estimated 50,000 to 70,000 hectares of arable land are destroyed annually through erosion, reflecting excessive population pressure and signifying a decline in total land resources. And rural population growth is only about 1.8 percent per annum, as opposed to 4.8 percent for the urban population, because an estimated 100,000 rural Moroccans leave the countryside each year for urban squatter settlements.[4]

Unfortunately, the current agricultural policy has not created the necessary economic development. Agricultural exports more than doubled during the period from 1969 to 1982, yet agricultural imports increased nearly eightfold during the same period (Table 14). This

[4] "La Population et l'agriculture," *Lamalif* 133 (1982): 24–25; "La Banque mondiale et l'agriculture marocaine," *LMA* 126 (1980): 9. Pascon notes that the rural exodus is composed of "les plus capables . . . les plus hardis, les talents, les jeunes et les capitaux. Peu à peu la campagne devient un desert culturel" (P. Pascon, "Agriculture, faillité et perspectives," *Lamalif* 145 [1983]: 20).

trend has continued. The result has been a growing strain on the national economy. In addition, Morocco's foreign debt has steadily mounted as a result of borrowing for dam and irrigation projects. Indeed, the country's foreign debt now exceeds its GDP, and nearly 40 percent of all export revenues are required to service this debt.[5] Morocco's political and economic future has been disastrously mortgaged to the fulfillment of a colonial vision.

Morocco's agricultural situation has the potential to develop into a severe crisis in the not-distant future.[6] Population growth will relentlessly increase the need for food imports. And Morocco will probably lose much of the European market for its agricultural exports—its primary market. The country's massive investment in export agriculture, in fact, is imperiled by the increasingly protectionist policy of the European Community resulting from the January 1986 entry into the EC of Spain and Portugal, agricultural competitors of Morocco. Spain's entry, in particular, ultimately may completely shut out Moroccan agricultural exports to the EC.[7] European agribusiness firms are already investing heavily in "winter garden" production in southern Spain. The gradual closing of European markets to Moroccan citrus and market garden exports will pose a major dilemma. At tremendous expense, Morocco has built or is now building the dams necessary to irrigate a million hectares. Yet it can't even sell what it now produces on its present 625,000 hectares of modern irrigated land. Unexportable surpluses are mounting annually.

It is unlikely that other sectors of the Moroccan economy will be able to compensate for the deteriorating agricultural sector. Morocco is experiencing a protracted economic recession. The demand for

[5] Only about $1 billion of Morocco's 1985 outstanding external debt of $13 billion was military-related. See *Middle East Economic Digest*, 13 August 1985, p. 14.

[6] For a fuller analysis of Morocco's present agricultural crisis, see W. D. Swearingen, "Morocco's Agricultural Crisis," in *The Political Economy of Morocco*, ed. I. W. Zartman (New York, 1987), pp. 234–254.

[7] U.S. Department of Agriculture, *Middle East and North Africa: Outlook and Situation Report*, Economic Research Service Report, 12 April 1985, p. 31. A mid-1985 EC proposal to deal with the "Moroccan question" involved a five-year transition plan that would gear agricultural quotas through 1990 to Moroccan export levels during the 1980 to 1984 period, a period of substantial decline over traditional levels. (European countries were already distancing themselves from Morocco in anticipation of Spain and Portugal's scheduled EC entry). For citrus, for example, imports from Morocco would be set at 342,000 metric tons (Morocco produced 1,020,000 tons in 1984); for tomatoes, imports would be set at 77,000 tons (Morocco produced 355,000 tons in 1983). However, this proposal had not yet been accepted by either EC foreign ministers or the Moroccan government as of the end of 1986. See *Economist* Intelligence Unit, *Country Profile: Morocco, 1986-87* (1986), p. 59.

phosphates, the country's major export, has been weak since 1977. Remittances from laborers abroad are not likely to increase, and may even significantly decrease. And Morocco's tourist industry, despite excellent potential, faces formidable Mediterranean and international competition. Further, it will remain ever vulnerable to disruption by outside political and economic factors. Growth in this sector will be slow, at best. Unfortunately, no other sectors of the Moroccan economy have the capacity to expand significantly in the near future.[8]

The Moroccan government will be compelled by growing food shortages, mounting trade deficits, increasing political problems, and pressure from international lenders to wage a sustained campaign to raise cereal production in the traditional agricultural sector. This campaign's goal will be to restore self-sufficiency in cereals and generate grain reserves as a hedge against future droughts. Such a goal is laudable, and such a campaign may be one of Morocco's few viable options. However, this campaign has little likelihood of success unless Morocco's policymakers glean lessons from past dryland development failures.[9]

This study has shown that past dryland development campaigns have failed for several reasons: (1) They were overly idealistic, poorly planned, and did not fully account for Morocco's sociopolitical realities; (2) they were overly interventionist, thereby forfeiting the popular support essential for their success; (3) they were effectively dropped by the government after only a couple of years, before positive results could be achieved; and (4) they attempted to develop traditional dryland agriculture without addressing one of its principal problems, the need for a comprehensive reform. The necessary reform would include strict limits on landholding sizes, land expropriation

---

[8] In 1984, exports of phosphates and phosphate products brought in foreign revenues of approximately 8.9 billion Dh, worker's remittances amounted to some 8.7 billion Dh, tourism generated net receipts of about 4.2 billion Dh, and citrus and market vegetable exports, including processed products, yielded approximately 1.7 billion Dh. The exchange rate in 1984 averaged about 8.8 Dh per $US. See ibid., pp. 41 and 53-55.

[9] One of the major objectives of the 1981–85 Five Year Plan was the development of dryland agriculture. Around 40 percent of government investment in agriculture was earmarked for this sector. A Plan Céréalier came into being in 1982. However, budget cuts, the momentum acquired by irrigation projects, the inefficiency of the Directions Provinciales de l'Agriculture (DPAs) charged with dryland development, and political considerations have ensured that there has been little change or improvement in the dryland sector. The Moroccan government is now seriously considering having the ORMVAs absorb the DPAs, a move that would seemingly guarantee that irrigation development retains priority.

and redistribution, a complete restructuring of land tenure systems and agricultural pricing policy, and a substantial broadening of credit opportunities.[10]

Morocco's leadership has not yet demonstrated that it has learned from past mistakes. With regard to agrarian reform, it is confronted with a particularly acute dilemma. It has used agricultural policy to garner support from the Moroccan elite. By changing policy, it would put this political support and its future in jeopardy. On the other hand, its future increasingly will be brought in question if it does not undertake a comprehensive reform.

Morocco's present agricultural problems have their roots in the colonial past. These problems have grown to ominous proportions today, however, because Morocco has never effectively broken with this past.

[10] The Moroccan government was in 1986 taking several steps that it viewed as agrarian reform. It was selling the SODEA and SOGETA lands to the Moroccan elite; it was liberalizing the trade code on agricultural imports into Morocco; it was dismantling all or part of the Office de Commercialization et de l'Exportation (OCE) to facilitate exports; it had suspended agricultural taxes until the year 2000; and it had somewhat broadened credit opportunities to small farmers, mainly "modern" small farmers.

Epilogue: Policy by Illusion

On the occasion of his birthday, 8 July 1985, His Majesty King Hassan II addressed the Moroccan nation.[1] Among other critical matters, the king spoke of the drought that had plagued the country during the first half of the 1980s.

> Dear people. . . . We have noticed that drought strikes Morocco once every 20 years. The drought we faced during the past 4 years was exceptional, the like of which occured only in the 16th century in the era of the Sa'diyeen. . . . Now, thank God, we have emerged from the difficult 4 years and will be entering the 20 rainy years. Within the 20 years, the population of Morocco will reach over 40 million. We will then face 3 or 4 years of drought, but it will not be like the present drought.

The Moroccan monarch revealed the reason for his confidence in the country's ability to withstand future droughts: He had initiated a campaign "to cultivate 1 million hectares of grain." Ten thousand tractors had been marshaled for this task, as well as the requisite fertilizer, seeds, and "good will." The success of the undertaking would save 1 billion centimes of hard currency per year, and enable Morocco to meet 75 percent of its grain needs instead of only 25 percent. Furthermore, it would "prove to all that Moroccans win when faced with a challenge."

Lest it be construed that the new million-hectare operation represented a major shift in agricultural policy, the king cautioned that, by itself, the initiative would provide only a partial defense against drought. He exhorted all government agencies involved with irrigation to strive to exploit existing water resources fully and to develop new resources. Through dryland and irrigation development efforts, "Thanks be to God, we will be safe from catastrophes like those we have seen."

[1] U.S. Foreign Broadcast Information Service, *Daily Report—Middle East and Africa* 5, no. 134 (12 July 1985) Q2–Q5.

Hassan II's birthday speech is a prime example of the authoritarian "dreams and deceptions" approach that has characterized dryland development in Morocco since World War II. The king's new initiative is at present still more rhetoric than reality. However, its strategy is basically identical to that employed in both the SMP campaign (1945–ca. 1947) and Operation Plow (1957–63), programs notable primarily for failure. Indeed, Operation Plow had exactly the same goal of 1 million hectares of improved grain production. Like its two predecessors, the new initiative involves extensive use of government machinery to plow traditional agricultural lands before the autumn rainy season.[2] Through this strategy, more land can be put into production, and higher yields can be obtained through better soil preparation and the introduction of fertilizer and improved seed varieties. This strategy is sound as far as it goes. However, to succeed it needs to be linked to a larger program of agrarian reform—something Morocco has never had. Past efforts have failed, in significant part, because they attempted to change the mechanics of production without altering the social, political, and economic matrix in which traditional cereal production in Morocco takes place. The new initiative appears to be recycling the errors of the past. Ten thousand tractors—as opposed to Operation Plow's one thousand tractors—will not by itself reap a tenfold harvest of success.

The king's vision, however, is fundamentally flawed. "Twenty rainy years" is pure fantasy. This fantasy derives from a faulty reading of the executive summary of a 1984 report on Morocco's drought, a summary that was itself in error.[3] A major conclusion of the report was that no predictions could be made about when drought would recur or how long it would endure. This was stated in the summary. However, the summary also noted that "the present drought, while undoubtedly severe, is not unique. Similar droughts occurred in 1935–38 and 1958–61."[4] From the twenty-year interval between 1938 and 1958, and between 1961 and the recent drought's onset in 1981, it could possibly be inferred by advisors wishing to please the king that drought would not again strike Morocco until the year 2004, twenty

[2] As noted earlier, a perennial problem for the majority of Morocco's peasants is their inability to begin planting until autumn rainfall has softened the earth. The limitations of traditional agricultural technology and the short duration of the autumn rainy season typically mean that much land cannot be put into production.

[3] T.M.L. Wigley and S. E. Nicholson, "Statistical Analysis of Precipitation Data," part III of "Drought in Morocco," unpublished report to the Conseil Supérieur de l'Eau, Morocco (May 1984).

[4] Ibid., p. 1.

years after the end of the recent drought. However, the summary neglected to mention *l'Année terrible*, 1945, Morocco's worst drought of the century from an agricultural point of view.[5] Furthermore, even a superficial inquiry into Morocco's environmental history reveals that drought strikes much more frequently than once every two decades. Since 1912, there have been some twenty-two drought years.[6] The average interval between droughts during this same period is a mere three years. This average has no precise predictive value. Yet it does suggest the extreme unlikelihood that Morocco can now expect twenty years of good harvests.

Unfortunately, the illusion of deliverance from drought has now been strengthened by subsequent bountiful harvests. In 1985, Morocco's cereal production reached 52.2 million quintals, the best harvest since 1976.[7] And in 1986, it rose to an astonishing 76.8 million quintals, the best harvest in Moroccan history.[8] Cereal production in 1986, in fact, represented a 91 percent increase over the yearly average for the 1974 to 1984 period.

These outstanding harvests, however, far from improving Morocco's agricultural situation, will tend to make it worse. This is because they appear to substantiate the rosy forecast of twenty rainy years, encouraging postponement of the critical reforms. Indeed, in a 10 October 1986 address to the Moroccan parliament, King Hassan boasted that the return of rain "should soon bring about self-sufficiency in grain production."[9] And in this same speech, he announced that as a result

[5] Total cereal production in 1945 amounted to only slightly over 5 million quintals. This was in an era when, during a good year, Morocco produced nearly 40 million quintals of cereals (for example: 1939, 1941). Cereal yields in 1945 averaged only 1.5 quintals per hectare, as opposed to 9.3 quintals/hectare in 1939 (see Fig. 2). It is interesting to compare the 1945 drought with the recent drought. The worst recent drought year was 1981, when total cereal production amounted to slightly over 21 million quintals and yields averaged 4.8 quintals/hectare. The total area planted in cereals has not significantly increased since the early 1940s (for example: 4.5 million hectares in 1941 versus slightly less than 4.7 million hectares in 1985).

[6] From 20 to 24 drought years, actually, depending on how "drought" is defined. See Introduction, note 15.

[7] *Economist* Intelligence Unit, *Quarterly Economic Review of Morocco* 1 (1986): 21. In 1976, total cereal production amounted to 56.6 million quintals.

[8] The 1986 cereal production figure is from the *Economist* Intelligence Unit, *Country Report: Morocco* 4 (1986): 20. The best previous harvest on record occurred in 1968, when total cereal production reached 63.2 million quintals. Cereal yields in 1986 attained 15.1 quintals/hectare, and the total cultivated area was slightly over 5 million hectares. Ibid.

[9] *Morocco News Summary*, published by the Embassy of the Kingdom of Morocco, Washington, D.C., n.d., unpaginated.

of abundant rain, he was implementing a plan to build "a dam per year . . . until the year 2000."[10] In such a way is policy built on illusion.

The truth is that these plentiful harvests represent only a momentary upswing in a dramatically fluctuating production history. The 1986 cereal harvest probably will prove to be as exceptional an event as the devastating 1945 drought. During the 1985–86 growing season, both the timing and the total amount of rainfall were nearly optimum throughout Morocco, a meteorological miracle. Inexorably, fat years will be followed by lean. And the precipitous long-term decline in per capita cereal production likely will continue.

Drought in Morocco, in fact, can be expected to become increasingly common for two partly non-climatological reasons. First, since 1984, cereal cultivation has been significantly expanded onto rangeland— marginal land traditionally not under plow for the very good reason that it usually is deprived of sufficient rainfall to sustain cultivation. Even during "normal" years, this land will be prone to drought. Morocco will soon become a new victim of the "drought follows the plow" phenomenon. Second, drought will occur more frequently because food production systems increasingly will be unable to keep pace with Morocco's rapidly growing population. Progressively smaller a shortage of rain, or infelicity of its occurrence, will constitute "drought" in the future.

Royal illusions may make for stirring birthday speeches, but they will not help feed the hungry. Morocco's erratic climate will remain indifferent both to the whims of the country's monarch and the ever-increasing needs of its people. Ultimately, only enlightened policy will help.

[10] Ibid. The "dam a year" statement refers both to large dams that have been included in the *politique des barrages* schedule for many years, as well as to more modest *petite* and *moyenne hydraulique* works.

Sources and Bibliography

This study is based principally on analysis of data gathered during a year of research in France and Morocco. Sources include government documents and publications, unpublished reports and theses, correspondence, and articles in newspapers and journals. Nearly all are in French: Documentation concerning agricultural policy in Morocco during the period covered in this study, 1912–86, is almost exclusively in French. Written sources were reinforced by interviews.

The following research centers and libraries were used extensively.

Centre des Hautes Etudes sur l'Afrique et l'Asie Moderne (CHEAM), Paris, France
  Documentation: Unpublished reports and *mémoires de stage* by Native Affairs officers and civil controllers.
Bibliothèque, Institut International d'Administration Publique (IIAP), Paris, France
  Documentation: Unpublished reports and *mémoires de stage* by colonial administrators. Also a good collection of published sources.
Collection "Afrique du Nord—Augustin Bernard," Bibliothèque, Institut de Géographie, Université de Paris, Paris, France
  Documentation: Rare published sources and some unpublished documents.
Bibliothèque, Centre de Recherches et d'Etudes sur les Sociétés Méditerranéennes (CRESM), Aix-en-Provence, France
  Documentation: Probably the world's largest collection of published sources on contemporary North Africa. Also some unpublished materials, mainly government documents.
Bibliothèque, Dépôt des Archives d'Outre-Mer, Aix-en-Provence, France
  Documentation: Rare published sources on the protectorate period.
Bibliothèque Générale et Archives de Rabat, Rabat Morocco
  Documentation: Protectorate archives, a near-exhaustive collection of published sources on both protectorate and contemporary periods in Morocco, and many valuable unpublished reports and *mémoires de stage*.
Centre National de Documentation (CND), Rabat, Morocco
  Documentation: Protectorate and contemporary government archives on microfiche.

Bibliothèque, Société d'Etudes et de Bibliographie Marocaines (SEBM), *French Embassy,* Rabat, Morocco
   Documentation: Published sources, often rare, in open stacks.
Bibliothèque, Chambre d'Agriculture de Rabat, Rabat, Morocco
   Documentation: A now-defunct library with probably the only extant complete collection of the Rabat Chamber's *Bulletins.* Also several extremely rare unpublished reports not found elsewhere.

A comment about the French protectorate archives is in order. The "official" protectorate archives relevant to this study are in repository in France and mostly are not available for consultation. They are closed both by a "time-lock" of commonly as much as 60 years and by the fact that the majority of older, theoretically available documents have not yet been organized, declassified, and made available to the public. In Morocco, however, many protectorate documents remain. It is not generally known that there is a warehouse containing French archives behind the Arabic archives at the Bibliothèque Générale in Rabat. These protectorate archives are officially closed to the public and purportedly have never been inventoried and arranged. I obtained special permission to gain access, and conducted a thorough search over a five-week period. I found these archives to be well organized, both chronologically and by administrative bureau. Many "dossiers" or cartons pertinent to this study were located, some with highly detailed information not available elsewhere. Each dossier contains up to fifty or more individual items: memoranda, reports, letters, and minutes of meetings. The following dossiers were particularly useful:

TRAVAUX PUBLICS SECTION
"Hydraulique, 1925–30": Various reports concerning government water development during the period indicated.
"Hydraulique, 1931": Includes a complete inventory of protectorate projects for water development to 1931, and correspondence and memos related to planned projects.
"No. 13, Agriculture et Colonisation" (1930): Various reports on Morocco's agricultural production and problems of colonization.

COMMERCE SECTION
"No. 33, Chambres d'Agriculture": Minutes of numerous meetings of the Rabat, Casablanca, Marrakech, Fez, and Meknes Chambers of Agriculture during the 1930s.

The Centre National de Documentation (CND) in Rabat, in addition, contains many French protectorate documents on microfiche. Various reports, letters, and memoranda from the archives of the Office de l'Irrigation aux Beni Amir–Beni Moussa and the Direction de l'Agriculture were located at the CND and used in this study, some stamped "confidentiel." Many difficult-to-find government documents from the contemporary period were also readily located at the CND.

The bulletins of the Rabat and Casablanca Chambers of Agriculture deserve particular mention. Extremely rare, these bulletins contain much invaluable archival material not yet accessible elsewhere. Morocco's Chambers of Agriculture were established by the colonial government to represent settler interests and lend assistance in policy formulation. Each was composed of roughly twenty prominent members of the agricultural community. These elite settlers exerted a powerful influence on the protectorate government. In fact, as this study has shown, they were often the real policymakers. The Rabat and Casablanca chambers represented approximately 70 percent of Morocco's settlers, including the bulk of the more prosperous private settlers. They were by far the most influential of the colonial Chambers of Agriculture, and were the only chambers that regularly published bulletins. Both the Rabat and Casablanca bulletins contain detailed minutes of chamber meetings. They therefore provide unequaled insight into the evolution of government agricultural policy. The Rabat bulletins, additionally, include verbatim copies of all correspondence between the chamber and the protectorate government. Much of this correspondence is so frank that it will remain classified and inaccessible for many years yet at the other end, in the official archives in France. Chamber of Agriculture bulletins were probably the single most valuable source of information for this study.

Select Bibliography of Unpublished Sources

Mémoires de stages and theses cited can be consulted at the institutions indicated; many are also held by the Bibliothèque Générale in Rabat. For reports, known locations are indicated in brackets when these differ from or are absent from the citations.

Barbarin, A. "La Protection de la petite propriété agricole dans la zone française du Maroc: étude du bien de famille." *Mémoire* no. 1569, 1950. Paris: CHEAM.

Bazin, H. "Un Problème de modernisation rurale au Maroc: l'intégration des terres collectives dans les associations syndicales du bassin inférieur du Sebou." *Mémoire* no. 1639, 1949. Paris: CHEAM.

Ben-Elkadi, M. "L'Evolution de l'exploitation des ressources hydrauliques au Maroc." *Mémoire*, 3d cycle, 1976. Rabat: Institut Agronomique Hassan II.

Blanc, L., H. Chapot, and G. Cuenot. "La Culture et la sélection des agrumes subtropicaux aux U.S.A. (Notes de mission, novembre 1950–janvier 1951)." Report, 1951. Rabat: Direction de l'Agriculture. [Rabat: Bibliothèque Générale.]

Bois, J. "La Surpopulation rurale des Doukkalas." *Mémoire* no. 300, 1938. Paris: CHEAM.

Boyer, B. "Les Grands Périmètres irrigués du Maroc: équisse d'une réforme foncière dans le cadre d'une politique de mise en valeur." *Mémoire*, 1960. Paris: Ecole Nationale d'Administration.

Cathary, M. "Tentative dans le périmètre de Marrakech, 1961–1963." *Mémoire* no. 4027, 1965. Paris: CHEAM.

Colombier, A. "La Gestion des grands périmètres d'irrigation au Maroc." *Mémoire*, 1953. Paris: Ecole Nationale d'Administration.

Comité National Marocain de la CIID. "Spécificités de l'aménagement hydro-agricole au Maroc." Report, 1979. Rabat: Institut Agronomique Hassan II.

Cosnier, H. "Intensification de la production agricole au Maroc en vue de sa contribution au ravitaillement de la France. Mission Henri Cosnier. Avril, mai, juin 1917." Report, 1917. [Rabat: Bibliothèque, Chambre d'Agriculture.]

Daillier, M. "Les Problèmes de remembrement posés par l'irrigation des terres 'Melk' dans les Abda." *Mémoire* no. 1893, 1951. Paris: CHEAM.

Dubarry, M. "Transplantation de populations sur un périmètre irrigué." *Mémoire* no. 2889, 1958. Paris: CHEAM.

El Kabir, A. "Les Tentatives de modernisation de l'agriculture marocaine." *Mémoire*, 1971. Paris: University of Paris.

Ezzaki, T. "L'Investissement d'infrastructure et ses implications en matière de politique du développement (le cas du Maroc)." *Mémoire*, 1977. Casablanca: Hassan II University.

Fournial, A. "Les Barrages en Afrique du Nord, leur utilisation hydraulique, agricole et industrielle." *Mémoire de stage*, 1946. Paris: IIAP.

Gayoso, A. "Agricultural Development Strategies in Morocco, 1957–1970." Report, 1970. Rabat: USAID.

Giscard d'Estaing, F. "L'Office de l'Irrigation au Beni Amir–Beni Moussa et la mise en valeur de la plaine du Tadla." *Mémoire de stage*, 1949. Paris: Ecole Nationale d'Administration.

Goujon, M. "Un Travail original de restauration des sols: la protection du périmètre irrigué des Doukkala." *Mémoire* no. 2332, 1955. Paris: CHEAM.

Laleye, A. "Barrages et développement économique au Maroc." *Mémoire*, 1971. Paris: IIAP.

Laxan, E. "L'Irrigation et la rémunération du travail agricole chez les Beni Amir." *Mémoire*, 1947. Paris: Ecole Nationale d'Administration.

Louafa, M. "La Politique hydraulique et le développement économique au Maroc." *Mémoire*, 1974. Paris: University of Paris.

Mingasson, C. "Aspects techniques, économiques et sociaux du développement en zone irriguée d'Afrique du Nord: le périmètre du Tadla." Doctoral thesis, 3d cycle. University of Strasbourg, 1964.

Oussalah, L. "Le Développement inégal au niveau national: Maroc utile/Maroc inutile." *Mémoire*, 1976. Aix-en-Provence: University of Aix–Marseille II.

Pilleboue, J. "Aspects de l'irrigation dans le Haouz de Marrakech." *Mémoire*, 3d cycle, Geography. University of Paris, 1962.

Renard, F. "Les Problèmes humains posés par l'irrigation dans le périmètre des Doukkala." *Mémoire de stage*, 1949. Paris: Ecole Nationale d'Administration.

Roché, P. "Exposés sur l'économie rurale et la modernisation au Maroc jusqu'en 1960." *Mémoire* no. 4255, 1968. Paris: CHEAM.

Schmidt, M. "Contribution à l'étude de l'évolution socio-économique d'une vieille paysannerie marocaine: le périmètre des Abda-Doukkala." Doctoral thesis, 3d cycle, University of Paris, 1966.

Soudho, D. "L'Evolution des structures foncières dans le Rharb entre 1965 et 1981: cas du secteur hydraulique S9 de la Première Tranche d'Irrigation." *Mémoire*, 3d cycle, 1981. Rabat: Institut Agronomique Hassan II.

Tallec, C. "L'Equipement hydraulique de la plaine des Beni Amir et ses incidences politiques." *Mémoire confidentiel* no. 556, red series, 1941. Paris: CHEAM.

United States Agency for International Development. "Morocco, Country Development Strategy Statement (FYs 1987–1991). Annex C, The Agricultural Sector in Morocco: A Description." Unpublished report, 1986. Washington, D.C.: USAID.

Vrolyk, Lt. "Le Paysannat indigène en Afrique du Nord." *Mémoire* no. 319, 1939. Paris: CHEAM.

Select Bibliography of Published Sources

Agourram, A. "L'Hydraulique agricole au Maroc." *Bulletin Economique et Sociale du Maroc* 31 (1969): 1–12.

Akbour, H. "La Réforme agraire: un mythe et quelques réalités." *Lamalif* 120 (1980): 30–37.

Amphoux, M. "Le Maroc et la crise économique." *Revue d'Economie Politique* 47, no. 1 (1933): 110–138.

Amphoux, M. "L'Evolution de l'agriculture européenne au Maroc." *Annales de Géographie* 42 (1933): 175–185.

Ancey, C. *Nos Interêts économiques au Maroc.* Paris: Edition du Journal "La Prime," 1918.

Ashford, D. E. "The Politics of Rural Mobilization in North Africa." *Journal of Modern African Studies* 7 (1969): 187–220.

Bauzil, V. "L'Hydraulique agricole au Maroc." *Bulletin Economique et Social du Maroc* 8 (1946): 371–380.

Belal, A., and A. Agourram. "Les Problèmes posés par la politique agricole dans une économie 'dualiste.' " *Bulletin Economique et Social du Maroc* 122 (1973): 1–36.

Benhadi, A. "La Politique marocaine des barrages." *Annuaire de l'Afrique du Nord, 1975* 14 (1976): 275–294.

Benhlal, M. "Politique des barrages et problèmes de la modernisation rurale dans le Gharb." *Annuaire de l'Afrique du Nord, 1975* 14 (1976): 261–273.

Bénier, C. "Essai statistique sur l'économie agricole marocaine." *Bulletin Economique et Social du Maroc* 74 (1957): 179–224 and 75 (1957): 322–382.

Bernard, A. "Rural Colonization in North Africa." In *Pioneer Settlement: Cooperative Studies*, pp. 221–235. Edited by W.L.G. Joerg. New York: American Geographical Society, 1932.

Berque, J., and J. Couleau. "Vers la modernisation du fellah marocain." *Bulletin Economique et Social du Maroc* 26 (1945): 18–26.

Berthault, P. *La Production des céréales en Afrique du Nord*. Paris: Edition du Comité Algérie-Tunisie-Maroc, 1928.

Betts, R. *Tricouleur: The French Overseas Empire*. London: Gordon and Cremonesi, 1978.

Bey-Rozet, L. *Notions d'arboriculture fruitière à l'usage des planteurs du Maroc*. Rabat, 1931.

Bidwell, R. *Morocco under Colonial Rule: French Administration of Tribal Areas, 1912–1956*. London: Frank Cass, 1973.

Bondis, Captain A. *La Colonisation au Maroc*. Rabat, 1932.

Bonnefous, M. *Perspectives de l'agriculture marocaine*. Bordeaux: E. Taffard, 1949.

Bouderbala, N. "Quelques données élémentaires sur l'évolution des structures agraires dans la plaine du Rharb." *Revue de Géographie du Maroc* 20 (1971): 119–124.

Bouderbala, N., J. Chiche, A. Herzenni, and P. Pascon. *La Question hydraulique: petite et moyenne hydraulique au Maroc*. Rabat, 1984.

Bouderbala, N., M. Chraibi, and P. Pascon. *La Question agraire au Maroc*, nos. 123–125. *Bulletin Economique et Social du Maroc*, 1974.

Bouderbala, N., M. Chraibi, and P. Pascon. *La Question agraire au Maroc II*, nos. 133–134. *Bulletin Economique et Social du Maroc*, 1977.

Branquec, Y. "La Propriété et la colonisation dans la zone française du Maroc." *Bulletin Economique et Social du Maroc* 7 (1945): 37–40, 131–137.

Brunschwig, H. *French Colonialism, 1871–1914: Myths and Realities*. New York: Frederick A. Praeger, 1966.

Burke, E., III. "The Image of the Moroccan State in French Ethnological Literature: A New Look at the Origin of Lyautey's Berber Policy." In *Arabs and Berbers*, pp. 175–199. Edited by E. Gellner and C. Micaud. Lexington, Mass.: D. C. Heath, 1973.

Burke, E., III. *Prelude to Protectorate in Morocco: Precolonial Protest and Resistance, 1860–1912*. Chicago: University of Chicago Press, 1976.

Burke, J. H. *The Citrus Industries of North Africa*. Foreign Agriculture Report no. 66. Washington, D.C.: USDA, January 1952.

Calary de la Mazière, M. "La Conquête agricole du Maroc." *Revue de Paris* 15 (1923): 686–697.

Canal, J. *Géographie générale du Maroc*. Paris: A. Challamel, 1902.

Cardi, G. "Un Problème d'irrigation, la mise en valeur de la région de Sidi Slimane." *Bulletin Economique et Social du Maroc* 7 (1945): 138–146.

Carle, G. "Notes sur l'agriculture au Maroc." *Revue de Botanique Appliquée et d'Agriculture Coloniale* 5 (1925): 338–343.

Carle, G., and J. Gattefosse. "Le Problème général de l'Extrême Sud marocain." *Revue de Géographie Marocaine* 21 (1937): 185–194.

Catherine, H. "L'Hydraulique au Maroc." *Bulletin de la Société de Géographie du Maroc* 8 (1919): 13–21.

Célérier, J. "Les 'Merjas' de la plaine du Sebou." *Hespéris* 2 (1922): 109–138, 209–239.

Célérier, J. "La Colonisation au Maroc." *Annales de Géographie* 38 (1929): 629–630.

Célérier, J. "Le Maroc, est-il un pays neuf?" *Revue de Géographie Marocaine* 8, nos. 3–4 (1929): 66–97.

Célérier, J. "La Disette dans le Maroc du Sud." *Annales de Géographie* 46 (1937): 544–546.

Célérier, J. "Travaux de petite hydraulique dans le Sud marocain." *Annales de Géographie* 47 (1938): 534–539.

Célérier, J. "La Modernisation du paysannat marocain." *Revue de Géographie Marocaine* 1 (1947): 3–29.

Célérier, J., and A. Charton. "Les Grands Travaux d'hydraulique agricole au Maroc." *Annales de Géographie* 34 (1925): 76–80.

Chabert, M. *L'Hydraulique au Maroc.* Rabat: H. Blanc, 1922.

Chabert, M. *L'Hydraulique au Maroc.* Casablanca: Imprimerie Réunis, 1946.

Cherif, O., et al. "Dossier: l'agriculture marocaine." *Afrique Agriculture* 34 (1978): 22–93.

Christian, P. *L'Afrique française.* Paris: Napoléan Chaix, 1846.

Cleaver, K. M. *The Agricultural Development Experience of Algeria, Morocco, and Tunisia: A Comparison of Strategies for Growth.* Staff Working Paper, no. 552. Washington, D.C.: World Bank, 1982.

Colliez, A. *Notre protectorat marocain: la première étape, 1912–1930.* Paris: M. Rivière, 1930.

Conac, F. "Irrigation moderne et agriculture irriguée au Maroc, analyses et réflexions." *Annales de Géographie* 94 (1985): 723–731.

Cosnier, H. *L'Afrique du Nord—son avenir agricole et économique.* Paris: Larose, 1922.

Cousin, A., and D. Saurin. *Le Maroc.* Paris: Figaro, 1905.

Couvreur, M. "Une Nouvelle Forme de gestion des terres recuperées au Maroc: la Société de Développement Agricole (SODEA)." *Méditerranée* 29 (1977): 97–102.

Couvreur-Laraichi, F. "Quelques Aspects de l'évolution récente du périmètre irrigué du Tadla." *Revue de Géographie du Maroc* 20 (1971): 125–133.

Daoud, Z. "Le Capitalisme agraire marocain." *Lamalif* 121 (1980): 24–33.

Daoud, Z. "L'Agriculture, le grand dilemme." *Lamalif* 159 (1984): 26–31.

Delannoy, H. "Le 'Code des Investissements Agricoles': nouveau cadre législatif de la transformation des campagnes marocaines." *Revue de Géographie du Maroc* 16 (1969): 151–157.

Delau, L., ed. *Le Maroc à la croissée des chemins*. Casablanca: Imprimerie Réunis, 1931.

Dresch, J. *L'Agriculture en Afrique du Nord*. Paris: Centre de Documentation Universitaire, 1956.

Dumont, R. *Etude des modalités d'action du Paysannat*. Cahiers de la Modernisation Rurale 3. Rabat: Société d'Etudes Economiques, Sociales et Statistiques, 1948.

Durand, P. "La Région de Marrakech et du sud marocain." *Revue de Géographie Marocaine* 6 (1927): 104–137.

Durand, P. "La Sécurité du Maroc central par l'eau." *Renseignements Coloniaux*, 1929, pp. 655–657.

Durand, P. "La Colonisation au Tadla." *Renseignements Coloniaux*, 1930, pp. 5–8.

Du Taillis, J. *Le Nouveau Maroc*. Paris: Société d'Editions Géographiques, Maritimes et Coloniales, 1923.

Duval, G. *L'Hydraulique au Maroc*. Paris: Edition Domat-Montchrestien, 1933.

Eickelman, D. *Moroccan Islam: Tradition and Society in a Pilgrimage Center*. Austin: University of Texas Press, 1976.

Eickelman, D. "Royal Authority and Religious Legitimacy: Morocco's Elections, 1960–1984." In *The Frailty of Authority*, pp. 181–205. Edited by M. J. Aronoff. New Brunswick, N.J.: Transaction Books, 1986.

"Exode rural." *Bulletin Economique et Social du Maroc* 19 (1955): 459–465.

Faugeras, J. *Oranges, citrons, pamplemousses: leur culture et leur commerce en Floride et en Californie*. Paris: Dunod, 1931.

Faure-Dère, R. *L'Hydraulique agricole au Maroc*. Tunis: Ecole Coloniale d'Agriculture, 1936.

Faust, M. *La Colonisation rurale au Maroc, 1919–1929*. Algiers: Ancienne Imprimerie V. Heintz, 1931.

Fazy, H. *Agriculture marocaine et protectorat*. Paris: Lecante, 1947.

Fogg, W. "The Sebou Basin." *Scottish Geographical Magazine* 47 (1931): 80–97.

Fourgous, M. J. *L'Avenir économique du Maroc*. Paris: Société de Géographie Commerciale de Paris, 1916.

Gadille, J. "La Colonisation officielle au Maroc." *Cahiers d'Outre-Mer* 8 (1955): 305–322.

Gadille, J. "L'Agriculture européenne au Maroc—étude humaine et économique." *Annales de Géographie* 66 (1957): 144–158.

Gallagher, C. F. "The Moroccan Economy in Perspective." *American Universities Field Staff Reports, North African Series* 12 (1966): 1–13.

Gallissot, R. "Le Maroc et la crise." *Revue Française d'Histoire d'Outre-Mer* 63 (1976): 477–491.

Garcin, P. *La Politique des contingents dans les relations franco-marocaines*. Paris: Recueil Sirey, 1937.

Garnier, L. "L'Industrie des agrumes aux U.S.A." *La Terre Marocaine*, 1949, pp. 189–193.

Garnier, L. "Les Irrigations." *La Terre Marocaine*, 1949, pp. 237–239.

Garnier, L. "Les Leçons d'une mission aux Etats-Unis." In *La Mise en valeur du Maroc*, pp. 13–17. Edited by F. Malet et al. Paris: Librairie Agricole, Horticole, Forestière et Menagère, 1949.

Garnier, L. "Rapport préliminaire de M. Louis Garnier, Ingénieur en Chef du Génie Rural au Maroc sur sa mission aux Etats-Unis." *Bulletin de la Chambre d'Agriculture de Rabat*, 1949, pp. 1746–1750, 1773–1784, 1870–1875.

Geertz, C., H. Geertz, and L. Rosen. *Meaning and Order in Moroccan Society: Three Essays in Cultural Analysis*. New York: Cambridge University Press, 1979.

Germain, J., and S. Faye. *Le Nouveau Monde français—Maroc, Algérie, Tunisie*. Paris: Plon-Nourrit, 1924.

Girault, A. *Principes de colonisation et de législation coloniale: les colonies françaises avant et depuis 1815*. Paris: Recueil Sirey, 1943.

Gottmann, J. "Economic Problems of French North Africa." *Geographical Review* 33 (1943): 175–196.

"Grands Périmètres d'irrigation au Maroc." *Notes Marocaines* 2 (1952): 4–10.

Graux, Lt. Col. *Le Maroc, sa production agricole*. Paris: Sirey, 1912.

Griffin, K. *Land Concentration and Rural Poverty*. New York: Holmes and Meier, 1976.

Grigory, S. "A propos du Projet Sebou au Maroc." *Maghreb-Machrek* 85 (1979): 61–65.

Guerin, P. *L'Arboriculture californienne*. Paris: Alcan, 1937.

Guillemet, P. "Hespérides." *Fruits et Primeurs de l'Afrique du Nord* 1: 7–8.

Guillemet, P. "La Colonisation nord-africaine, l'éxemple de la Californie." *Renseignements Coloniaux*, 1931, pp. 105–108, 475–476.

Guillemet, P. "Au Maroc, le problème de l'eau." *Renseignements Coloniaux*, 1934, pp. 141–144.

Guillemet, P. "Regards sur l'hydraulique agricole au Maroc." *La Terre Marocaine* 54 (1934): 11–23.

Hamdouch, B. "La Dépendance alimentaire du Maroc." *Lamalif* 132 (1982): 20–29.

Hodgson, R. W. "L'Industrie et les possibilités de l'arboriculture fruitière en Afrique du Nord française." *Fruits et Primeurs de l'Afrique du Nord* 118 (1941): 167–168.

Hoffherr, R. *L'Economie marocaine*. Paris: Recueil Sirey, 1932.

Hoisington, W. A., Jr. *The Casablanca Connection: French Colonial Policy, 1936-1943*. Chapel Hill, N.C.: University of North Carolina Press.

Houston, J. M. "Irrigation in French Morocco." *Times Review of Industry*, December 1953, pp. 102, 105.

Houston, J. M. "The Significance of Irrigation in Morocco's Economic Development." *Geographical Journal* 120 (1954): 314–328.

Joly, F. "La Modernisation rurale au Maroc." *Annales de Géographie* 55 (1946): 210–213.

Joly, F. "Donnèes sur l'agriculture marocaine." *Cahiers d'Outre-Mer* 1 (1948): 97–99.

Jourdan, P. "Impressions sur les agrumes en Californie, été 1953." *Fruits et Primeurs de l'Afrique du Nord* 252 (1953): 435–442.

Jouve, A. M. "L'Evolution des superficies équipées et irriguées dans les grands périmètres irrigués de 1957 à 1977." *Hommes, Terre et Eaux* 4 (1972): 55–61.

Jouve, A. M. "Démographie et céréaliculture: évolution comparée de la démographie et de la céréaliculture au Maroc depuis le début du siècle." *Revue de Géographie du Maroc* 4 (1980): 5–19.

Kann, R. *Le Protectorat marocain.* Nancy: Berger-Levrault, 1921.

Kanya-Forstner, A. S. "French Expansion in Africa: The Mythical Theory," pp. 277–294. In *Studies in the Theory of Imperialism.* Edited by R. Owen and B. Sutcliffe. London: Longman, 1972.

Kloet, H. van der. *Inégalités dans les milieux ruraux: possibilités et problèmes de la modernisation agricole au Maroc.* Geneva: UNRISD, 1975.

Knight, M. M. *Morocco as a French Economic Venture.* New York: D. Appleton-Century, 1937.

Laborde, F. "La Colonisation nord-africaine: l'exemple de la Californie." *Renseignements Coloniaux*, 1930, pp. 659–662; 1931, pp. 209–212.

Lacarelle, F. *Rapport sur l'activité de l'expérimentation fruitière et maraîchère du Maroc.* Casablanca: Imprimerie Réunis, 1934.

Lahlimi, A. "Modèle colonial et impasse agraire au Maghreb—cas du Maroc." In *Les Temps moderne du Maghreb*, pp. 334–353. Paris: Les Temps Moderne, 1977.

Lauriac, R. *Le Maroc, terre d'agrumes.* Casablanca, Imprimerie Réunis, 1938.

Lawless, R. I. "Progress and Problems in the Development of Maghreb Agriculture." *Maghreb Review* 3 (1976): 6–11, 22.

Lebault, G. "Le Maroc, Californie française." *La Terre Marocaine*, 1928, pp. 368–369.

Lebault, G. "Avons-nous une politique fruitière?" *Bulletin de la Chambre d'Agriculture de Casablanca* 1 (1930): 15–16.

Lebault, G. "Le Problème de l'eau au Maroc." *Bulletin de la Chambre d'Agriculture de Casablanca* 4 (1930): 9–14.

Lebault, G. "L'Office Marocain de Contrôle et d'Exportation." *La Terre Marocaine* 12 (1931): 2–4.

Lebault, G. "Pour notre équipement agricole." *Bulletin de la Chambre d'Agriculture de Casablanca* 16 (1931): 3–4.

Lebault, G. "Rapport sur la politique fruitière et hydraulique du Protectorat." *Bulletin de la Chambre d'Agriculture de Rabat* 7 (1933): 50–56.

Lebault, G. "La Politique de l'hydraulique au Maroc." In Proceedings: *Congrès*

International d'Arboriculture Fruitière et de Pomologie, 20 janvier–1 février, 1934, pp. 129–133. Casablanca, 1934.

Le Coz, J. "Les Agrumes marocains." *Notes Marocaines* 19 (1960): 51–96.

Le Coz, J. *Le Rharb, fellahs et colons,* 2 vols. Rabat: CURS et al., 1964.

Le Coz, J. "Le Troisième Age agraire du Maroc." *Annales de Géographie* 77 (1968): 385–413.

LeGray, J. "Une Oeuvre franco-marocaine." *Revue Politique et Parlementaire* 631 (1953): 162–176.

Le Moigne, Y. "Hydraulique et irrigations au Maroc." In Proceedings: *Congrès de l'Outillage Economique Colonial et des Communications, 20–25 juillet 1931, Paris, organisé par l'Union Coloniale Française.* Paris: Imprimerie de la Sécuritas, 1931.

Le Moigne, Y., and J. Bourcart. "Un Projet d'utilisation d'un fleuve marocain: l'Oum er Rbia." *Revue de Géographie Physique et de Géologie Dynamique* 6 (1933): 5–42.

Leveau, R. *Le Fellah marocain: défenseur du trône.* 2d ed. Paris: Presses de la Fondation Nationale des Sciences Politiques, 1985.

Leveau, R. "Public Property and Control of Property Rights: Their Effects on Social Structure in Morocco." In *Property, Social Structure and Law in the Modern Middle East,* pp. 61–84. Edited by A. E. Mayer. Albany: State University of New York Press, 1985.

Louis, G. *Sources d'eau, sources d'or, sources d'hommes (un reportage de la "Vigie Marocaine" en Californie, juin 1931).* Casablanca: Imprimerie Réunis, 1932.

Lucien-Graux, Dr. *Le Maroc économique—rapport à Monsieur le Ministre du Commerce et de l'Industrie.* Paris: Librairie Ancienne Honoré Champion, 1928.

Malet, F. "Une Oeuvre de quarante ans: l'équipment et la mise en valeur du Maroc agricole." In *La Mise en valeur du Maroc,* pp. 4–8. Edited by F. Malet. Paris: Librairie Agricole, Horticole, Forestière et Menagère, 1949.

Marais, O. "Le Maroc." In *Terre, paysans et politique,* pp. 271–301. Edited by H. Mendras and Y. Tavernier. Paris: SEDEIS, 1969.

Marchal, L. "Les Principes, les méthodes et les buts de la modernisation rurale au Maroc." *Bulletin d'Information du Maroc,* 1946, pp. 303–321.

Maréchal, J. "Les Dépenses du protectorat pour la mise en valeur du Maroc entre 1928 et 1936." *Bulletin Economique du Maroc* 12 (1936): 90–96.

Marthelot, P. "Histoire et réalité de la modernisation du monde rural au Maroc." *Tiers-Monde* 2 (1961): 137–168.

Marthelot, P. "Les Implications humaines de l'irrigation moderne en Afrique du Nord." *Annuaire de l'Afrique du Nord* 1 (1962): 127–154.

Martin. "La Question hydraulique dans la région de Marrakech." *Revue de Géographie Marocaine* 6 (1927): 50–72.

Martin, J., H. Jover, J. Le Coz, G. Maurer, and D. Noin. *Géographie du Maroc.* Paris: Hatier, 1967.

Mas, P. de. *Marges marocaines*. The Hague: NUFFIC/IMWOO/PROJET REM-
    PLOD, 1978.

Mas, P. de. "The Place of Peripheral Regions in Moroccan Planning." *Tijd-
    schrift voor Economische en Sociale Geografie* 69 (1978): 86–94.

Mas, P. de. "Opinion à propos du Projet Sebou." *Le Maroc Agricole* 122
    (1980): 20–32.

Mazières, E. A. de. *La Culture des céréales dans l'Afrique du Nord (au Maroc)*.
    Casablanca: Imprimerie Française, n.d.

Merriam, J. G. "Morocco's Commitment to Agrarian Reform and Rural De-
    velopment: An Examination." *Maghreb Review* 8, nos. 3–4 (1983): 77–
    84.

Miège, E. "Les Cultures complémentaires au Maroc." *Bulletin Economique du
    Maroc* 14 (1936): 283–297.

Miège, E. "Les Agrumes au Maroc." *Revue de Botanique Appliquée et d'Agricul-
    ture Tropicale* 17 (1937): 865–882.

Miègeville, Dr. "La Situation économique de la région de Béni Mellal." *Revue
    de Géographie Marocaine* 6 (1927): 3–49.

Miller, J. A. *Imlil: A Moroccan Mountain Community in Change*. Boulder,
    Colo.: Westview, 1984.

Mingasson, C. "Le Périmètre d'irrigation du Tadla." *Annales Algériennes de
    Géographie* 1 (1966): 41–65; 2 (1966): 82–119.

Morocco. *L'Agriculture marocaine 20 ans après l'indépendence*. N.p.: Ministère
    de l'Agriculture et de la Réforme Agraire, 1975.

Morocco. *L'Equipement hydraulique du Maroc*. Rabat: Travaux Publics, 1954.

Morocco. *L'Irrigation au Maroc*. Rabat: Ministère de l'Agriculture et de la
    Réforme agraire, 1975.

Morocco. *Major Dams in Morocco*. N.p.: Public Works, 1973 (English edition).

Morocco. *Plan quinquennal, 1960–1964*. N.p.: Division de la Coordination
    Economique et du Plan, 1960.

Morocco. *Three-Year Plan, 1965–1967*. N.p.: Division de la Coordination
    Economique et du Plan, 1965 (English edition).

Morocco. *Plan quinquennal, 1968–1972*. N.p.: Division de la Coordination
    Economique et du Plan, 1968.

Morocco. *Plan de développement économique et social, 1973–1977*. N.p.: Secré-
    tariat d'Etat au Plan, 1973.

Morocco. *Plan de développement économique et social, 1978–1980*. N.p.: Direc-
    tion du Plan et du Développement Régional, 1978.

Morocco. *Plan de développement économique et social, 1981–1985*. N.p.: Minis-
    tère du Plan et du Développement Régional, 1981.

Moulièras, A. *Le Maroc inconnu*, vol. I: *Exploration du Rif*. Paris: Librairie
    Coloniale et Africaine, 1895.

Naciri, M. "Les Expériences de modernisation de l'agriculture au Maroc." *Re-
    vue de Géographie du Maroc* 11 (1967): 102–114.

Naciri, M. "Inégalites dans les milieux ruraux au Maroc." *Bulletin Economique
    et Social du Maroc* 136–137 (1977): 193–200.

Noin, D. *La Population rurale du Maroc.* 2 vols. Paris: PUF, 1970.

Noin, D. "Morocco." In *World Atlas of Agriculture*, vol. 4: *Africa*, pp. 377–387. Novara: Instituto Geografico de Agostini, 1976.

Normandin, A. "Une Grande Oeuvre française: l'utilisation agricole des eaux au Maroc." *Annales des Ponts et Chaussées*, 1939, pp. 315–329.

Nouvel, J. "La Crise agricole de 1945–1946 au Maroc et ses conséquences économiques et sociales." *Revue de Géographie Humaine et d'Ethnologie* 1 (1949): 87–90.

Oved, G. "Contribution à l'étude de l'endettement de la colonisation agricole au Maroc." *Revue Française d'Histoire d'Outre-Mer* 63 (1976): 492–505.

Papy, L. "Une Réalisation française au Maroc: les secteurs de modernisation rurale." *Cahiers d'Outre-Mer* 36 (1956): 325–349.

Pascon, P. *Le Haouz de Marrakech.* 2 vols. Rabat: CURS, 1977.

Pascon, P. "Sur les terres collectives, l'état n'a plus d'idées." *Lamalif* 112 (1980): 22–23.

Pascon, P. "Agriculture, faillité et perspectives." *Lamalif* 145 (1983): 18–20.

Payne, R. "Food Deficits and Political Legitimacy: The Case of Morocco." In *Africa's Agrarian Crisis: Roots of Famine*, pp. 153–172. Edited by S. Commins, M. Lofchie, and R. Payne. Boulder, Colo.: Lynne Reinner, 1986.

Penet, P. *Les Richesses hydrauliques du Maroc occidental.* Grenoble: J. Rey, 1918.

Popp, H. "Les Périmètres irrigués du Gharb." *Bulletin Economique et Social du Maroc* 138–139 (1979): 157–177.

Popp, H. *La Question hydraulique: effets socio-géographiques de la politique des barrages au Maroc.* Rabat, 1984.

"Population de l'Agriculture." *Lamalif* 133 (1982): 24–25.

Poupart, J. M. "Les Problèmes de l'eau à Marrakech." *Cahiers d'Outre-Mer* 2 (1949): 38–52.

Pourtauborde, J. "L'Irrigation de la plaine des Béni Amir–Béni Moussa." *La Terre Marocaine*, 1950, pp. 443–451.

"Problèmes de l'eau en Afrique du Nord (première partie, 'L'Equipement hydraulique du Maroc')." *Documentation Française*, Notes et Etudes Documentaires no. 1.170, 22 July 1949, pp. 2–16.

"Projets et problèmes de l'agriculture marocaine." *Maghreb* 24 (1967): 27–39.

Qarouach, M. *L'Agriculture marocaine face au deuxième élargissement de la CEE.* Casablanca: Presses des Editions Maghrébines, 1983.

Raki, A. "Dualisme rural—cas du Gharb." *Bulletin Economique et Social du Maroc* 122 (1973): 65–82.

Raynal, R. "Problèmes et bilan de l'agriculture marocaine." *Cahiers d'Outre-Mer* 4 (1951): 342–362.

Reclus, E. *North-West Africa*, vol. 11: *The Earth and Its Inhabitants.* New York: D. Appleton, 1887.

Richemont, F. de. "Une Politique agraire pour l'Afrique du Nord." *Revue Politique et Parlementaire* 174 (1938): 257–263.

Rossano, J. "La Colonisation européenne dans le Haouz de Marrakech." *Cahiers d'Outre-Mer* 7 (1954): 342–366.

Sayigh, Y. A. *The Economies of the Arab World: Development since 1945.* New York: St. Martin's Press, 1978.

Seddon, D. *Moroccan Peasants: A Century of Change in the Eastern Rif, 1870–1970.* Folkestone, Kent: Dawson, 1981.

Segrè, C. G. *Fourth Shore: The Italian Colonization of Libya.* Chicago: University of Chicago Press, 1974.

Sermaye, J. "L'Irrigation de la plaine des Béni-Amir fait naître un paysannat marocain." *Annales Coloniales,* 11 July 1938, pp. 1, 3.

Sermaye, J. "La Politique de l'eau au Maroc français." *L'Illustration,* 22 October 1938, pp. 249–252.

Sonnier, A. "Considérations sur la condition juridique des merdjas du Gharb." *Revue de Géographie Marocaine,* 1931, pp. 33–38.

Sonnier, A. "Contribution à l'étude du régime juridique des eaux au Maroc." *Revue de Géographie Marocaine,* 1931, pp. 307–325.

Sonnier, A. *Le Régime juridique des eaux au Maroc.* Paris: Recueil Sirey, 1933.

Sonnier, A. "Les Merjas de la plaine du Gharb." *Bulletin de la Chambre d'Agriculture de Rabat,* 1935, pp. 480–488.

Stewart, C. F. *The Economy of Morocco, 1912–1962.* Cambridge, Mass.: Harvard University Press, 1964.

Surugue, P. "La Renaissance du paysannat marocain." *Renseignements Coloniaux,* 1939, pp. 162–170.

Swearingen, W. D. "Not a Drop of Water to the Sea: The Colonial Origins of Morocco's Present Irrigation Programme." *Maghreb Review* 9, nos. 1–2 (1984): 26–38.

Swearingen, W. D. "In Pursuit of the Granary of Rome: France's Wheat Policy in Morocco, 1915–1931." *International Journal of Middle East Studies* 17 (1985): 347–363.

Swearingen, W. D. "Morocco's Agricultural Crisis." In *The Political Economy of Morocco,* pp. 234–254. Edited by I. W. Zartman. New York: Praeger, 1987.

Tessler, M. "Continuity and Change in Moroccan Politics. Part I: Challenge and Response in Hassan's Morocco." *UFSI Reports* no. 1, Africa (1984).

Tessler, M. "Continuity and Change in Moroccan Politics. Part II: New Troubles and Deepening Doubts." *UFSI Reports* no. 2, Africa (1984).

Trintignac, R., and M. Brayard. "De Los Angeles à Rabat: rapport de la Mission Officielle Californie-Mexique (1930)." *La Terre Marocaine,* 1932: no. 18, pp. 26–32; no. 19, pp. 15–43; no. 20, pp. 10–19; no. 21, pp. 9–16; no. 22, pp. 7–23. 1933: no. 24, pp. 8–20; no. 25, pp. 6–30; no. 26, pp. 18–29; no. 28, pp. 7–19; no. 30, pp. 13–37; no. 32, pp. 15–32; no. 33, pp. 6–26.

Vaffier-Pollet, E. "L'Agriculture et l'élévage au Maroc." *Renseignements Coloniaux,* 1906, pp. 205–209.

Van Wersch, H. J. "Rural Development in Morocco: *Opération Labour.*" *Economic Development and Cultural Change* 17 (1968): 33–49.

Vidi. "La Colonisation nord-africaine, l'exemple de la Californie." *Revue Politique et Parlementaire* 144 (1930): 422–431.

Villeneuve, M. *La Situation de l'agriculture et son avenir dans l'économie maro-caine*. Paris: R. Pichon et R. Durand Auzias, 1971.

Waterbury, J. *The Commander of the Faithful: The Moroccan Political Elite, a Study in Segmented Politics*. New York: Columbia University Press, 1970.

Weisgerber, F. "Le Problème de l'eau au Maroc." *Revue Française d'Outre-Mer* 763 (1939): 55–60.

World Bank. *Morocco: Economic and Social Development Report*. Washington, D.C.: World Bank, 1981.

World Bank. *The Economic Development of Morocco*. Baltimore: Johns Hopkins University Press, 1966.

World Bank. *The World Bank Annual Report, 1985*. Washington, D.C.: World Bank, 1985.

Y. "L'Hydraulique agricole au Maroc." *Revue Générale des Sciences Pures et Appliquées*, 15 April 1914, pp. 354–356.

Zartman, I. W. "Farming and Land Ownership in Morocco." *Land Economics* 39 (1963): 187–198.

Index

Library of Congress Cataloging-in-Publication Data

Swearingen, Will D. (Will Davis), 1946–
Moroccan mirages.

Bibliography: p.
Includes index.
1. Agriculture—Economic aspects—Morocco—History.
2. Agriculture and state—Morocco—History. I. Title.
HD2121.S94 1987   338.1'0964   87-6981
ISBN 0–691–05505–X (alk. paper)
ISBN 0–691–10236–8 (LPE)